601 WORDS

YOU NEED TO KNOW TO PASS YOUR EXAM

Fourth Edition

by

MURRAY BROMBERG
Principal Emeritus
Andrew Jackson High School
Queens, New York

JULIUS LIEBB
Former Assistant Principal, English
Andrew Jackson High School
Queens, New York

BARRON'S

All inquiries should be addressed to:
Barron's Educational Series, Inc.
250 Wireless Boulevard
Hauppauge, New York 11788
www.barronseduc.com

ISBN-13: 978-0-7641-2816-5
ISBN-10: 0-7641-2816-7

Library of Congress Catalog Card No. 2004043773

Library of Congress Cataloging-in-Publication Data

Bromberg, Murray.
    601 words you need to know to pass your exam /
  by Murray Bromberg, Julius Liebb. — 4th ed.
        p.   cm.
      Includes index.
      ISBN 0-7641-2816-7 (pbk. : alk. paper)
      1. Vocabulary tests—Study guides.   I. TItle: Six hundred and one words
  you need to know to pass your exam. II. Liebb, Julius.   III. Title.

  PE1449.B6437   2005
  428.1'076—dc22   2004043773

PRINTED IN THE UNITED STATES OF AMERICA

9 8 7 6 5 4 3

CONTENTS

Unit I

Unit II

Unit III

Unit IV

INTRODUCTION

People who are planning to take Scholastic Aptitude Tests (SATs, PSATs), Graduate Record Exams (GREs), Miller Analogies Tests (MATs), and other standardized tests commonly study long lists of vocabulary words in preparation for the verbal portion of such tests. Although that is commendable, it is not economical. There are just too many words to study—and not enough time before a test to master all of them.

With that challenge in mind, we have carefully chosen 601 words that testmakers are fond of using. By concentrating on words at the level most commonly tested on the major exams, we have been able to produce a compact, manageable assortment of functional vocabulary words. Naturally, no one—not even the testmakers themselves—can predict precisely which words will turn up on a specific exam, but the words we've selected deal with topics and concepts considered vital for today's students. Mastering them will be a valuable step toward readiness for your upcoming exam.

This book was designed for the high school or college student who wants to be ready for an upcoming standardized test. It is also useful for the adult who is seeking self-improvement through independent study. This fourth edition contains expanded exercises, updated sample sentences, new illustrations, and a Vocabulary Roundup that features the new words in context in interesting articles.

Testmakers who thought they could stump you with *etiology, jejune, leitmotif,* and *baleful* will be in for a surprise when you get through with *601 Words You Need to Know to Pass Your Exam.*

NOTE: The answers to all exercises are at the back of the book.

PRONUNCIATION KEY*

a	asp, fat, parrot		ə	represents
ā	ape, date, play, break, fail			
ä	ah, car, father, cot			a in ago
				e in agent
e	elf, ten, berry			i in sanity
ē	even, meet, money, flea, grieve			o in comply
				u in focus
i	is, hit, mirror			
ī	ice, bite, high, sky		ər	perhaps
ō	open, tone, go, boat		ch	chin, catcher, arch, nature
ô	all, horn, law, oar		sh	she, cushion, dash, machine
o͞o	ooze, tool, crew, rule		zh	azure, leisure, beige
oo	look, pull, moor, wolf		ŋ	ring, anger, drink
yo͞o	use, cute, few			
yoo	cure, globule		H	German ich
oi	oil, point, toy			
ou	out, crowd, plow			
u	up, cut, color, flood			

---

*Pronunciation Key, excerpted with permission of Macmillan USA, a Simon & Schuster Macmillan Company, from WEBSTER'S NEW WORLD DICTIONARY, Third College Edition. Copyright © 1988, 1991, 1994 by Simon & Schuster, Inc.

Words from Proper Names

Should you be pleased to be called a *maverick?*

Who might issue a *philippic* against a *philanderer?*

Why would *Procrustean* be an interesting name for a mattress company?

Is it acceptable to boast about a *Pyrrhic* victory?

Which literary figure do you recognize in the word *quixotic?*

---

jingoist
lothario
maverick
nemesis
philanderer
philippic
procrustean
protean
Pyrrhic
quixotic
saturnine
solecism
spoonerism
sybarite
tawdry

1. **jingoist** (jiŋ'-gō-ist)—one who boasts about his patriotism and favors a warlike foreign policy. In 1877, British Prime Minister Disraeli sent the fleet to Gallipoli to slow up the Russians. A singer wrote a ditty called "By Jingo" in honor of that action.
   a. The senator lost because his constituents rejected his *jingoistic* policies.
   b. *"Jingoism,"* to paraphrase Samuel Johnson, "is the last refuge of a scoundrel."

2. **lothario** (lō-ther'-ē-ō)—rake; seducer; lover. Lothario was an amorous character in an eighteenth-century play, *The Fair Penitent.*
   a. The aging playboy thought of himself as a sophisticated *lothario.*
   b. I tried out for the role of the young *lothario,* but they cast me as the butler.

3. **maverick** (mav'-ər-ik)—one who acts independently. Samuel Maverick was a Texas rancher who refused to brand his cattle as others were doing.
   a. When you defend unpopular causes, you get the reputation of being a *maverick.*
   b. The president said that he didn't want yes-men or *mavericks* in his cabinet.

4. **nemesis** (nem'-ə-sis)—agent of retribution; just punishment. In Greek mythology, the goddess Nemesis punished pretentiousness with her sword and avenging wings.
   a. No matter how great a team we fielded, little Calhoun Tech always proved to be our *nemesis.*
   b. Math is my *nemesis,* constantly reminding me that I'm not as bright as I think I am.

5. **philanderer** (fi-lan'-dər-er)—one who makes love insincerely; one who engages in passing love affairs. The word comes from the Greek *philandros* ("man-loving") but gained its current usage because many English playwrights gave the name to their romantic leads.
   a. When Mrs. Greene wanted to find out if her husband was a *philanderer,* she hired a detective.
   b. At the age of 40, Eric switched from part-time *philanderer* to full-time, domesticated husband.

6. **philippic** (fi-lip'-ik)—bitter verbal attack. Philip II of Macedon wanted to make Greece into a monarchy. He was opposed by the great orator, Demosthenes, who denounced Philip in devastating speeches that came to be known as *philippics.*
   a.   My *philippic* against higher taxes was reported on the local radio station.
   b.   The leader of the rent strike mounted the platform to deliver an effective *philippic* against the management.

7. **procrustean** (prō-krus'-tē-ən)—designed to secure conformity; drastic. An ancient Greek robber named Procrustes tied his victims to a bed and then, to make them fit the bed, stretched the short ones and hacked off the limbs of the taller ones.
   a.   Our mayor takes various suggestions and gives them a *procrustean* treatment to fit his philosophy.
   b.   Your *procrustean* attitude does not allow for disagreement.

8. **protean** (prōt'-ē-ən)—changeable; taking on different forms. In Greek mythology, Proteus was a sea god who could change his appearance at will.
   a.   I resent your *protean* propensity for changing your mind whenever you feel like it.
   b.   The stage designer received an award for his *protean* construction that lent itself to the play's various moods.

9. **Pyrrhic victory** (pir'-ik)—a victory that is exceptionally costly. Pyrrhus defeated the Romans in 279 B.C. but his losses were terribly heavy.
   a.   The workers seemed to triumph at the end of the strike but it was a *Pyrrhic victory.*
   b.   Although we won the championship, it was a *Pyrrhic victory* because of the crippling injuries we suffered.

10. **quixotic** (kwik-sät'-ik)—romantically idealistic; impractical. The Spanish novelist, Cervantes, brought this word into our language when he wrote *Don Quixote.* His hero went forth foolishly to tilt against windmills and help the downtrodden.
    a.   Margo's *quixotic* behavior was upsetting to her family because she had always been so level-headed.
    b.   The City Planning Commission's ideas were labeled *quixotic* by the skeptical editors.

11. **saturnine** (sat'-ər-nīn)—sluggish; gloomy; grave. The planet Saturn is so far from the sun that it was thought of as cold and dismal.
    a.   Uncle Dave's constant *saturnine* expression drove my lively Aunt Pearl up the wall.
    b.   While awaiting the jury's verdict, my pessimistic client had a *saturnine* appearance.

12. **solecism** (säl'-ə-siz'm)—substandard use of words; violation of good manners. This word derives from the Greek inhabitants of the colony of Soloi who used a slangy dialect.
    a.   There are some word forms that my teacher rejects as *solecisms* but I feel are acceptable.
    b.   "Ain't she sweet" is a *solecism*—ain't it?

13. **spoonerism** (spōōn'-ər-iz'm)—an unintentional exchange of sounds. Reverend Spooner of New College, Oxford, occasionally twisted his words around when he got excited so that "conquering kings" came out as "kinkering congs."
    a.   My cousin collects *spoonerisms* that he hears on the radio, and he hopes to publish them.
    b.   The candidate's unfortunate *spoonerism* shocked his elderly audience and cost him their votes.

14. **sybarite** (sib'-ə-rīt)—one who is fond of luxury and soft living. Sybaris was a fabulously wealthy Italian city, symbolic of the good life.
    a.   Rudy was criticized for living as a *sybarite* while others of his family were starving.
    b.   The *sybarites* in Roman depictions are often eating grapes.

15. **tawdry** (tô'-drē)—cheap; gaudy; showy. This word can be traced to St. Audrey. Scarves called "St. Audrey's laces" were sold in England where the local people changed the pronunciation to *tawdry.* The quality of the scarves, which at first was good, deteriorated when they were mass produced for the peasant trade.
    a.   Marlene's *tawdry* taste in clothing was an embarrassment to her boyfriend.
    b.   The jewelry at Tiffany's can hardly be described as *tawdry.*

EXERCISES

I. Which Word Comes to Mind?

In each of the following, read the statement, then circle the word that comes to mind.

1. You want to rip into your neighbor for his bigoted remarks

   (philanderer, *philippic*, protean)

2. A newspaper editorial calls for us to send the fleet to intimidate a Caribbean country

   (*jingoism*, spoonerism, solecism)

3. All the girls wear pantsuits except Betsy who prefers dresses

   (*maverick*, saturnine, nemesis)

4. I heard of a scheme that would provide $10,000 for each American family

   (lothario, Pyrrhic victory, *quixotic*)

5. Everyone at the meeting was forced to change his or her mind in order to agree with the chairman's philosophy

   (tawdry, sybarite, *procrustean*)

6. It's unusual for a fashion editor to have such gaudy taste in jewelry

   (*tawdry*, saturnine, protean)

7. Mark boasted of having been engaged seven times

   (philippic, *lothario*, jingoist)

8. The singer was fond of saying he always did it his way

   (*maverick*, solecism, spoonerism)

9. Ted likes caviar and imported champagne

   (*sybarite*, nemesis, philanderer)

10. The senator blasted his opponent in a fiery speech

    (quixotic, procrustean, *philippic*)

II. True or False?

In the space provided, indicate whether each statement is true or false.

_T_ 1. No one welcomes a *Pyrrhic victory*.
_T_ 2. A *jingoist* is a hawk rather than a dove.
_F_ 3. "I don't know nothing" is a *spoonerism*.
_F_ 4. A *nemesis* is something like a jinx.
_F_ 5. Going along with the majority is a *maverick's* way.
_F F_ 6. A *tawdry* garment is tasteful.
_T_ 7. By Ed's *saturnine* expression, we knew that the news was bad.
_F_ 8. The prison diet of bread and water was in keeping with the *sybarite's* lifestyle.
_T_ 9. The class was shocked at the professor's use of a *solecism*.
_T_ 10. Placing a man on the moon was once considered a *quixotic* idea.

III. Fill in the Blank

Insert one of the new words in the proper space in each sentence below.

1. My cousin tried to diet, but desserts proved to be his __nemesis__.
2. Charley, a born __maverick__, always votes against the majority.
3. The usually level-headed Kyra came up with a __quixotic__ suggestion that was totally out of character.
4. Andrea thought she looked elegant, but we found her appearance to be __tawdry__.
5. At the end of a one-hour __philippic__ against taxes, the candidate received thunderous applause.
6. The __jingoist__ had contempt for anyone he thought lacked patriotic spirit.
7. After my tongue-tied __spoonerism__, I apologized to our hostess and left.
8. With fifty servants to wait on him, the Roman emperor was a true __sybarite__.
9. Considering himself a __lothario__, Uncle Don proposed to every widow in town.
10. Myrtle's __saturnine__ expression was the result of a chronic stomach condition.

IV. What's the Antonym?

Which of the new words is most nearly *opposite* in meaning to the one provided?

1. conformist __maverick__
2. eulogy __saturnine__ Phyrric Victory
3. tasteful __tawdry__
4. lively __saturnine__
5. practical __quixotic__
6. constant __protean__
7. faithful husband __philanderer__
8. conservative __procrustean__
9. political dove __jingoist__
10. democratic __jingoist__

V. Matching

Match the word in column A with its correct definition in column B by writing the letter of that definition in the space provided.

	A		B
C	1. jingoist	a.	interchange of initial sounds
J	2. lothario	b.	changeable
D	3. maverick	c.	super-patriot
G	4. nemesis	d.	nonconformist
I	5. philanderer	e.	impractical
N	6. philippic	f.	language error
M	7. procrustean	g.	retribution
B	8. protean	h.	fond of high living
L	9. Pyrrhic victory	i.	unfaithful lover
E	10. quixotic	j.	rake
O	11. saturnine	k.	gaudy
F	12. solecism	l.	too costly
A	13. spoonerism	m.	designed to secure conformity
H	14. sybarite	n.	bitter verbal attack
K	15. tawdry	o.	sluggish

Don Quixote = quixotic

Appearances and Attitudes (I)

What is the relationship of *bilious* to a body fluid?

Why might a *lachrymose* person need tissues?

Would you prefer a waiter who was *complaisant* or *churlish?*

Should we applaud or hiss *craven* actions?

Is it a good idea to submit your manuscript to a *captious* editor?

---

acidulous
avaricious
baleful
bellicose
bilious
bumptious
captious
churlish
complaisant
contrite
convivial
craven
debonair
dyspeptic
lachrymose

1. **acidulous** (ə-sij'-oo-ləs)—somewhat acid or sour.
   a. Joan's father took an *acidulous* view of her plans to get married.
   b. He is the kind of *acidulous* critic who hates every new book that is published.

2. **avaricious** (av-ə-rish'əs)—excessively greedy.
   a. The *avaricious* broker was prosecuted by the attorney general.
   b. In the first part of *A Christmas Carol,* Scrooge is portrayed as an *avaricious* employer.

3. **baleful** (bāl'-fəl)—deadly; sinister.
   a. I saw the *baleful* look on the gang leader's face, and I knew we were in for trouble.
   b. Overhead, the *baleful* clouds were announcing a storm's approach.

4. **bellicose** (bel'-ə-kōs)—warlike; of a quarrelsome nature.
   a. Although our landlord sometimes sounds *bellicose,* he is actually very soft-hearted.
   b. Our ambassador often has to ignore *bellicose* statements from the prime minister.

5. **bilious** (bil'-yəs) bad-tempered; bitter. It comes from the French word *bilis* ("bile"), the fluid secreted by the liver.
   a. Twenty years in his company's complaint department gave Ted a *bilious* attitude toward the public.
   b. I overlooked Cynthia's *bilious* remarks because I know that she is bad-tempered until she has had her morning coffee.

6. **bumptious** (bump'-shəs)—arrogant; disagreeably conceited.
   a. My uncle's *bumptious* personality has caused him to be fired from several good jobs.
   b. In his *bumptious* fashion, Mario felt that every girl was madly in love with him.

7. **captious** (kap'-shəs)—critical; quick to find fault; quibbling.
   a. I don't mind criticism from Professor Torres, but his *captious* comments about my term paper did not endear him to me.
   b. The gardeners hate to work for Mrs. Lyons because of her *captious* eye.

8. churlish (churl'-ish)—rude; surly. This adjective comes from "churl," the old word for a peasant.
   a. We were barred from the restaurant because some of our team members had behaved in a *churlish* fashion.
   b. Harry's allowance was cut off by his parents as punishment for his *churlish* table manners.

9. complaisant (kəm-plaʹzʹnt)—willing to please; tending to consent to others' wishes.
   a. Every employee at the state agency acts in an admirable, *complaisant* way.
   b. Uriah Heep adopted a *complaisant* pose as a cover-up for his hostility.

10. contrite (kən-trītʹ)—crushed in spirit by a feeling of guilt.
   a. Because Judge Dooly believed that the prisoner was *contrite,* he gave him a light sentence.
   b. When the fraternity members realized the horror of their actions, they were truly *contrite*.

11. convivial (kən-vivʹ-ē-əl)—festive; sociable.
   a. All of the shoppers contributed to the *convivial* atmosphere at the mall.
   b. New Orleans at Mardi Gras time is world-famous for its *convivial* qualities.

12. craven (kraʹ-vən)—cowardly.
   a. Even the most *craven* animal will turn courageous when its young are threatened.
   b. Lieutenant Rader's *craven* behavior under fire resulted in his court-martial.

13. debonair (deb-ə-nerʹ)—courteous, gracious and having a sophisticated charm; suave; urbane. In Old French the words were *de bon aire* ("of a good race or breed").
   a. Uncle Edward, with his top hat at a jaunty angle, was the model of a *debonair* gentleman.
   b. Driving up in a sporty foreign car, my brother impressed the neighbors with his *debonair* appearance.

14. dyspeptic (dis-pepʹ-tik)—grouchy; gloomy; a person who suffers from dyspepsia or indigestion.
   a. Eric's *dyspeptic* analysis of our chances for success was discouraging.
   b. Our local newspaper features two columnists—one with a *dyspeptic* viewpoint, the other with an incurable optimism.

15. lachrymose (lakʹ-rə-mōs)—sad; mournful; inclined to shed many tears.
   a. Most television soap operas have *lachrymose* themes.
   b. The funniest Ringling Brothers Circus clown has a *lachrymose* expression painted on his face.

EXERCISES

I. Which Word Comes to Mind?

In each of the following, read the statement, then circle the word that comes to mind.

   1. A defendant's attitude that impresses the jury

          (debonair, contrite, acidulous)

   2. An ill-tempered waiter

          (complaisant, craven, churlish)

3. Scrooge

   (baleful, avaricious, bumptious)

4. A person suffering from indigestion

   (dyspeptic, bellicose, captious)

5. An angry boss insulting his workers

   (lachrymose, bilious, convivial)

6. Someone with a chip on his or her shoulder

   (bellicose, craven, complaisant)

7. A tearful movie

   (captious, lachrymose, churlish)

8. Stealing from the blind man

   (bumptious, craven, dyspeptic)

9. After the prank, the college boys apologize

   (contrite, convivial, bilious)

10. Giving someone a hotfoot as a practical joke

   (churlish, debonair, acidulous)

II. True or False?

In the space provided, indicate whether each statement is true or false.

F 1. A *craven* leader inspires respect in his followers.
T 2. Citizens are pleased to see a criminal who is *contrite*.
T 3. *Captious* people often split hairs.
T 4. It's difficult for a gawky 14-year-old to look *debonair*.
F 5. By displaying proper etiquette, one can expect to be praised for one's *churlishness*.
T 6. The children's *lachrymose* behavior at the funeral was understandable.
T 7. Arthur's *bumptious* remarks at the dinner embarrassed his roommate.
F 8. We always maintained a *bellicose* relationship with our good neighbor, Canada.
T 9. The *acidulous* reviews led the producers to close the play after two performances.
T 10. The tone at most New Years parties is quite *convivial*.

III. Fill in the Blank

Insert one of the new words in the proper space in each sentence below.

1. The entire audience was sobbing as the curtain came down on the _lachrymose_ ending.
2. Some patriots labeled the refusal to join the army as a _churlish_ action.
3. I hate dining with _captious_ people who criticize everything the chef prepares.
4. Our normally peaceful terrier turns _bellicose_ whenever the letter carrier arrives.
5. The choral singing and the beautiful decorations lent a _convivial_ flavor to our party.
   debonair

6. The manufacturer's _avaricious_ intentions led him to jail.

7. Benjy's _convivial_ attitude endeared him to his teammates.

8. At game time, the nervous coach displayed a _craven_ demeanor.

9. Rocco's _baleful_ glare intimidated me.

10. I like to tease _bumptious_ characters who are swollen by their imagined importance.

IV. What's the Antonym?

Which of the new words is most nearly *opposite* in meaning to the one provided?

1. peaceful   _bellicose_
2. happy   _lachrymose_
3. congenial   _baleful_
4. contrary   _complaisant_
5. polite   _churlish_
6. sweet-tempered   _bilious_
7. humble   _bumptious_
8. well-mannered   _churlish_
9. heroic   _craven_
10. charitable   _avaricious_

V. Matching

Match the word in column A with its correct definition in column B by writing the letter of that definition in the space provided.

A	B
____ 1. acidulous	a. arrogant
____ 2. avaricious	b. cowardly
____ 3. baleful	c. surly, rude
____ 4. bellicose	d. sour
____ 5. bilious	e. greedy
____ 6. bumptious	f. festive
____ 7. captious	g. grouchy
____ 8. churlish	h. sinister
____ 9. complaisant	i. sad
____ 10. contrite	j. overwhelmed with guilt
____ 11. convivial	k. courteous
____ 12. craven	l. polite
____ 13. debonair	m. bad-tempered
____ 14. dyspeptic	n. critical
____ 15. lachrymose	o. warlike

Words About Groups

Does *genealogy* have a connection to the gene pool?

Are we likely to find *esprit de corps* where there is *camaraderie?*

What is the connection between *liaison* and *ligature?*

Why wouldn't you publish the names of the members of your *cabal?*

Where are we more likely to find a *cortege*—at the florist's or at a funeral?

---

cabal
camaraderie
caste
clandestine
cortege
detente
echelon
ecumenical
elite
esprit de corps
genealogy
hierarchy
hobnob
liaison
rapprochement

1. **cabal** (kə-bal')—a clique; a small group joined in a secret intrigue; a conspiracy. This French word was formed from the initials of Charles II's ministers (Clifford, Arlington, Buckingham, Ashley, Lauderdale); *cabal* ultimately derives from the Hebrew word *qabbalah,* which referred to a mystical interpretation of the Scriptures.
   a. The *cabal* met to formulate plans for the overthrow of the Bolivian government.
   b. When the *cabal's* membership list was disclosed, it put an end to their activities.

2. **camaraderie** (käm'-ə-räd'-ər-ē)—comradeship; good fellowship. Two soldiers sharing the same room (in German, *kammer*) usually developed a loyal and warm friendship. The Communist Party adopted the word *comrade* to denote a fellow member.
   a. A beautiful *camaraderie* developed among the actors in the cast of *Cats.*
   b. The good fellowship award was given to the beauty pageant contestant who contributed most to the *camaraderie* of all the girls.

3. **caste** (kast)—a distinct social class or system. Hindu society is traditionally divided into four major hereditary *castes,* each class separated from the others by restrictions in marriage and occupation.
   a. Satindra was a member of the untouchable *caste.*
   b. The union leader spoke angrily about a *caste* system at the factory.

4. **clandestine** (klān-des'tin)—concealed, secret.
   a. F.B.I. agents were taping the proceedings of the *clandestine* meeting.
   b. When the *clandestine* arrangements were uncovered, everyone was embarrassed.

5. **cortege** (kôr-tezh')—a group of attendants accompanying a person; a ceremonial procession. It is not surprising that *cortege* is related to court, a place where followers and ceremonies abound.
   a. The funeral *cortege* of the Spanish dictator is said to have stretched for two miles.
   b. Some actors never travel without a *cortege* of agents to publicize their every word and deed.

6. **detente** (dā-tänt')—a relaxing or easing, especially of international tension. After the Cold War years following World War II, the U.S. embarked on a policy of closer ties with Russia; hence was born the policy of *detente.*

    a.   With the help of the United Nations, the two belligerent countries reached a *detente*.
    b.   Even in our personal relationships, we can often accomplish more with *detente* than with obstinacy.

7. **echelon** (esh'-ə-län)—a level of command or authority or rank; a steplike formation of ships, troops, or planes. Coming to English through several languages, the word *echelon* has descended a ladder starting with the Latin word *scale,* which indeed means ladder, and explains why we still "scale a ladder."
    a.   The command *echelon* was unaware that the fighting troops were being attacked.
    b.   Starting at the lowest *echelon,* the dynamic Ms. Steinem worked her way to the top of her profession.

8. **ecumenical** (ek-yoo-men'-i-k'l)—universal; general; fostering Christian unity throughout the world. The idea of *ecumenism,* as well as the spirit of brotherhood, was fostered by the far-reaching policies of Pope John XXIII (1958–63).
    a.   The influence of Pope John's *ecumenical* pronouncements is still being felt today.
    b.   We must work not merely for our selfish interests but for the *ecumenical* welfare.

9. **elite** (i-lēt')—the best or most skilled members of a given social group. The word is related to *elect* and suggests that some people are born with "a silver spoon in their mouth" or, at least, are entitled to special privileges. *Elite* is also used as an adjective.
    a.   The *elite* of the city teams vied for the honor of being chosen to travel to Cuba.
    b.   I attended an *elite* gathering of authors and was much impressed by the level of their language.

10. **esprit de corps** (es-prē'-də-kôr')—a sense of union and of common interests and responsibilities. The French expression literally means "spirit of feeling as one body." It implies not only a camaraderie but a sense of pride or honor shared by those involved in an undertaking.
    a.   Their coach established an *esprit de corps* that was powerful enough to catapult the team to the Rose Bowl.
    b.   Were it not for the amazing *esprit de corps* among the surviving members of the patrol, they would never have been able to accomplish their mission.

11. **genealogy** (jē'-nē-äl'-ə-jē)—lineage; science of family descent. Though our hereditary character is transmitted through genes in our chromosomes, that does not assure us that our *genealogy* has provided us with the most desirable traits. Much can and does happen as the generations pass.
    a.   The young African-American man proudly displayed his *genealogical* chart, which linked him with African royalty.
    b.   Of course, if we trace our *genealogy* back far enough, we will find that we all share some common ancestors.

12. **hierarchy** (hī-ə-rär'-kē)—a group of persons or things arranged in order rank, or grade; a system of church government by clergymen in graded ranks. The Greek word *hierarkhes* meant "high priest." From there it was a small step to the designation of the entire church leadership as a *hierarchy.* With the loss of temporal power by the church after the Middle Ages, the word now refers to any arrangement by authority or position.
    a.   The political *hierarchy* in our country begins with the voter in the polling booth.
    b.   To learn the operation of a newspaper, it is necessary to examine the entire *hierarchy* of jobs from copyboy to editor.

13. **hobnob** (häb'-näb')—to associate on very friendly terms. The title of the novel *To Have and Have Not* is an exact translation of the original meaning of *hobnob.* This word was formed by a combination of the Old English words *habban* ("to have") and *navban* ("not to have"). The modern meaning suggests the egalitarian idea of friendship not based on one's possessions.
    a.   Juanita's vivacious temperament allowed her to *hobnob* with people in all walks of life.
    b.   Calvin's parents refused to let him *hobnob* with the worst elements in the neighborhood.

14. liaison (lē'-ə-zän)—the contact maintained between military or naval units in order to undertake concerted action; a similar connection between the units of any organization; an illicit relationship between a man and a woman. This word is a cousin to *ligature,* a connection on the physical level similar to the connection made on an informational level by a *liaison.*

a. The elected sophomore served as a *liaison* between the council and his class.

b. Having been appointed chief *liaison* officer, Colonel Marks assumed responsibility for the flow of information.

15. rapprochement (ra-prōsh'-män)—a reestablishing of cordial relations. If there is to be an end to war, people and nations must learn to meet each other, to approach each other on common grounds. That is what this word implies, a coming together in friendship and trust.

a. After months of secret negotiations, a *rapprochement* was reached between the warring factions.

b. Doctor Welby attempted to bring about a *rapprochement* between mother and son.

EXERCISES

I. Which Word Comes to Mind?

In each of the following, read the statement, then circle the word that comes to mind.

1. The superpowers agree to work together on questions of world trade.

(cabal, echelon, rapprochement)

2. A young man breaks the engagement because his fiancee cannot afford a dowry

(caste, liaison, hierarchy)

3. Firemen risk their lives to rescue a trapped buddy

(cortege, camaraderie, genealogy)

4. He associates informally with our town's high society

(detente, clandestine, hobnob)

5. The sermon ended with a call for universal brotherhood and recognition of individual worth

(ecumenical, elite, esprit de corps)

6. A funeral procession of hundreds of mourners

(cortege, clandestine, cabal)

7. Police arrest a group of men who were plotting an assassination

(cabal, rapprochement, detente)

8. You receive an offer of a framed history of your ancestors

(echelon, genealogy, caste)

9. Speaking a foreign language made the French student invaluable as a link between our two countries

(esprit de corps, liaison, hierarchy)

10. Stepping in between the two warring factions, we got them to agree to a cease-fire

(elite, hobnob, detente)

II. True or False?

In the space provided, indicate whether each statement is true or false.

_____ 1. The *cabal* holds a public forum to discuss the issue.
_____ 2. *Detente* involves risks and compromises by both sides.
_____ 3. A member of the *elite* feels that the world is his oyster.
_____ 4. *Esprit de corps* denotes a stronger bond than *camaraderie.*
_____ 5. A *liaison* serves a purpose similar to that of a go-between.
_____ 6. The gossip columnist frequently *hobnobs* with move stars.
_____ 7. We paid an expert to research our family's *genealogy.*
_____ 8. Entering into a *rapprochement,* the cousins continued their bitter fight.
_____ 9. The producer wanted a young *caste* for his new musical.
_____ 10. Arnold joined his company's *hierarchy* when he became a vice-president.

III. Fill in the Blank

Insert one of the new words in the proper space in each sentence below.

1. At the highest _____ in our company sit the founder and his two trusted advisers.

2. We formed a _____ group to avoid needless duplication among the three committees.

3. The former society reporter used to _____ with the rich and famous.

4. Baseball managers strive to develop a winning _____ in their locker room lectures.

5. Laden with floral displays, the funeral _____ wound its way into the cemetery.

6. All members of the failed _____ were arrested last night.

7. I picked up the phone in order to bring about a _____ with my twin sister.

8. A study of our _____ revealed our descent from Spanish royalty.

9. Promoted to cardinal, the bishop became part of the church's _____ .

10. As a member of the _____ group, Hedley was invited everywhere.

IV. What's the Antonym?

Which of the new words is most nearly *opposite* in meaning to the one provided?

1. commoners   _____

2. dissension   _____

3. hostility   _____

4. parochial   _____

5. withdraw   _____

6. breaking off   _____

7. disorganization   _____

8. equality   _____

9. ill will   _____

10. open   _____

V. Matching

Match the word in column A with its correct definition in column B by writing the letter of that definition in the space provided.

A	*B*
____ 1. cabal	a. resumption of harmonious relations
____ 2. camaraderie	b. arrangement by rank
____ 3. caste	c. pal around
____ 4. cortege	d. conspiracy
____ 5. clandestine	e. family tree
____ 6. detente	f. worldwide
____ 7. echelon	g. most qualified, best
____ 8. ecumenical	h. procession
____ 9. elite	i. connection
____ 10. esprit de corps	j. steplike formation of troops
____ 11. genealogy	k. secret
____ 12. hierarchy	l. class system
____ 13. hobnob	m. relaxation of tension
____ 14. liaison	n. group loyalty
____ 15. rapprochement	o. friendship

Sounds Italian

Which is the faster tempo—*allegretto* or *adagio?*

Is *fortissimo* a title given to a high-ranking officer?

Does *libretto* refer to the words or the music?

Which requires more than one note, a *crescendo* or an *arpeggio?*

Which indicates musical skill—*bravura, intaglio,* or *imbroglio?*

---

adagio
arpeggio
bravura
contralto
crescendo
falsetto
fortissimo
imbroglio
intaglio
largo
libretto
limbo
salvo
staccato
vendetta
virago

1. **adagio** (ə-dä'-jō)—slowly, in music. The plural, *adagios,* refers to a slow movement in music or a slow ballet dance requiring skillful balancing.
    a. The second movement of the symphony was played in *adagio* tempo.
    b. The ballerina executed the *adagios* in the pas de deux with exquisite grace and beauty.

2. **arpeggio** (ärpej'-ē-ō, -pej'-ō)—the playing of the tones of a chord in rapid succession rather than simultaneously.
    a. The sound of the *arpeggio* simulates the music of a harp.
    b. The lively composition concluded with a series of crashing *arpeggios.*

3. **bravura** (brə-vyoor'-ə)—in music, a florid passage requiring great skill and spirit in the performer; a display of daring; a brilliant performance (used as a noun and as an adjective).
    a. Verdi is noted for his stunning *bravuras.*
    b. The more dangerous the stunts, the more the crowd cheered the *bravura* performances.

4. **contralto** (kən-träl'-tō)—the lowest female voice or part, between a soprano and a tenor; a woman having such a voice.
    a. The famous singer had a rich and powerful *contralto* voice.
    b. Though sopranos are the traditional prima donnas of the music world, many people prefer the fullness and melodiousness of the lower-pitched *contralto* voice.

5. **crescendo** (krə-shen'-dō, -sen'-dō)—a gradual increase in the volume or intensity of sound; a music passage played in *crescendo. Crescendo* is also used as a verb.
    a. The natives' chants *crescendoed* to a piercing frenzy.
    b. The gale reached its *crescendo* at dawn.

6. **falsetto** (fôl-set'-ō)—a typically male singing voice, marked by artificially produced tones in an upper register that go beyond the voice's normal range.
    a. The thief, speaking in *falsetto,* was able to convince the maid to open the door.
    b. The cantor's skill at a sustained *falsetto* won the admiration of the congregants.

7. **fortissimo** (fôr-tis'-ə-mō)—a very loud passage, sound or tone. The word is also used as an adverb.
   a. The "1812 Overture" ends with a *fortissimo* of crashing cymbals, rolling drums and roaring cannons.
   b. The deafening *fortissimo* of the storm's passage was followed by a silence broken only by the melancholy dripping of raindrops from the tree branches.

8. **imbroglio** (im-brōl'-yō)—a confused or difficult situation; a confused heap or tangle. The original Latin word describes the situation best—*in broglio* ("entangled in a bush").
   a. The derelict sat beside the *imbroglio* comprised of all his meager belongings.
   b. Accepting two dates for the same evening placed Nanette in an *imbroglio* she could not easily resolve.

9. **largo** (lär'-gō)—in a slow, solemn manner (a direction in music); a slow, broad movement (noun).
   a. The music depicting the army's retreat was played in *largo*.
   b. The *largo* movement began with the echoes of hope and ended in the anguished tones of despair.

10. **libretto** (li-bret'-ō)—the text of an opera or other dramatic musical work. It is the Italian diminutive of *libro* ("book").
    a. In the most famous team that produced light opera, Gilbert wrote the *librettos* and Sullivan the music.
    b. The *librettos* of many popular musicals would be quickly forgotten were it not for the memorable music they are wedded to.

11. **limbo** (limb'-ō)—a state of neglect; an intermediate place. Souls that are kept from heaven through circumstance such as a lack of baptism are said to be in limbo.
    a. Hal's application to Yale was in *limbo* because it was incomplete.
    b. Uncertain funding for the league kept the teams in *limbo*.

12. **salvo** (sal'-vō)—a simultaneous discharge of firearms; a sudden outburst of cheers or the like. It is not surprising to find that words like *salutation, salutary, salve,* and *salvation* are related to *salvo* since the Latin *salve* ("hail"), and *salvus* ("safe or well"), form the ancestry of both strands of meaning.
    a. The new play received *salvos* of praise from the leading critics.
    b. The continuous *salvos* from the enemy artillery failed to dislodge the tenacious defenders from their mountaintop positions.

13. **staccato** (stə-kä'-tō)—music performed with a crisp, sharp attack to simulate rests between successive tones; composed of abrupt, distinct, emphatic parts or sounds. This word is from the Old French word *destachier* ("detach") and is contrasted with *legato*.
    a. From the distance, we heard the *staccato* beat of rain on a tin roof.
    b. The *staccato* click of Miss Benton's heels sounded on the tile floor as she hurried to answer the door.

14. **vendetta** (ven-det'-ə)—blood feud; a prolonged feud marked by bitter hostility. This is the Italian word for revenge and is related to *vindicate,* our meaning for which is "to avenge."
    a. The *vendetta* between the McCoys and the Hatfields became a tradition of American mountain folklore.
    b. The *vendetta* to defend the family honor has become outmoded with the loosening of family ties.

15. **virago** (və-rä'-gō)—a scold; a noisy, tyrannizing woman.
    a. Quiet and demure, Janet turned out to be a genuine *virago* after the marriage.
    b. Shakespeare's Katherine was the *virago* who met her match in "The Taming of the Shrew."

EXERCISES

I. Which Word Comes to Mind?

In each of the following, read the statement, then circle the word that comes to mind.

1. A musical direction

    (largo, falsetto, contralto)

2. A volley of rockets

    (salvo, adagio, limbo)

3. An embarrassing situation

    (fortissimo, libretto, imbroglio)

4. A scrawny boy seeking to get even with a bully

    (vendetta, bravura, arpeggio)

5. Machine-gun fire

    (crescendo, virago, staccato)

6. I'm going to get you for that

    (largo, vendetta, fortissimo)

7. The story of *Carmen*

    (libretto, arpeggio, falsetto)

8. Sudden loud music drowned out our conversation

    (fortissimo, staccato, limbo)

9. A female singer with a surprisingly deep voice

    (bravura, falsetto, contralto)

10. A scolding woman

    (imbroglio, virago, adagio)

II. True or False?

In the space provided, indicate whether each statement is true or false.

  ✓ 1. A *contralto* has a higher-pitched voice than a soprano.
  ✗ 2. If your case is in *limbo*, it is being taken care of.
  ✗ 3. A man singing in *falsetto* has probably hit a wrong note.
  ✗ 4. A *virago* is difficult to get along with.
  ✓ 5. A participant in a *vendetta* tends to harbor unreasonable hatred.
  ✓ 6. A sergeant barked out his commands in *staccato* fashion.
  ✓ 7. With a *salvo* of fireworks, the celebration ended.
  ✗ 8. I requested a *largo* tempo because the music was too slow and solemn.
  ✓ 9. Applause for the winning candidate reached a *crescendo.*
  ✓ 10. Parents were called to school to settle the *imbroglio* that had developed between their children.

III. Fill in the Blank

Insert one of the new words in the proper space in each sentence below.

1. Mr. Evans, our guidance counselor, was helpful in resolving the _vendetta_
2. The _bravura_ rendition of the difficult étude was highly praised by the music critics.
3. Reports from the battle zone were interrupted by _staccato_ bursts of gunfire.
4. The _libretto_ of the new opera failed to match the quality of the music.
5. With a _arpeggio_ of noise, the seventy-six trombones concluded their presentation.
6. The ugly _vendetta_ between the families ended in violence.
7. At the grave, an honor guard fired off a rifle _salvo_ .
8. Elsa purposely raised her normal voice to an artificial _cresendo_
9. Spain's foremost matador put on a _bravura_ performance.
10. The _staccato_ commands from headquarters were brief, fast, and furious.

IV. What's the Antonym?

Which of the new words is most nearly *opposite* in meaning to the one provided?

1. quickly — _largo_
2. soprano —
3. friendly relations — _vendetta_
4. diminuendo —
5. softly — _fortissimo_
6. smooth — _staccato_
7. decrease in volume — _crescendo_
8. basso —
9. even-tempered woman — _virago_
10. a resolved situation — _imbroglio_

V. Matching

Match the word in column A with its correct definition in column B by writing the letter of that definition in the space provided.

	A		B
F	1. adagio	a.	spirited or showy passage in music
O	2. arpeggio	b.	predicament
A	3. bravura	c.	a mounting in intensity
H	4. contralto	d.	disconnected
C	5. crescendo	e.	state of neglect
D	6. falsetto	f.	slowly
N	7. fortissimo	g.	slow and solemn
B	8. imbroglio	h.	lower than soprano
G	9. largo	i.	salute
J	10. libretto	j.	text of an opera
K	11. limbo	k.	artificial tones
I	12. salvo	l.	a scold
M	13. staccato	m.	bitter quarrel
M	14. vendetta	n.	extremely loud
L	15. virago	o.	tones of a chord played in rapid succession

SOME CRESCENDO!

Jobs and Professions

Would you resent being sent to see an *alienist*?

Is a *lapidary* similar to a dromedary?

What's the proper name for an eye specialist?

Where would you go with a bad case of acne?

In what way does an *internist* differ from an intern?

---

alienist
amanuensis
beadle
charlatan
cosmetologist
dermatologist
entomologist
graphologist
internist
lapidary
ophthalmologist
ornithologist
osteopath
pharyngologist
physiologist

1. **alienist** (āl'-yən-ist)—a doctor who specializes in mental disease. Alienation, referring to mental derangement or insanity, comes from the Latin word, *alienato* ("separation"). The question, "Have you taken leave of your senses?" shows the relationship to *alienist*.
   a. The defense lawyer hired an *alienist* to testify to his client's insanity.
   b. Dr. Fowler, an *alienist,* is annoyed with people who confuse his title with the word alien.

2. **amanuensis** (ə-man-yoo-wen'-sis)—secretary; one who copies something. It comes from the Latin *manus* ("hand") and *ensis* ("relating to"). In ancient times a scribe was known as an *amanuensis.*
   a. When illiteracy was widespread, people used the services of an *amanuensis* to write letters for them.
   b. My secretary likes to tease people by telling them she is a professional *amanuensis.*

3. **beadle** (bē'-d'l) minor official. *Beadle* comes from an Old French word that meant "messenger"—a man who preceded a procession. The functionary carrying a mace (symbolic club) at the head of a university procession is a *beadle.*
   a. Mr. Bumble in Dickens' *Oliver Twist* is the most famous *beadle* in literature.
   b. When the president arrived to address the joint meeting of Congress, he was ushered in by a pompous *beadle.*

4. **charlatan** (shar'lə–tən)—a quack; one who is not what he claims to be.
   a. The "doctor" proved to be a *charlatan*, and was sent to jail.
   b. It's amazing that so many intelligent people were taken in by the *charlatan.*

5. **cosmetologist** (käz-mə-täl'-ə-jist)—an expert in cosmetics. When a woman applies cosmetics she is putting herself in order. The Latin word *cosmos* means order in the sense of an orderly universe. Since such order was equated with beauty, when a *cosmetologist* helps to apply makeup, she is maintaining the classical connection between the two.
   a. Our school hired a *cosmetologist* to teach the girls how to look beautiful.
   b. It was ironic that the least attractive woman in the room was a *cosmetologist.*

6. **dermatologist** (dur-mə-täl'-ə-jist)—a doctor who specializes in skin problems. From the Greek *derma* ("skin"). Your epidermis is your outer layer of skin.
   a. Dr. Zweben chose to be a *dermatologist* because patients rarely die of their skin ailments.
   b. Harold went to a *dermatologist* to investigate the strange discoloration on his arm.

7. **entomologist** (en-tə-mäl'-ə-jist)—a specialist in the study of insects. In Greek, *entomos* means "cut up." Insects' bodies appear to be divided into sections or "cut up."
   a. My professor invited an *entomologist* to lecture on "Roaches I Have Known."
   b. Eddie loved to play with insects when he was a kid, and interestingly enough, he grew up to be an *entomologist*.

8. **graphologist** (gra-fäl'-ə-jist)—a handwriting analyst. In Greek, *graphos* means "to write." *Graphologists* are often hired as entertainers today, analyzing the handwriting of guests at a party and describing their character traits and aptitudes.
   a. Because my handwriting tends to slope upward, *graphologists* say I'm an optimist.
   b. Even though Rachel's own handwriting is poor, it didn't stop her from becoming a *graphologist*.

9. **internist** (in-tur'-nist)—doctor who specializes in internal medicine. In Latin, *internus* means "inward." *Internists* are noted as diagnosticians, not surgeons.
   a. The *internist* in our medical group is loath to prescribe drugs.
   b. Charles consulted a Park Avenue *internist* to find out why he was having pain.

10. **lapidary** (lap'-ə-der-ē)—an expert in precious stones. Julius Caesar used the word *lapis* when he meant stone. Lapidaries cut, polish, and engrave stones.
    a. After the *lapidary* had washed the mud off the stone, he realized its true value.
    b. "You've got rocks in your head," joked the *lapidary's* neighbor.

11. **ophthalmologist** (äf-thal-mäl'-ə-jist)—a doctor who treats eyes and their diseases. From the Greek *ophthalmos* ("eye"). Oculist is a synonym for *ophthalmologist*. An optometrist prescribes eyeglasses; an optician makes or sells eyeglasses.
    a. It took an *ophthalmologist* to discover that Aunt Rose had a detached retina.
    b. Ethel's *ophthalmologist* saved her from blindness by treating her glaucoma promptly.

12. **ornithologist** (ôr-nə-thäl'-ə-jist)—an expert in the branch of zoology dealing with birds. It is from the Greek *ornis* ("bird").
    a. Audubon didn't have a degree as an *ornithologist,* but his paintings of birds displayed his vast knowledge of them.
    b. The Museum of Natural History hired an *ornithologist* to supervise their bird displays.

13. **osteopath** (äs'-tē-ə-path)—one who treats ailments by placing pressure on bones and nerves. From the Greek *osteo* ("bone") and *pathos* ("suffering").
    a. Uncle Henry always said that an *osteopath* was a respectable chiropractor.
    b. By manipulating my son's bones, the *osteopath* attempted to reduce his fever.

14. **pharyngologist** (far-in-gäl'-ə-jist)—a doctor who specializes in diseases of the pharynx, the cavity of the alimentary canal leading from the mouth and nasal passages to the larynx and esophagus.
    a. During a routine examination, the *pharyngologist* discovered that the heavy smoker had a possible mouth cancer.
    b. I laughingly accused the *pharyngologist* of putting his foot in his mouth.

15. **physiologist** (fiz-ē-äl'-ə-jist)—a biologist who deals with the functions and vital processes of living organisms. It comes from the Greek *physis* ("nature") and *logos* ("discourse").
    a. Alvin, our school's Science Award winner, is planning to be a *physiologist*.
    b. After working with laboratory mice, I decided to become a *physiologist*.

EXERCISES

I. Which Word Comes to Mind?

In each of the following, read the statement, then circle the word that comes to mind.

1. You need treatment for a tennis elbow

    (alienist, ophthalmologist, *osteopath*)

2. Someone may have forged your signature

    (*graphologist*, cosmetologist, lapidary)

3. "Gnats to you!"

    (*entomologist*, charlatan, pharyngologist)

4. Teenagers frequently suffer from acne

    (beadle, *dermatologist*, amanuensis)

5. "Hey, man, you're for the birds!"

    (*ornithologist*, internist, physiologist)

6. A psychiatrist testifies at a trial

    (graphologist, beadle, *alienist*)

7. You go for a routine physical examination

    (charlatan, internist, *amanuensis*)

8. A sapphire is being appraised by an expert

    (*lapidary*, ornithologist, graphologist)

9. Something got stuck in your throat

    (*pharyngologist*, cosmetologist, dermatologist)

10. Test for glaucoma

    (ornithologist, *ophthalmologist*, physiologist)

II. True or False?

In the space provided, indicate whether each statement is true or false.

_____ 1. An *alienist* can give you an opinion about someone's emotional stability.
_____ 2. X-rays are usually employed by a competent *amanuensis*.
_____ 3. The *lapidary* knew that the opals would make a great necklace.
_____ 4. If you have blurred vision, you should consult an *ophthalmologist*.
_____ 5. All doctors are abvious *charlatans*.
_____ 6. An *osteopath* is more similar to a chiropractor than he is to a physiologist.
_____ 7. Estée Lauder, Helena Rubenstein, and Max Factor deal with *cosmetologists*.
_____ 8. You seek out a *dermatologist* to analyze your handwriting.
_____ 9. A competent *amanuensis* is worth a great deal to a busy executive.
_____ 10. An *ornithologist,* you might say, is for the birds.

III. Fill in the Blank

Insert one of the new words in the proper space in each sentence below.

1. The expensive mascara was recommended by a trained _cosmetologist_
2. An _entomologist_ was hired as a technical advisor for the film *The Grasshopper Giants*.
3. To relieve my chronic back pain, I consulted an _osteopath_
4. Our talkative parrot was personally trained by a(an) _ornithologist_
5. Harold's _dermatologist_ warned him to stay out of the sun to avoid skin cancer.
6. My little brother was taken to a _laryngologist_ when he complained of trouble swallowing.
7. We hired a _lapidary_ from Tiffany's to cut the diamond expertly.
8. Detailed testimony from a(an) _physiologist_ convinced the jury that the defendant had been temporarily insane.
9. A _graphologist_ entertained at my cousin's party, analyzing everyone's handwriting.
10. The tear in Martha's retina was diagnosed by a(an) _ophthalmologist_

IV. Extra Letters

In each of the vocabulary words below there is an extra letter. Put all the extra letters together and you will be able to spell out a word taught in a previous lesson. Its meaning is "slowly."

cosmetoalogist   alienist
beaddle   graphrologist
lapsidary   entotomologist

V. Matching

Match the word in column A with its correct definition in column B by writing the letter of that definition in the space provided.

	A		B
6	1. alienist	a.	beauty expert
M	2. amanuensis	b.	quack
H	3. beadle	c.	handwriting expert
B	4. charlatan	d.	psychiatrist
A	5. cosmetologist	e.	stone cutter
F	6. dermatologist	f.	skin specialist
J	7. entomologist	g.	eye specialist
C	8. graphologist	h.	minor official
L	9. internist	i.	expert on birds
E	10. lapidary	j.	knows about insects
K	11. ophthalmologist	k.	manipulates bones and nerves
I	12. ornithologist	l.	doctor of internal medicine
G	13. osteopath	m.	biologist who studies vital functions
N	14. pharyngologist	n.	treats diseases of the pharynx
D	15. physiologist	o.	secretary

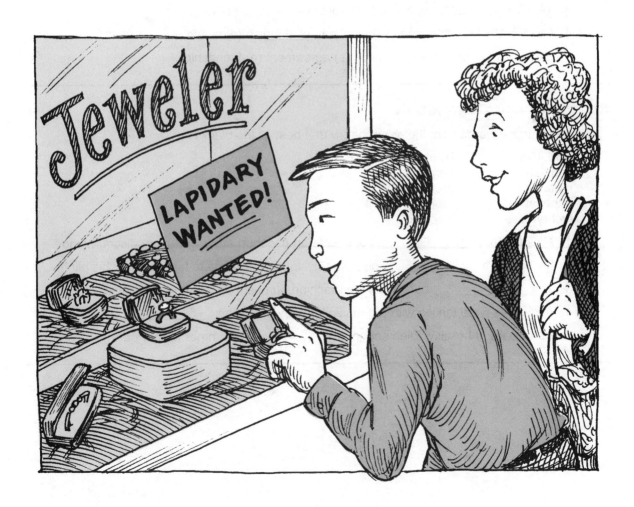

Unit I
(LESSONS 1–5)

Mini Review

I.   Antonyms

Circle the word that most nearly expresses the *opposite* meaning of the word in capital letters.

1. MAVERICK: (a) dynamo (b) conformist (c) steed (d) illusionist

2. SATURNINE: (a) dramatic (b) analytical (c) upbeat (d) rebellious

3. BELLICOSE: (a) rigid (b) peaceful (c) flexible (d) dormant

4. CRAVEN: (a) complacent (b) grasping (c) scholarly (d) heroic

5. ELITE: (a) athletic (b) sickly (c) ordinary (d) talented

II.   Synonyms

Circle the word that most nearly expresses the *same* meaning as the word printed in capital letters.

1. VENDETTA: (a) terror (b) feud (c) religion (d) miracle

2. AMANUENSIS: (a) psychiatrist (b) composer (c) director (d) secretary

3. TAWDRY: (a) gaudy (b) sinister (c) troublesome (d) pensive

4. DEBONAIR (a) lightheaded (b) practical (c) sluggish (d) suave

5. CABAL: (a) conspiracy (b) tension (c) agreement (d) friendship

III.   Sentence Completion

Select those words from the group below that best fill the blanks.

acidulous	libretto
churlish	nemesis
hierarchy	protean
internist	rapprochement
lachrymose	staccato

1. Miss Moore's _____ comments on my short story were very discouraging.

2. My brother's _____ plea was designed to get me to feel sorry for his plight.

3. The _____ burst from the machine gun sent us scurrying for cover.

4. Audiences were thrilled with the music but they hated the _____ .

5. After years of hostility, Ellen sought a _____ with her former partner.

Mythology (I)

Does a *Cassandra* speak the truth?

Is a *bacchanal* a wedding song or a riotous feast?

Why would one feel safe with a *palladium?*

What was *Narcissus'* undoing?

What color is *iridescent?*

Adonis
aegis
bacchanal
Cassandra
cornucopia
cupidity
erotic
herculean
hydra
iridescent
narcissism
odyssey
Olympian
palladium
phoenix

1. **Adonis** (ə-dän'-is)—an exceptionally handsome young man; a plant with solitary red or yellow flowers. Adonis was beloved by both Aphrodite, the goddess of love, and Persephone, the queen of the dead. He was killed by a boar in a hunting expedition and from his life's blood sprang up a crimson flower.
    a. Brad Pitt was considered an *Adonis* of the film world.
    b. Though he was once the *Adonis* of the Broadway stage, Johnny found his popularity short-lived.

2. **aegis** (ē'-jis)—sponsorship, protection. In Greek mythology the aegis was the shield of Zeus, lent to him by Athena.
    a. The science fair was staged under the *aegis* of Microsoft.
    b. We felt relieved to learn that the school trip would be under the *aegis* of the Parents Association.

3. **bacchanal** (bak'-ə-n'l)—a follower of Bacchus (Greek, Dionysus), the god of wine; a drunken reveler; an orgy. Early Greek drama developed in connection with the festival honoring this god.
    a. The *bacchanal* lasted into the late hours of the night.
    b. The *bacchanalian* scene in the play was so realistic the audience began to wonder what was really in the wine glasses.

4. **Cassandra** (kə-san'-dre)—a daughter of King Priam and Queen Hecuba of Troy who had the gift of prophecy but was cursed by Apollo so that her prophecies, though true, were fated never to be believed; one who prophesies doom or disaster. The Trojans thought Cassandra was insane and disregarded her predictions. Among these were the revelation that Troy would be destroyed if Paris went to Sparta, and that there were armed Greeks in the Wooden Horse. If either of these prophecies had been heeded, Troy would have been saved.
    a. The general said, "If we remain militarily strong, we need not be concerned with the *Cassandras* who see only tragedy."
    b. Since Marge had ignored her work all term, it took no *Cassandra* to predict her inevitable failure.

5. **cornucopia** (kôr-ne-kō'-pē-ə)—abundance; horn of plenty. Named after the horn of the goat Amalthea that suckled the infant Zeus, the horn is always full of food and drink in endless supply.
    a. The people of the Third World still look for a *cornucopia* of riches that will end hunger and suffering in their lands.
    b. The spendthrift cannot expect a *cornucopia* of merchandise to cater to his fanciful tastes.

6. **cupidity** (kyoō-pid'-i-tē)—excessive desire for wealth. In Roman mythology Cupid was the god of love, represented by a winged boy with a bow and arrow. It has come to mean "avarice."
   a. The company president was accused of *cupidity* that led to outright theft.
   b. What started out as honest ambition for Harry later became out-and-out *cupidity*.

7. **erotic** (i-rät'-ik)—concerning sexual love and desire; amatory. Eros was the Greek god of love.
   a. *Erotic* literature is no longer subject to the censor's pen.
   b. Genuine love between a man and a woman involves respect and regard for one another that go far beyond mere *erotic* sensations.

8. **herculean** (hur-kyə-lē'-ən, hur-kyoō'-lē-ən)—tremendously difficult and demanding; resembling Hercules in size, power, or courage. Hercules was the son of Zeus and Alcmene who won immortality by performing Twelve Labors demanded by the jealous Hera.
   a. Digging the tunnel was a *herculean* task.
   b. With *herculean* courage, the wounded airman brought the crippled plane back to the safety of the carrier.

9. **hydra** (hī'-drə)—the nine-headed serpent slain by Hercules; a persistent or many-sided problem that presents new obstacles as soon as old ones are solved. The *hydra* had to be slain by Hercules as one of his Twelve Labors. This monster grew two heads for each one cut off. Hercules finally destroyed the *hydra* by cauterizing the necks as he cut off the heads.
   a. Economists are struggling to solve the *hydra*-headed problems of inflation without creating the evils of recession.
   b. In a bizarre series of accidents that, *hydra*-like, seemed to grow one from the other, the team slipped from first to last place in the latter part of the season.

10. **iridescent** (ir'-i-des'-ənt)—displaying lustrous colors like those of the rainbow. Iris was a messenger of the gods and regarded as the goddess of the rainbow.
    a. The fashion show featured an *iridescent* display of color in the most modern styles.
    b. The prelude was as *iridescent* as a prism in a morning room.

11. **narcissism** (nar'-si-siz'-m)—excessive admiration of oneself; egocentrism. Narcissus was a youth who, having spurned the love of Echo, fell in love with his own image reflected in a pool, and after wasting away from unsatisfied desire was transformed into the flower that bears his name. The plant, incidentally, has narcotic effects (from the Greek *narke*, "numbness").
    a. Psychoanalysts consider *narcissism* an infantile level of personality development.
    b. Some people have such exaggerated opinions of themselves that they border on *narcissism*.

12. **odyssey** (äd'-i-sē)—a long series of wanderings, especially when filled with notable experiences or hardships. *The Odyssey,* called "the greatest tale of all time," is the second epic of Homer. It recounts the wanderings and adventures of Odysseus after the fall of Troy, and his eventual return home to his faithful wife Penelope.
    a. My travels last summer were so extensive and exciting I am thinking of writing my own *odyssey.*
    b. The child's harrowing *odyssey* began with the outbreak of the war and did not end till he was reunited with the surviving members of his family many years later.

13. **Olympian** (ō-lim'pē-ən)—pertaining to the twelve gods of the ancient Greek pantheon whose abode was Mt. Olympus; majestic; incomparably superior; pertaining to the Olympic games. Olympus, the highest mountain in Greece, is located in northern Greece (Macedonia). It is sometimes used synonymously with "Heaven" or "the Sky."
    a. A turn of the road brought us to a landscape of *Olympian* beauty.
    b. An *Olympian* disregard for everyday matters does not become a person running for office.

14. **palladium** (pə-lā'-dē-əm)—anything believed to provide protection or safety; a safeguard or guarantee of the integrity of social institutions. Palladion was the fabled statue of Pallas Athena that assured the safety of Troy as long as it remained within the city.
    a. The Bill of Rights is the *palladium* of American civil liberties.
    b. After four successive championships, the coach began to regard the silver trophy as a *palladium* that guaranteed continued victories.

15. **phoenix** (fē'-niks)—a person or thing of peerless beauty or excellence; a person or thing that has become renewed or restored after suffering calamity or apparent annihilation. The phoenix was a mythical bird of great beauty, fabled to live 600 years in the Arabian desert, to burn itself on a funeral pyre, and to rise from its ashes to live through another cycle. It is an emblem of immortality.

  a. We seldom reflect upon our *phoenix*-like ability to wake each day refreshed and imbued with new energy.

  b. The fighter acquired the nickname *Phoenix* when he rallied after several knockdowns and virtual defeat to win the title.

EXERCISES

I. Which Word Comes to Mind?

In each of the following, read the statement, then circle the word that comes to mind.

1. Stung by Cupid's arrow

   (hydra, Cassandra, **erotic**)

2. A sumptuous feast

   (narcissism, **cornucopia**, odyssey)

3. Joseph's coat of many colors

   (**iridescent**, cupidity, palladium)

4. Superhuman feats of strength

   (Adonis, aegis, **herculean**)

5. Wine, women, and song

   (Olympian, **bacchanal**, phoenix)

6. Admiring himself in the mirror

   (**narcissism**, cupidity, palladium)

7. The male model appeared on several magazine covers

   (aegis, herculean, **Adonis**)

8. This year, designers are using vivid rainbow colors

   (**iridescent**, erotic, bacchanal)

9. Story of the journey of Ulysses

   (**odyssey**, Olympian, palladium)

10. From last place to first place

   (**phoenix**, narcissism, aegis)

II. True or False?

In the space provided, indicate whether each statement is true or false.

_F_ 1. *Phoenix* and *palladium* both suggest permanence.
_T_ 2. A stick-in-the-mud would be unlikely to engage in an *odyssey.*
_F_ 3. A *narcissist* is a lover of flowers.
_T_ 4. A *bacchanal* would likely attend every wedding feast but his own.
_F_ 5. *Cassandra's* song would probably be a top seller.
_T_ 6. The happy month held a *cornucopia* of good news for the family.
_T_ 7. I refuse to deal with *iridescent* complaints.
_T_ 8. After his plastic surgery, Ronnie was a regular *Adonis.*
_T_ 9. The president said, "Bringing peace to the Middle East is a *herculean* task."
_T_ 10. Feeding the *hydra* was very costly.

III. Find the Impostor

Find and circle the one word on each line that is not related to the other three.

1. Cassandra	dramatic	~~prophetic~~	doomsday
2. baccalaureate	revelry	bacchanal	dionysian
3. wisdom	metallic	palladium	safety
4. luxuriant	cornucopia	corpulent	~~plethora~~
5. ~~erotic~~	~~wandering~~	digression	desultory

IV. Fill in the Blank

Insert one of the new words in the proper space in each sentence below.

1. When the package was opened, out poured a veritable *cornucopia* of goodies.
2. Filling fifty bags of leaves from our lawn in two hours proved to be a *herculian* task.
3. Like the *phoenix* , our last place team rose from the ashes to become champions.
4. The designer filled her dark showroom with *iridescent* fabrics, which brightened it considerably.
5. As I read the autobiography, I followed the author's *odyssey* from poverty to riches.
6. Receiving an Academy Award is akin to scaling *Olympian* heights.
7. Although he had been an ordinary looking teenager, Maxwell developed into a genuine *bacchanal*
8. When smallpox destroyed the model's good looks, she was cured of her *narcissism*
9. I always anticipate a victory but my sister remains a *Cassandra*
10. Roger's *cupidity* led him to break the law.

V. Matching

Match the word in column A with its correct definition in column B by writing the letter of that definition in the space provided.

	A		B
M	1. Adonis	a.	reveler
K	2. aegis	b.	greed
A	3. bacchanal	c.	adventurous journey
J	4. Cassandra	d.	superior
G	5. cornucopia	e.	a thing of beauty par excellence
B	6. cupidity	f.	increasingly troublesome situation
N	7. erotic	g.	profusion
O	8. herculean	h.	sponsorship
F	9. hydra	i.	multi-colored
I	10. iridescent	j.	prophetess of doom
K	11. narcissism	k.	vanity
C	12. odyssey	l.	safeguard
D	13. Olympian	m.	extraordinarily handsome man
L	14. palladium	n.	filled with desire
E	15. phoenix	o.	mighty

Social Sciences

What does *anthropomorphism* have to do with Walt Disney?

Is an *archetype* similar to a prototype?

What do *demography* and *epidemiology* have in common?

Is there any connection between sublime and *subliminal*?

Why might you invite an *extrovert* to your party?

---

aberrant
anthropomor-
  phism
archetype
authoritarian
catharsis
demography
epidemiology
euthanasia
extrovert
psychic
psychopath
psychotherapy
schizophrenia
subliminal
trauma

1. **aberrant** (a-ber'-ənt)—deviating from what is normal or typical. It comes from the Latin *aberrare* ("to go astray").
    a. For two months the prison psychologists studied the murderer's *aberrant* behavior.
    b. The L.A. Rams' *aberrant* performance in the football game worried their coach.

2. **anthropomorphism** (an-thrə-pə-môr'-fiz'm)—attributing human shape to gods, objects, animals. The Greek *anthropo* is a combining form that means "man" or "human."
    a. In a fit of *anthropomorphism,* the poet called his cat his bride.
    b. Movie cartoons frequently deal in *anthropomorphism,* wherein inanimate objects are given the power of speech.

3. **archetype** (är'-kə-tīp)—model; original pattern; prototype. One meaning of the Greek prefix *arch* is "main" or "chief."
    a. R. Buckminster Fuller's sketch became the *archetype* for future geodesic domes.
    b. The brothers hated Joseph because he was constantly being held up to them as the *archetype* of juvenile perfection.

4. **authoritarian** (ə-thôr-ə-ter'-i-ən)—characterized by unquestioning obedience to authority. An *authoritarian* figure is one who rejects individual freedom of judgment and action.
    a. The principal reason for Donna's anger was her father's *authoritarian* stance.
    b. One of the explanations for the tribe's survival was their acceptance of an *authoritarian* system.

5. **catharsis** (kə-thär'-sis)—the relieving of the emotions by art; the alleviation of fears by bringing them to consciousness. This Greek word has played an important role in theater, as well as in psychiatry.
    a. The Aristotelian concept of tragic theater is that the audience is purified by means of the drama's *catharsis.*
    b. After the emotional *catharsis,* my psychiatrist felt that I was cured.

6. **demography** (di-mäg'-rə-fē)—the science of vital statistics, as of births, deaths, population, etc. It comes from the Greek root *demos* ("the people") and *graph* ("to write").
    a. We applied *demography* to help win our case with the Housing Commission.
    b. *Demographic* studies convinced the Board of Education that a desegregation attempt might be counter-productive at this time.

7. **epidemiology** (ep-ə-dē-mē-äl'-ə-jē)—the branch of medicine that investigates the causes and controls of epidemics. This word is composed of two Greek roots meaning "among the people."
   a. We turned to *epidemiology* to find the cause of Legionnaires' Disease.
   b. A professor of *epidemiology* at Baylor University isolated the cause of the sleeping sickness outbreak.

8. **euthanasia** (yo͞o-thə-nā'-zhə)—method of causing death painlessly; mercy killing. In Greek, it means "happy death."
   a. I spoke against *euthanasia* in our classroom debate on mercy killing.
   b. After realizing that their daughter was incurably ill, the Reynolds family changed their minds about *euthanasia*.

9. **extrovert** (eks'-trə-vurt)—a person who is active and expressive; a person who is outgoing. The opposite is *introvert.*
   a. Following his psychoanalysis, my withdrawn, shy brother became an *extrovert.*
   b. It's strange, but in the presence of his mother the *extrovert* became an introvert.

10. **psychic** (sī'-kik)—of the psyche or mind; beyond natural or known physical processes. All of our words that begin with *psych* come from the Greek *psychikos* ("of the soul").
    a. The jury wanted hard facts, not so-called *psychic* evidence.
    b. In this science fiction film, *psychic* powers were stimulated in humans after they had drunk a special potion.

11. **psychopath** (sī'-kə-path)—a person afflicted with a mental disorder. The Greek root *path* means "suffering" or "disease."
    a. Our police force was searching for the homicidal *psychopath* who had slain six children.
    b. I was suspicious of Doctor Bonheim's claim that he could cure any *psychopath.*

12. **psychotherapy** (sī-kō-ther'-ə-pē)—using forms of mental treatment to cure nervous disorders. *Therapy* comes from the Greek *therapeia* ("one who serves or treats medically").
    a. The specialists decided that hypnosis was the form of *psychotherapy* that would help their patient.
    b. Some old-fashioned country doctors prefer aspirin to *psychotherapy.*

13. **schizophrenia** (skiz-ə-frē'-ni-ə)—a mental disorder characterized by delusions of persecution and omnipotence. Some victims of this disease are said to have a "split personality."
    a. Psychiatrists sometimes refer to Dr. Jekyll and Mr. Hyde when explaining *schizophrenic* behavior.
    b. It is now thought that *schizophrenia* may be the result of a chemical imbalance in the system.

14. **subliminal** (sub-lim'-ə-n'l)—below the threshold of conscious perception. *Limen* is a Latin word meaning "threshold."
    a. The *subliminal* effect of the rapidly-flashed pictures of popcorn was that the audience headed for the refreshment counter.
    b. In our art gallery, we rely on soft music and incense to create a *subliminal* appeal.

15. **trauma** (trô'-mə)—an emotional experience that has a lasting psychic effect. The Greek word *trauma* means "wound."
    a. For weeks after the operation, Adele suffered from severe *trauma.*
    b. The *trauma* caused by Eric's return to his old neighborhood was quite intense.

EXERCISES

I. Which Word Comes to Mind?

In each of the following, read the statement, then circle the word that comes to mind.

1. A nurse is suspected of having given an overdose of drugs to a cancer-ridden patient

   (subliminal, euthanasia, anthropomorphism)

2. Researchers examine the tissues of the corpses

   (epidemiology, psychotherapy, psychic)

3. Man bites dog

   (aberrant, authoritarian, catharsis)

4. The government issues statistics on the ten fastest growing cities

   (schizophrenia, extrovert, demography)

5. A citizen of Hiroshima continues to have nightmares

   (archetype, trauma, psychopath)

6. The life of the party

   (catharsis, extrovert, trauma)

7. Dr. Jekyll and Mr. Hyde

   (schizophrenia, epidemiology, demography)

8. Commands from a dictator

   (subliminal, psychic, authoritarian)

9. A family asks the doctors to "pull the plug"

   (archetype, catharsis, euthanasia)

10. A Walt Disney show

    (trauma, anthropomorphism, subliminal)

II. True or False?

In the space provided, indicate whether each statement is true or false.

_____ 1. *Psychotherapy* is used to treat muscles that have *atrophied*.
_____ 2. *Aberrant* behavior is always welcomed by society.
_____ 3. *Subliminal* suggestions tend to be subtle ones.
_____ 4. *Psychopaths* and *schizophrenics* can be cured quickly today.
_____ 5. Jupiter throwing his lightning bolts across the sky is an example of *anthropomorphism*.
_____ 6. Her lawyer claimed that camp experiences led to Helen's *trauma*.
_____ 7. Our family operates on democratic principles because Dad is an *authoritarian* figure.
_____ 8. The supermarket owners studied the neighborhood's *demography* before building the new store.
_____ 9. Europe's Black Plague is a fruitful study for *epidemiologists*.
_____ 10. *Euthanasia* deals with young people in China.

III. Fill in the Blank

Insert one of the new words in the proper space in each sentence below.

1. It was obvious to the emergency room doctor that the patient had undergone a serious _____ .

2. Concern over the so-called "mercy killing" led the clergymen to organize a symposium on _____ .

3. The classroom was run in an _____ fashion because the teacher scorned democratic principles.

4. We were confounded by the _____ results of the test in which the poorest students received the highest grades.

5. Study of our neighborhood's projected _____ will help us to plan for the influx of new families.

6. We usually refer to people with multiple personalities as suffering from _____ .

7. The psychologist advanced the theory that the deranged murderer was a _____ .

8. As an uninhibited _____ , Larry was the life of the party.

9. Since I am dedicated to eliminating infectious diseases, I plan to major in _____ .

10. Following a _____ in the final act, the playwright created a happy ending.

IV. What's the Antonym?

Which of the new words is most nearly *opposite* in meaning to the one provided?

1. democrat   _____
2. normal   _____
3. conscious   _____
4. shy one   _____
5. poor example   _____

V. Matching

Match the word in column A with its correct definition in column B by writing the letter of that definition in the space provided.

A	*B*
_____ 1. aberrant	a. medical research into epidemics
_____ 2. anthropomorphism	b. an outgoing person
_____ 3. archetype	c. attributing human shape to nonhumans
_____ 4. authoritarian	d. beyond natural processes
_____ 5. catharsis	e. use of mental treatment to cure disorders
_____ 6. demography	f. split personality
_____ 7. epidemiology	g. model
_____ 8. euthanasia	h. deviating from the normal
_____ 9. extrovert	i. emotional experience with a lasting effect
_____ 10. psychic	j. person with a severe mental disorder
_____ 11. psychopath	k. science of vital statistics
_____ 12. psychotherapy	l. subconscious
_____ 13. schizophrenia	m. mercy killing
_____ 14. subliminal	n. relieving of emotions
_____ 15. trauma	o. giving orders

"Carrying anthropomorphism too far?"

From Sunny Spain

What would be your weakness if you had a "*mañana* complex"?

Where are you likely to see a *flotilla?*

Why is Don Quixote often called a *grandee?*

Who are the probable residents of the *barrio?*

Is a football stadium the right place for an *aficionado* of the sport?

---

aficionado
barrio
bonanza
bravado
desperado
flotilla
grandee
hacienda
lariat
machismo
mañana
palmetto
renegade
siesta
torero

1. **aficionado** (ə-fish-ə-nä'-dō)—a fan; devotee. Although this word originally described bull-fighting fans, it is now used to refer to devotees of all sports.
   a. Pablo used to be a bull-fighting *aficionado* but grew tired of the bloodshed.
   b. When I was an *aficionado* of baseball, I knew every player's batting average.

2. **barrio** (bär'-ē-ō)—part of the city where Spanish-speaking people live; ghetto.
   a. Even after he became rich, Jose would return to the *barrio* for a home cooked meal.
   b. The two Spanish-speaking candidates campaigned actively for votes in the *barrio.*

3. **bonanza** (bə-nan'-ze)—rich pocket of ore; any source of wealth. In Spanish it means "fair weather at sea." A popular television program of the 1960s was entitled *"Bonanza."*
   a. The old mine turned out to be a *bonanza* for its owners.
   b. With this unexpected *bonanza,* Paul retired to the good life in Florida.

4. **bravado** (brə-vä'-dō)—pretended courage.
   a. In a display of *bravado,* the prisoner asked for a cigarette before being hanged.
   b. The poodle's *bravado* frightened the big dog away.

5. **desperado** (des-pə-rä'-dō)—bold outlaw; dangerous criminal. The relationship to our word "despair" is apparent. One who is without hope can be a dangerous criminal.
   a. The FBI men went into the woods to flush out the *desperado.*
   b. We were warned that the escaped *desperadoes* were heavily armed.

6. **flotilla** (flō-til'-ə)—a small fleet. The Spanish word *flota* means "fleet." *Flotilla,* then, is a diminutive form of *flota.*
   a. The colorful *flotilla* sailed out to meet the great ocean liner.
   b. Our slow vessel was swiftly overtaken by the pirate *flotilla.*

7. **grandee** (gran-dē')—a nobleman of the highest rank.
   a. A cocktail party was held in honor of the visiting *grandee* from Madrid.
   b. We were taken on a personal tour of his family's castle by the Spanish *grandee.*

8. **hacienda** (hä-sē-en'də)—large estate; country house. The Old Spanish word *facienda* meant "estate." The change from *f* to *h* is apparent in many words.
   a.   Expecting a broken down farm house, Edith was delighted to see the beautiful *hacienda*.
   b.   At the end of the cattle round-up, we gathered at the *hacienda* for a party.

9. **lariat** (lar'ē-it)—lasso; a rope used for tethering grazing horses. *Reata* is "rope" in Spanish.
   a.   The cowboy star twirled his lariat in television appearances.
   b.   The rodeo star snaked his *lariat* over the calf's head and brought the animal to a halt.

10. **machismo** (mä-chēz'-mō)—manly self-assurance; masculine drive; virility.
   a.   A male chauvinist harbors feelings of *machismo*.
   b.   With a strong sense of *machismo*, Reynaldo refused to allow his wife to get a job.

11. **mañana** (mä-nya'-nä)—tomorrow; at some indefinite time in the future. There is a pejorative twist to *mañana,* suggesting laziness.
   a.   Dorothy wanted the job done immediately, but *mañana* was good enough for her husband.
   b.   If you keep waiting for *mañana,* you may find that it never comes.

12. **palmetto** (pal-met'-ō)—small palm tree.
   a.   The terrible storm bent the *palmetto* almost to the ground.
   b.   We hid in the *palmetto* grove where the others could not find us.

13. **renegade** (ren'-ə-gād)—deserter; turncoat; traitor. In Spanish, the word *renegado* means "to deny."
   a.   One of the most notorious *renegades* in American history is Benedict Arnold.
   b.   Angry at being humiliated, the soldier deserted and became a *renegade.*

14. **siesta** (sē-es'-tə)—midday nap. In Spanish and Latin American countries, businesses often close at midday to allow for *siesta* time.
   a.   Following my *siesta,* I always feel refreshed.
   b.   In Mexico we had to wait until the end of the *siesta* before we could resume our shopping.

15. **torero** (tə-rer'-ō)—bullfighter on foot. The *toreador* was a bullfighter on horseback, but that term is no longer used since all bullfighters today are *toreros.*
   a.   The *torero's* beautiful costume is called "The Suit of Lights."
   b.   After his great performance, the *torero* was awarded the ears and tail of the bull.

EXERCISES

I. Which Word Comes to Mind?

In each of the following, read the statement, then circle the word that comes to mind.

1. You go to see a performance of the opera "Carmen"

(lariat, flotilla, torero)

2. The calendar pictures a man asleep under a tree next to a lawn mower

(barrio, bravado, mañana)

3. A young man starts a fight to impress his girlfriend

(machismo, siesta, renegade)

4. You win the lottery

         (aficionado, bonanza, palmetto)

5. There is a wild police chase after the bank robber

         (desperado, grandee, hacienda)

6. The FBI arrests a man for selling U.S. secrets to a foreign country

         (aficionado, renegade, grandee)

7. Stores in Spain close for two hours after lunch

         (siesta, hacienda, palmetto)

8. The Niña, the Pinta, and the Santa Maria

         (flotilla, barrio, mañana)

9. David stands up to Goliath

         (desperado, lariat, bravado)

10. A bull-fighting fan shouts, "Ole!"

         (bonanza, aficionado, barrio)

II. True or False?

In the space provided, indicate whether each statement is true or false.

_____ 1. A truly courageous person does not have to resort to *bravado.*

_____ 2. Feminists have contempt for those men who display *machismo.*

_____ 3. Ordinarily a *grandee* might take a *siesta* in his *hacienda.*

_____ 4. The Spanish Armada was too awesome to be described as a *flotilla.*

_____ 5. A *lariat* can be the high point of a Spanish meal when it is seasoned properly.

_____ 6. The spectators applauded the *torero* for his fearlessness.

_____ 7. We bought an expensive *barrio* as a wedding gift.

_____ 8. Our winning lottery ticket proved to be a *bonanza.*

_____ 9. General Parker promised amnesty for any *renegade* who turned himself in.

_____ 10. Because of his lifelong philanthropy, the *desperado* was honored at a White House ceremony.

III. Fill in the Blank

Insert one of the new words in the proper space in each sentence below.

1. Since Teddy is an _____ of baseball, we got him two tickets to the World Series.

2. Refreshed by her _____ , Maria was ready to go to work.

3. As fish prices declined, the _____ of shrimp boats was cut in half.

4. Our new mayor proposed to tear down sections of the _____ and build middle-income housing.

5. The _____ was caught up on a horn of the bull and badly injured.

6. With unexpected _____ , the young man confronted the bully.

7. Movie cowboys generally are proficient with a _____ .

8. "Au revoir, so long, ciao, _____ ," she said as her taxi pulled away.

9. A photograph of the _____ appeared on the Most Wanted list in our post office.

10. On Navy Day, we stood upon the pier to watch the _____ sail into the harbor.

IV. What's the Antonym?

Which of the new words is most nearly *opposite* in meaning to the one provided?

1. cowardice   _____

2. patriot   _____

3. today   _____

4. weakness   _____

5. lawman   _____

6. loss   _____

7. state of alertness _____

8. shack   _____

9. peon   _____

10. wealthy neighborhood _____

V. Matching

Match the word in column A with its correct definition in column B by writing the letter of that definition in the space provided.

	A		*B*
____ 1. aficionado		a.	ghetto
____ 2. barrio		b.	pretended courage
____ 3. bonanza		c.	nobleman
____ 4. bravado		d.	large estate
____ 5. desperado		e.	midday nap
____ 6. flotilla		f.	prosperity, source of wealth
____ 7. grandee		g.	small palm tree
____ 8. hacienda		h.	bullfighter
____ 9. lariat		i.	deserter
____ 10. machismo		j.	devotee
____ 11. mañana		k.	virility
____ 12. palmetto		l.	tomorrow
____ 13. renegade		m.	small fleet
____ 14. siesta		n.	lasso
____ 15. torero		o.	bold outlaw

Time on Our Hands

How many years are there in a *score? A generation?*

With which war is *antebellum* usually associated?

If someone comes to you *anon*, is he making haste?

How often do *biennial* publications appear?

What do family resemblances have to do with *atavism?*

anachronism
anon
antebellum
antediluvian
atavism
augury
biennial
chronology
diurnal
eon
ephemeral
epoch
generation
score
tercentenary

1. **anachronism** (ə-nak'-rə-niz'm)—anything that is out of place in time. It is formed by the combination of the Greek roots *ana* ("against') and *chronos* ("time").
   a. The author was guilty of an *anachronism* when he described a frontier family with a washing machine.
   b. Paramount Pictures hired my uncle as a technical advisor to look out for *anachronisms.*

2. **anon** (ə-nän')—soon; shortly. Used as an abbreviation, *anon.* means "anonymous."
   a. I'm busy right now but I'll come to see you *anon.*
   b. Peter promised to be here *anon* but he's a terrible liar.

3. **antebellum** (an'-ti-bel'-əm)—before the war; especially before the American Civil War. This word is formed from the Latin prefix *ante* ("before") and the root *bellum* ("war").
   a. *Gone With the Wind* shows us one version of the *antebellum* South.
   b. In *antebellum* Mississippi, slave auctions were widely attended.

4. **antediluvian** (an-ti-də-lōō'-vē-ən)—old-fashioned; before the flood. The Latin word for "flood" is *diluvium.*
   a. It is futile to try to change my grandmother's *antediluvian* ideas.
   b. Mitchell wore an *antediluvian* suit that caused the whole neighborhood to snicker.

5. **atavism** (at'-ə-viz'm)—reversion to a primitive type; resemblance to a remote ancestor. The Latin *atavus* means "father of a great-grandfather."
   a. The pictures of David and his grandfather, both at age 16, confirmed my belief in *atavism.*
   b. Sylvia was an *atavistic* throwback to her frugal ancestors.

6. **augury** (ô'-gyər-ē)—the art of prophecy; an omen. The original Latin word *augur* means "priest who presides at fertility rituals."
   a. If I had the power of *augury,* I would know which stocks are good investments.
   b. You might rely on *augury*, but I prefer to deal with facts.

7. **biennial** (bī-en'-ē-əl)—happening every two years. *Biennial* should not be confused with *biannual,* which means "twice a year."
   a. Since our annual meeting was so poorly attended, we plan to switch to a *biennial* one in the future.
   b. A *biennial* plant lasts two years, producing flowers and seed the second year.

8. **chronology** (kr-nol'-ə-jē)—arrangement of events in time; determination of dates.
   a. According to the investigator's *chronology*, the suspect's alibi did not make sense.
   b. In terms of *chronology*, Eddie's birthday came before his sister's.

9. **diurnal** (dī-ur'-n'l)—daily; of the daytime. *Diurnal* is contrasted with *nocturnal.*
   a. My brother is a *diurnal* creature, usually in bed by 7:00 P.M.
   b. The custodian's *diurnal* chore was to raise the flag in front of the school.

10. **eon** (ē'-ən)—long, indefinite period of time; thousands of years.
    a. *Eons* ago, dinosaurs roamed this part of the country.
    b. You will have to wait an *eon* before they consent to your proposal.

11. **ephemeral** (i-fem'-ər-əl)—short-lived; transitory. *Ephemeros* is a Greek word meaning "for the day."
    a. "Fame is *ephemeral*," sighed the forgotten movie star.
    b. The novelist used to belittle his newspaper articles because of their *ephemeral* nature.

12. **epoch** (ep'-ək)—noteworthy period. It comes from a Greek word meaning "pause"—almost as if mankind takes time out before entering a new, important phase.
    a. We are living in the nuclear *epoch* when even tiny nations have the power to destroy.
    b. The Wright brothers' flight started an amazing *epoch* in the history of aviation.

13. **generation** (jen-ə-rā'-shən)—the period of time between the birth of one group and that of its offspring. A *generation* is about 30 years.
    a. At our last family reunion, four *generations* were present.
    b. We find it very difficult to relate to the people of our grandparents' *generation.*

14. **score** (skôr)—twenty people or objects; twenty years. It comes from the Greek word for a "scratch" or "mark" used in keeping tallies.
    a. Mr. Schultz came to this country three *score* years ago.
    b. A *score* or more years ago, a trolley car used to run down this street.

15. **tercentenary** (tur-sen-ten'-ər-ē)—a period of 300 years. *Ter* is the Latin prefix for "three" and *centenary* means "hundred."
    a. In 1997 we celebrated the *tercentenary* of our town, founded in 1697.
    b. On the *tercentenary* of Shakespeare's birth, an enormous festival was held in London.

EXERCISES

I. Which Word Comes to Mind?

In each of the following, read the statement, then circle the word that comes to mind.

1. The candidate was criticized because his proposals were hopelessly out-of-date.

    (epoch, antediluvian, diurnal)

2. Emperor Nero looking at his wristwatch

    (tercentenary, ephemeral, anachronism)

3. A young man following in his grandfather's footsteps

    (anon, atavism, score)

4. You meet your old classmates every two years at a reunion

    (antebellum, chronology, biennial)

5. Your fortune is told by a gypsy

    (augury, generation, eon)

6. They had been married for two decades

    (eon, score, diurnal)

7. The painter believed that everyone was entitled to fifteen minutes of fame

    (ephemeral, epoch, tercentary)

8. Many inventions were introduced during the Industrial Revolution

    (anon, epoch, atavism)

9. Plantation life was a feature of the South in the early 1800s

    (antebellum, generation, anachronism)

10. My family chore is to walk the dog each day

    (biennial, antediluvian, diurnal)

II. True or False?

In the space provided, indicate whether each statement is true or false.

____ 1. Abraham Lincoln's "Four *score* and seven" was 87 years.

____ 2. *Ephemeral* is the opposite of "permanent."

____ 3. Historians study the *chronology* of events.

____ 4. Cotton was the great crop of the *antebellum* South.

____ 5. The United States will have its *tercentenary* celebration in 2076.

____ 6. An entire *generation* has grown up using personal computers.

____ 7. To show a modern man driving up in a new car is an *anachronism*.

____ 8. Dinner will be served *anon.*

____ 9. The frightening *augury* lashed out at the startled travelers.

____ 10. Our previous *biennial* reunion was in 2004 so we expect the next one in 2006.

III. Fill in the Blank

Insert one of the new words in the proper space in each sentence below.

1. We spotted an _____ in the movie when Julius Caesar looked at his wristwatch.

2. In the next decade, our company will issue five _____ journals.

3. Industrialization spelled the end of an era for the _____ southern states.

4. The Beatles started a musical _____ that has gained worldwide acceptance.

5. Because of the _____ gap, Roger found it difficult to relate to his grandson.

6. My grandfather's _____ notions need updating.

7. With the evident power of _____ , Liza could predict the future.

8. Guido's interest in stamp-collecting proved to be _____ because he sold his entire collection.

9. It seemed to take an _____ before the traffic jam allowed us to get moving again.

10. Breakfast was preceded invariably by a _____ prayer that helped Roy get through the rest of the day.

IV. What's the Antonym?

Which of the new words is most nearly *opposite* in meaning to the one provided?

1. now   _____

2. boring period   _____

3. modern   _____

4. permanent   _____

5. nightly   _____

6. something relevant   _____

7. every two years   _____

8. postwar   _____

9. an instant   _____

10. an advance   _____

V. Matching

Match the word in column A with its correct definition in column B by writing the letter of that definition in the space provided.

A

_____ 1. anachronism
_____ 2. anon
_____ 3. antebellum
_____ 4. antediluvian
_____ 5: atavism
_____ 6. augury
_____ 7. biennial
_____ 8. chronology
_____ 9. diurnal
_____ 10. eon
_____ 11. ephemeral
_____ 12. epoch
_____ 13. generation
_____ 14. score
_____ 15. tercentenary

B

a. short-lived
b. before the flood
c. twenty years
d. reversion to an older type
e. every two years
f. something misplaced in time
g. period of 300 years
h. soon, in a short while
i. thousands of years
j. thirty years
k. daily
l. arrangement of events
m. noteworthy period
n. before the war
o. an omen

Short but Challenging Words

With whom does one usually make a *tryst?*

Is *shunt* a contraction of two words?

Does *svelte* refer to a kind of material or a person's appearance?

What emotion is expressed by *quailing?*

Is *knell* a method of prayer or an evil omen?

---

abut
bane
deign
eke
knell
mete
moot
mulct
plumb
quail
roil
shunt
svelte
thrall
tryst

1. **abut** (ə-but')—border on; adjoin.
    a. The new structure will *abut* on the golf course.
    b. I bought the house because it *abuts* on my parents' home.

2. **bane** (bān)—cause of death, ruin or distress. Obviously, you would avoid *baneful* herbs, like *baneberry,* and even shun *baneful* superstitions that could be equally harmful.
    a. Poor study habits were the *bane* of Walter's academic career
    b. Gambling was the *bane* of Peter's existence.

3. **deign** (dān)—to think it beneath one's dignity; condescend; give. Related to the same Latin root, *dignitas,* as *deign* are *dignity, dignify, dignitary,* and *indignant,* all of which comment on one's worthiness.
    a. Charles would not *deign* to discuss his failure with us.
    b. I have applied for employment to several companies, but they have not *deigned* to reply.

4. **eke** (ēk)—to supplement; to manage to make a living with difficulty; to use frugally. *Eke* can be traced to the Latin *augere* and the Greek *auxanein,* which in turn give us words like *augment* and *auxiliary.*
    a. The sharecroppers *eked* out a living by farming a small piece of land.
    b. Mr. Hernandez *eked* out his income by working at night.

5. **knell** (nel)—to ring in a slow, solemn way; toll; to call or announce by a mournful ringing; an omen of death or failure. The opening line of Gray's famous elegy, "The curfew tolls the *knell* of parting day," sets the mournful, reflective mood of the poem.
    a. The president's veto meant the *knell* of all the valiant efforts to tighten gun controls.
    b. With bells *knelling* in farewell, the long funeral procession wound through the dusty town toward the cemetery.

6. **mete** (mēt)—to allot, distribute or apportion. Tennyson's famous line amply illustrates the sense of measuring out: "I *mete* and dole unequal laws unto a savage race."
    a. Some people *mete* out their friendship by the drop; others, by the cupful.
    b. The authorities *meted* out punishment to the instigators of this brawl.

7. moot (mo͞ot)—discussion or argument of a hypothetical law case; debatable; so hypothetical as to be meaningless. Law students sharpen their skills in a *moot* court where hypothetical cases are tried.
   a.   The Supreme Court decision on capital punishment has made the deterrent effect of the death penalty a *moot* question.
   b.   The class becomes impatient when Howard engages the teacher in discussing *moot* points.

8. mulct (mulkt)—to punish by a fine or by depriving of something; to extract by fraud or deceit. It is from the Latin *mulcta* ("a fine.").
   a.   The petty official was suspected of having *mulcted* this treasury of thousands of dollars during his term of office.
   b.   The judge *mulcted* the defendant with a heavy fine besides imposing a jail sentence for his part in the bank swindle.

9. plumb (plum)—perfectly vertical; directly; to test or sound with a *plumb* line (measure); to discover the facts of; to fathom, solve or understand. A lead weight (Latin *plumbum,* "lead") was used at the end of the *plumb* line. The chemical symbol for lead is Pb.
   a.   It is not easy to *plumb* the intention of a fickle person.
   b.   Shallow ideas should be *plumbed* and discarded.

10. quail (kwāl)—to draw back in fear; lose heart or courage; cower. A *quail* is also a partridge-like bird mentioned in the Bible as the source of the meat sent to the Israelites in the desert. The definition of the verb to *quail* is related to the Latin word *coagulare* ("coagulate"), describing what seems to happen physically when the blood "runs cold."
   a.   The stout heart does not *quail* though the enemy be fierce and the battle unequal.
   b.   The lone sailor *quailed* before the mighty waves roaring toward his flimsy raft.

11. roil (roil)—to make a liquid cloudy or muddy; to stir up or agitate; to make angry; rile. Some authorities believe the word comes from the Old French word for "rust" or "mud," or the Latin *ruber* ("red"). Others frankly admit the origin is unknown. But we can offer some interesting synonyms: *annoy, fret, ruffle, exasperate, provoke.*
   a.   The delay in the announcement of the winner *roiled* the entire party.
   b.   We watched the lake *roil* beneath the pounding rain.

12. shunt (shunt)—to move or turn to one side; to shift or switch from one track to another. The word may be related to *shun,* which also has the sense of turning away.
   a.   The surgeon *shunted* the blood circulation around the heart so that the rupture could be repaired.
   b.   The freight train was *shunted* to another track just in time to avoid the hurtling passenger train.

13. svelte (svelt)—slender and graceful; suave; polished. The derivation from the Latin *evellare* ("to pull out"), implies that the *svelte* figure has, been "drawn out" like a heated glass tube.
   a.   Jennie maintained her *svelte* figure with a sensible diet, regular exercise, and, of course, a hereditary gift.
   b.   Not every person with a *svelte* manner should be considered devious and dishonest.

14. thrall (thrôl)—a slave or bondman; a person under the moral or psychological domination of something or someone; slavery. Performers who *enthrall* their audiences captivate their attention.
   a.   Mr. Hyde was in the *thrall* of morbid fantasies that plagued his waking moments.
   b.   The workers were held in *thrall* by the poor economic conditions that denied them upward mobility.

15. tryst (trist)—an appointment, as by lovers; to meet. In Scotland the word refers to a market, but the Old French *triste* ("hunting rendezvous") suggests that the Gallic hunters were not always after wild game.
   a.   The *trysting* place at the college remained a guarded secret among the fraternity members.
   b.   Martha came home very late from the *tryst,* bleary-eyed but happy.

EXERCISES

I. Which Word Comes to Mind?

In each of the following, read the statement, then circle the word that comes to mind.

1. The impoverished family barely survived the winter

    (mulct, moot, eke)

2. To each according to his due

    (thrall, mete, roil)

3. A house of terror for its inhabitants

    (quail, abut, deign)

4. Romeo and Juliet meet at the Friar's cell

    (knell, tryst, shunt)

5. Drink was his undoing

    (svelte, plumb, bane)

6. A detour off the main road

    (plumb, thrall, shunt)

7. Most models diet strenuously to keep their slender figure

    (svelte, abut, mulct)

8. The town rings a bell at curfew time

    (knell, deign, mete)

9. Children annoying their nanny

    (roil, shunt, tryst)

10. She worked like a slave in her aunt's household

    (moot, thrall, plumb)

II. True or False?

In the space provided, indicate whether each statement is true or false.

_____ 1. The lovers' *tryst* was uncovered by a gossip columnist.

_____ 2. The best time to appeal to someone for a favor is after he has been *roiled* up.

_____ 3. The *knelling* of bells has a somber, saddening effect.

_____ 4. Some girls are anxious to have a *svelte* figure.

_____ 5. A person found guilty of a serious crime in *moot* court must serve at least the minimum sentence.

_____ 6. Drugs and alcohol proved to be the *bane* of Peter's life.

_____ 7. Mrs. Miller was so angry that she would not *deign* to read my poem.

_____ 8. The greedy stockbroker *mulcted* his firm into bankruptcy.

_____ 9. It was difficult for the poor farmers to *eke* out a living.

_____ 10. Judge Medowar has *meted* out justice in his courtroom for twenty years.

III. Synonyms and Antonyms

Indicate whether the following pairs of words are the same, opposite, or unrelated in meaning by writing S, O, or U in the space provided.

_____ 1. thrall—master

_____ 2. moot—questionable

_____ 3. tryst—confidence

_____ 4. mete—assign

_____ 5. roil—soothe

IV. Anagrams

In four of the following, add or subtract a letter from the word, then rearrange the letters to form the new word whose meaning is given. In the last one, simply rearrange the given letters.

1. eke + one letter = timid _____

2. mete + one letter = rhythm _____

3. moot + one letter = power source _____

4. svelte – one letter = marker _____

5. loir = stir up _____

V. Matching

Match the word in column A with its correct definition in column B by writing the letter of that definition in the space provided.

	A		B
_____	1. abut	a.	agitate
_____	2. bane	b.	meeting
_____	3. deign	c.	toll
_____	4. eke	d.	curse
_____	5. knell	e.	fascination
_____	6. mete	f.	dole
_____	7. moot	g.	willowy
_____	8. mulct	h.	condescend
_____	9. plumb	i.	cheat
_____	10. quail	j.	barely survive
_____	11. roil	k.	recoil
_____	12. shunt	l.	border on
_____	13. svelte	m.	test
_____	14. thrall	n.	switch to another track
_____	15. tryst	o.	debatable

Swollen to Svelte

Unit I
(Lessons 1–10)

Review

A. The Out-of-Place Word

In each of the following groups, find and circle the one vocabulary word that is out of place. You should be able to explain what the other three words have in common.

1. amanuensis, graphologist, nemesis, osteopath
2. antebellum, score, biennial, thrall
3. dyspeptic, philippic, bilious, baleful
4. barrio, odyssey, grandee, flotilla
5. anachronism, bacchanal, narcissism, phoenix
6. farrier, trauma, extrovert, psychopath, lachrymose
7. philanderer, quixotic, solecism, echelon
8. adagio, salvo, vendetta, siesta
9. palladium, contrite, acidulous, craven
10. epidemiology, euthanasia, demography, lapidary

B. Rearranging Words

Rearrange the following groups of words using the first letter of each word to spell out one of the new words taught in this unit.

1. grandee, intaglio, tryst, jingoist, staccato, imbroglio, nemesis, Olympian

   _____

2. atavism, internist, odyssey, genealogy, detente, aberrant

   _____

3. roil, thrall, catharsis, ornithologist, graphologist, elite, erotic

   _____

4. torero, lapidary, Adonis, andante, imbroglio, rapprochemont

   _____

5. osteopath, sybarite, crescendo, maverick, lachrymose, ecumenical, iridescent, subliminal

   _____

C. Getting Satisfaction

Where would you go with the following? Circle the correct answer.

1. A backache

   (cosmetologist, demographer, palladium, osteopath)

2. A desire to have your character analyzed

   (anthropomorphist, graphologist, amanuensis, narcissist)

3. Plans for a funeral

   (tryst, cortege, archetype, flotilla)

4. An idea to overthrow someone in power

   (palmetto, cabal, catharsis, vendetta)

5. A case of acne

(*dermatologist, pharynologist, physiologist, amanuensis*)

6. To find out about your roots

(*genealogy, vendetta, physiologist, epoch*)

7. To determine the value of a precious stone

(*graphologist, palladium, augury, lapidary*)

8. A vision problem

(*ophthalmologist, contralto, protean, sybarite*)

9. A 300-year celebration

(*ancahronism, tercentary, phoenix, generation*)

10. A search for a nonconformist

(*libretto, beadle, maverick, philippic*)

D. Making Pairs

From the group below, find the pairs of words that have something in common and record them in the spaces provided. You should be able to find ten such pairs and list them numerically. The first two have been done for you.

lothario ___1___	Cassandra ___2___	desperado _____	Olympian ____
augury ___2___	philanderer ___1___	dyspeptic _____	sybarite _____
renegade _____	acidulous _____	herculean _____	phoenix _____
protean _____	contralto _____	elite _____	ornithologist __
libretto _____	esprit de corps _____	camaraderie _____	bacchanal ____

E. Cliché Time

Which of the words from this unit fit into the following familiar expressions? Choose the correct word from the choices given and record it in the space provided.

1. The _____ of my existence

(*eon, bane, trauma, nemesis*)

2. The noise reached a _____ .

(*epoch, palladium, knell, crescendo*)

3. We won but it was a _____ victory.

(*Pyrrhic, baleful, quixotic, protean*)

4. A _____ burst of machine gun fire

(*moot, staccato, maverick, tawdry*)

5. Where the _____ meet to eat

(*saturnine elite, svelte, contrite*)

Medical Science

Why would anyone want a *cadaver?*

Is "Tarzan of the *Simians*" an appropriate movie title?

What do *mastectomy* and *vasectomy* have in common?

Is the army slang term, "gold brick," synonomous with any of the fifteen vocabulary words below?

Which of the medical terms below could a poet use to describe a hill?

---

abscess
aphasia
arteriosclerosis
benign
biopsy
cadaver
carcinogen
comatose
etiology
malingerer
mastectomy
prosthesis
simian
therapeutic
vasectomy

1. **abscess** (ab'-ses)—swollen, inflamed area of body tissues. It is from the Latin *abscessus* ("to go from"). It was originally thought that the humors (liquids) went from the body into the swelling.
   a. Dr. Harris discovered the *abscess* under my gum that had accounted for my pain.
   b. When Helen's *abscess* was lanced, she felt immediate relief.

2. **aphasia** (e-fā'-zhə)—loss of the power to use or understand words, usually caused by brain disease or injury.
   a. Fortunately, Jeff's *aphasia* passed quickly, and by evening he was chattering away normally.
   b. The doctors believed that the *aphasia* that followed Justice Douglas' stroke would lead to his retirement.

3. **arteriosclerosis** (är-tir'-ē-ō-sklə-rō-sis)—a thickening and hardening of the walls of the arteries, as in old age.
   a. In my aunt's case, *arteriosclerosis* restricted the flow of blood to her brain, and she endured several strokes.
   b. Researchers at geriatric institutes are seeking ways to improve the blood flow in patients who suffer from *arteriosclerosis.*

4. **benign** (bi-nīn')—beneficial; not malignant.
   a. When Dr. Kolitz told us the tumor was *benign*, we breathed a sigh of relief.
   b. Carol's *benign* personality made many friends for her.

5. **biopsy** (bī-äp-sē)—the cutting out of a piece of tissue for diagnostic examination by microscope.
   a. While his surgeon awaited the results of the *biopsy,* the patient lay asleep on the operating table.
   b. June's family opened the champagne bottles for a celebration when the *biopsy* showed the tumor was benign.

6. **cadaver** (kə-dav'-ər)—dead body; corpse for dissection. It is from the Latin word *cadere,* which means "to fall."
   a. Medical students used to pay grave robbers for the *cadavers* they stole.
   b. The unclaimed *cadaver* lay in the morgue for an entire month.

7. carcinogen (kär-sin'-ə-jən)—any substance that causes cancer.
a.   We were shocked to learn that Donny's pajamas were sprayed with a chemical suspected of being a *carcinogen.*
b.   The Evans family moved to the coast when it was reported that our community's drinking water was filled with *carcinogens.*

8. comatose (kom'-ə-tōs)—as if in a coma; lethargic. The Greek word *coma* means "deep sleep."
a.   Hal remained *comatose* after having been struck on the head.
b.   Trading was nonexistent on the Stock Exchange floor, and the business community seemed in a *comatose* state.

9. etiology (ēt-ē-äl'-ə-jē)—the science of the causes and origins of disease.
a.   Dr. James Parkinson spent many years tracing the *etiology* of palsy.
b.   Thanks to medical science, we now know a great deal about the *etiology* of many diseases.

10. malingerer (ma-liŋ'-gər-ər)—one who fakes illness and pretends to be suffering.
a.   General Patton struck the alleged *malingerer* across the face.
b.   The doctors decided to frighten the *malingerer* back into good health.

11. mastectomy (mas-tek'-tə-mē)—the surgical removal of a breast.
a.   After viewing the special x-rays, the breast surgeon recommended an immediate *mastectomy.*
b.   Aunt Lorraine made a quick recovery after her *mastectomy.*

12. prosthesis (präs'-thə-sis)—replacement for a missing part of the body.
a.   Ethel's broken hip could not be pinned but would require a *prosthesis.*
b.   Learning to walk with the new *prosthesis* would only be successful if Sergeant Yates had motivation and will power.

13. simian (sim'-ē-ən)—of or like a monkey or an ape.
a.   Ira's long arms and body posture gave him a *simian* appearance.
b.   The *simian* experts at the zoo objected to the experimental surgery being performed on the apes.

14. therapeutic (ther-ə-pyo͞ot'-ik)—curative; serving to heal.
a.   A long vacation was the only *therapeutic* treatment prescribed for Myra.
b.   Scientists have found that aspirin has *therapeutic* possibilities that we had not appreciated.

15. vasectomy (vas-ek'-tə-mē)—the surgical removal of the duct that conveys the male sperm—the *vas deferens.*
a.   Both husband and wife agreed that a *vasectomy* would be their best form of contraception.
b.   A simple *vasectomy* can be performed in a physician's office without anaesthesia.

EXERCISES

I. Which Word Comes to Mind?

In each of the following, read the statement, then circle the word that comes to mind.

1. Eugene O'Neill's play, *The Hairy Ape*

     (vasectomy, biopsy, simian)

2. The Federal Drug Administration's report on harmful food additives

     (aphasia, carcinogen, prosthesis)

3. Breast surgery

     (etiology, malingerer, mastectomy)

4. Days of anxious waiting for the unconscious patient to awaken

     (abscess, comatose, therapeutic)

5. A disease of old age

     (cadaver, arteriosclerosis, etiology)

6. Malignant or benign

     (comatose, biopsy, aphasia)

7. Visit to the morgue

     (cadaver, abscess, simian)

8. A great pretender

     (etiology, malingerer, carcinogen)

9. Walking with a wooden leg

     (prosthesis, comatose, arteriosclerosis)

10. Vigorous exercise

     (therapeutic, carcinogen, aphasia)

II. True or False?

In the space provided, indicate whether each statement is true or false.

_____ 1. Good news can serve as a *therapeutic* drug for many patients.

_____ 2. Speech therapy is prescribed for many people who suffer from *aphasia.*

_____ 3. When the government suspects the presence of a *carcinogen* in a food, it increases sales and distribution.

_____ 4. A wooden leg was a common *prosthesis* years ago.

_____ 5. Most motion picture horror stories have at least one *cadaver* to boast about.

_____ 6. After the doctor drained my *abscess,* I immediately felt better.

_____ 7. While awaiting the results of the *biopsy,* Eleanor fainted.

_____ 8. Snakes have a traditional *simian* characteristic.

_____ 9. Researchers are at work on the *etiology* of lung cancer.

_____ 10. In a *comatose* state, Manute was able to resume his basketball career.

III. Find the Words

Somewhere in this box of letters, reading up, down, across, or diagonally, four vocabulary words that were taught in this lesson are hidden. As you locate each one, draw a circle around it.

A	L	B	R	A	K	R	Y
S	P	O	M	W	E	H	S
J	U	H	X	V	Z	Y	P
B	L	P	A	O	K	T	O
X	G	D	E	S	S	W	I
D	A	F	T	G	I	N	B
C	E	S	I	M	I	A	N

IV. Extra Letters

In each of the vocabulary words below there is an extra letter. Put all of the extra letters together, and you will be able to spell out two words taught in a previous lesson; their meanings are "cause of distress" and "to manage with difficulty."

combatose   proesthesis

siamian   vasecktomy

abescess   carecinogen

diurnnal

V. Matching

Match the word in column A with its correct definition in column B by writing the letter of that definition in the space provided.

A	B
_____ 1. abscess	a. replacement for a part of the body
_____ 2. aphasia	b. one who pretends to be ill
_____ 3. arteriosclerosis	c. contraceptive surgery
_____ 4. benign	d. curative
_____ 5. biopsy	e. examination of body tissue
_____ 6. cadaver	f. hardening of the arteries
_____ 7. carcinogen	g. mild
_____ 8. comatose	h. science of the causes and origins of disease
_____ 9. etiology	i. removal of a breast by surgery
_____ 10. malingerer	j. cancer-causing substance
_____ 11. mastectomy	k. illness affecting speech and understanding
_____ 12. prosthesis	l. dead body
_____ 13. simian	m. ape-like
_____ 14. therapeutic	n. inflamed area in body tissues
_____ 15. vasectomy	o. unconscious

Animal World

Is an elephant a *saurian,* an *ursine,* or neither?

What do *felines* and *vulpines* have in common?

Which denotes the animal with the worst "table manners"—*behemoth, vulpine,* or *porcupine?*

To which animal is a *vixenish* woman compared?

Would a racing fan best be described as a *saurian,* an *equine,* or a *bovine* fancier?

---

behemoth
bestial
bovine
carnivorous
equine
feline
harbinger
leonine
porcine
predator
saurian
ursine
vixen
vulpine

1. **behemoth** (bi-hē'-məth)—huge animal; something enormous.
    a. When the *behemoth* charged at us, we were terrified.
    b. The millionaire investor pulled off a *behemoth* of a real estate deal.

2. **bestial** (bes'chəl)—savage; like an animal.
    a. The *bestial* crime stunned the entire neighborhood.
    b. Uncle Archer was criticized for his *bestial* table manners.

3. **bovine** (bō'-vīn,-vin,-vēn)—an ox, cow, or related animal; having oxlike qualities; slow, dull, stupid, or stolid.
    a. People with *bovine* temperaments may be dependable but they are not exciting company.
    b. Because of their easygoing nature, *bovine* creatures have been domesticated to serve mankind faithfully.

4. **carnivorous** (kär-niv'-ər-əs)—flesh eating.
    a. Ellen gave up her *carnivorous* ways for the life of a vegetarian
    b. The *carnivorous* eagle swooped down upon his helpless prey.

5. **equine** (é-kwīn, ek'-wīn)—a horse; of, like, or characteristic of a horse.
    a. The zebra belongs to the *equine* group.
    b. Although the glory of the *equines* in the development of the West has ended, horses still play an important part in the world of sports.

6. **feline** (fē'-līn)—a member of the family that includes lions, tigers, jaguars, and wild and domestic cats; resembling or suggestive of a cat, as in suppleness, slyness, treachery, or stealthiness.
    a. When Maria heard herself described as *feline,* she did not know if the speaker referred to her sleekness or her tendency to gossip.
    b. She walked with a *feline* grace that was a pleasure to behold.

7. **harbinger** (här'-bin-jər)—forerunner.
    a. The robin is a certain *harbinger* of spring.
    b. A troop of elephants was a *harbinger* of the circus's arrival.

8. **leonine** (lē'-ə-nīn)—of, pertaining to, or characteristic of a lion. Like Felix the cat and Bossie the cow, Leo the lion takes his name from the original Latin.
    a. Flagrant injustice always evoked a *leonine* rage in the senator.
    b. Emitting a huge *leonine* sigh, old Mr. Carew shuffled back to his seat.

9. **porcine** (pôr'-sīn)—of or pertaining to swine or pigs; piglike. The cartoon character Porky Pig derives his name from the Latin *porcus,* pig.
   a.   A bald, *porcine* old man sat on the bench greedily eating a huge lunch.
   b.   Reverend Tolliver's sermon stressed the point that *porcine* pleasures ill become the nobility of the soul.

10. **predator** (pred'-ə-tər)—an animal that preys on others; one who abuses others for his own gain.
    a.   The lion was the chief *predator* in that part of the jungle.
    b.   Putting small shopkeepers out of business was the *predator's* delight.

11. **saurian** (sôr'-ē-ən)—of or having the characteristics of lizards; a lizard. The names of the prehistoric animals, like the dinosaur and the brontosaur, used combining forms with the Greek root *saurios* ("lizard").
    a.   The flesh-eating *saurians* walked on their hind legs, the planteaters on all fours.
    b.   *Saurians* include a wide range of reptiles from the gentle chameleon to the ferocious crocodile.

12. **ursine** (ur'-sīn)—of or characteristic of a bear. The constellations Ursa Major and Ursa Minor, popularly called the Big Dipper and the Little Dipper, appeared to the ancients to have the outlines of a "Great Bear" and a "Little Bear."
    a.   Contrary to popular belief, the *ursine* habit of hibernating is interrupted several times by periods of wakefulness.
    b.   Using the *ursine* appetite for sweets as an incentive, trainers have taught bears to appear to be "reading" as they turn pages looking for honey.

13. **venomous** (ven'-ə-môs)—malicious, spiteful, poisonous.
    a.   A bite from that *venomous* snake could be fatal.
    b.   In a *venomous* attack, the columnist destroyed the actor's reputation.

14. **vixen** (vik'-sən)—a female fox; a quarrelsome shrewish, or malicious woman. Vixen may also be used as an adjective.
    a.   Petruchio knew the secret of turning a *vixen* into an obedient and loving housewife.
    b.   Margot's *vixen* temperament shows in her refusal to yield to even the most reasonable suggestion to end the quarrel.

15. **vulpine** (vul'-pīn, -pin)—of, resembling, or characteristic of a fox; clever, devious, or cunning. The famous play *Volpone,* or *The Fox,* was an early seventeenth-century drama by Ben Jonson.
    a.   Sherlock Holmes, as a successful detective, possessed certain *vulpine* qualities that gave him the edge over his adversaries.
    b.   Fables sometimes represent *vulpine* characters as coming out second best in spite of their cunning.

EXERCISES

I. Which Word Comes to Mind?

In each of the following, read the statement, then circle the word that comes to mind.

1. A lizard crawled into view

    (bovine, saurian, equine)

2. The sour-grapes fable

    (equine vulpine, leonine)

3. *Taming of the Shrew*

    (vixen, vulpine, feline)

4. A sloppy eater

    (behemoth, bestial, ursine)

5. Smokey Bear

    (ursine, carnivorous, harbinger)

6. The Adam and Eve story

    (vixen, ovine, vulpine, venomous)

7. The Kentucky Derby

    (feline, equine, porcine)

8. Meow

    (bovine, feline, saurian)

9. MGM movies start with the lion's roar

    (leonine, ursine, behemoth)

10. In 2003 the United States and Great Britain had to deal with "mad cow" disease

    (harbinger, vulpine, bovine)

II. True or False?

In the space provided, indicate whether each statement is true or false.

_____ 1. *Felines* and *saurians* have much in common.

_____ 2. Both lions and tigers can be described as *leonine*.

_____ 3. Horse racing would be impossible without *equines*.

_____ 4. An aquarium would house many *ursine* creatures.

_____ 5. A *bovine* and *equine* animal make a natural pair.

_____ 6. Overeaters are often described as *porcine*.

_____ 7. Because Lou loved dogs, he received an award from the *Feline* Society of America.

_____ 8. *Vulpine* milk is taken from brown cows only.

_____ 9. The actor who starred as a vampire was given a *leonine* appearance.

_____ 10. We rely on our *saurian* animals for warm woolen garments.

III. Find the Impostor

Find and circle the one word on each line that is not related to the other three.

1. equity	equine	equerry	equestrian
2. ephemeral	fleeting	feline	transient
3. shrew	vexing	virago	vixen
4. bullish	matador	terrain	taurine
5. mare	foal	equine	fowl

IV. Anagrams

In each of the following, subtract one or more letters from the word, then rearrange the letters to form the new word whose meaning is given.

1. ursine – one letter = awakened _____

2. vixen – two letters = disallow _____

3. bovine – two letters = skeleton component_____

4. feline – two letters = river _____

5. saurian – two letters = a plastic wrap _____

V. Matching

Match the word in column A with its correct definition in column B by writing the letter of that definition in the space provided.

A	B
____ 1. behemoth	a. flesh eating
____ 2. bestial	b. relating to swine
____ 3. bovine	c. lionlike
____ 4. carnivorous	d. sluggish
____ 5. equine	e. resembling a cat
____ 6. feline	f. animal that preys on others
____ 7. harbinger	g. lizard
____ 8. leonine	h. ill-tempered woman
____ 9. porcine	i. savage
____ 10. predator	j. devious
____ 11. saurian	k. bearlike
____ 12. ursine	l. big animal
____ 13. venomous	m. pertaining to a horse
____ 14. vixen	n. forerunner
____ 15. vulpine	o. poisonous

Identity crisis

Countdown—Words with Numbers

Is a *millennium* the same as, more than, or less than a million?

In what profession is it important to follow *protocol?*

Is *bicameral* a double-strength lens or a legislative system?

In what way is the word *decimate* linked to a mutiny?

What is the *penultimate* letter of a word?

---

ambiguous
atonement
bicameral
Decalogue
decimate
dichotomy
double-think
millennium
nihilism
penultimate
primeval
protocol
quatrain
quintessence
untrammeled

1. **ambiguous** (am-big'yōo-əs)—subject to more than one interpretation; indefinite.
   a. Anita's *ambiguous* reply left all of us confused.
   b. The president's press secretary was the master of the *ambiguous* phrase.

2. **atonement** (ə-tōn'-mənt)—amends for wrong-doing; expiation. The theological use of this word can be readily understood if it is interpreted to mean "being at one" with God, taking the proper action to correct an injury or repair a relationship.
   a. The Day of *Atonement,* the holiest day of the Jewish year, is observed by fasting and prayer.
   b. How, ask the environmentalists, can we make *atonement* for the crime of poisoning the atmosphere?

3. **bicameral** (bī-kam'-ə-rəl)—composed of two houses, chambers or branches. It is easy to identify the prefix *bi,* which we find in *bicentennial, biceps,* and *binomial.* The second part, obviously related to *camera,* tells us that photography, like the legislature, requires a chamber in which to function.
   a. The *bicameral* system of government in the U.S. arose as a compromise between the advocates of a strong national government and the supporters of states rights.
   b. The House of Lords in England, though nominally making Parliament *bicameral,* does not wield the same power as the House of Commons.

4. **Decalogue** (dek'-ə-lôg)—the Ten Commandments. The precepts spoken by God to Israel on Mt. Sinai are the basis of Mosaic Law.
   a. The *Decalogue* remains the most sublime declaration of man's relationship with his Creator and his fellow human beings.
   b. Some believe that modern society has paved the way for its own destruction by transgressing the sacred *Decalogue.*

5. **decimate** (des'-ə-māt)—to destroy a great number or proportion of. The word is traceable to the cruel punishment for mutiny—selecting by lot and killing one in every ten people. The same Latin root, *decem* ("ten"), gives us *decimals, decade,* and even *December* (the tenth month if you begin, as the Romans did, with March).
   a. Besides causing enormous destruction of property, the violent earthquake *decimated* the city's population.
   b. The ecological imbalance has *decimated* many species of animal life and brought some to the brink of extinction.

6. **dichotomy** (dī-kŏt'-ə-mē)—division into two usually contradictory parts or opinions. The Greek root means something cut in two. In modern usage the word has special significance in logic (a division into mutually exclusive groups) and in botany (a branching into two equal subdivisions).
    a. There is a clear *dichotomy* of opinion on the subject of abortion.
    b. Dolores and Irv's *dichotomy* of viewpoints on mercy killing has caused many a heated battle.

7. **double-think** (dub'-əl-think)—the belief in two contradictory ideas at the same time. This, as well as other forms of Newspeak, was formulated by George Orwell in his novel, *1984.*
    a. "War is peace" is an example of *double-think.*
    b. Is *double-think* self-deception or ignorance?

8. **millennium** (mə-len'-ē-əm)—a span of a thousand years; a period of general righteousness and happiness, especially in the indefinite future.
    a. The last fifty years of this *millennium* have wrought the greatest changes in the history of civilization.
    b. Our pastor said that we can bring the *millennium* in our lifetime if we treat each other with a spirit of generosity and forgiveness.

9. **nihilism** (nī'-ə-liz'm)—total rejection of established laws and institutions; total destructiveness toward the world and oneself. The *nihilist* adopts the extreme position that nothing exists or can be communicated; hence, he lives in a lonely, empty world.
    a. Since Max has turned toward *nihilism,* we are afraid that he will do something antisocial.
    b. We must counter the folly of *nihilism* by improving the quality of life without yielding to despair because of our slow progress.

10. **penultimate** (pi-nul'-tə-mit)—next to the last. The Latin *paene* ("almost") and *ultimus* ("last") combine to form this word.
    a. *Y* is the *penultimate* letter of our alphabet.
    b. The *penultimate* scene of the play had the audience sitting on the edge of their seats.

11. **primeval** (prī-mē'vəl)—original; belonging to the first or earliest ages. It is important to differentiate between primeval and its synonyms; *prime* "first in numerical order" and *primitive* "suggesting the simplicity of original things." Other synonyms are *pristine* and *primordial.*
    a. Longfellow's "Hiawatha" begins with the sonorous tones of "This is the forest *primeval."*
    b. Many characteristics of the *primeval* forms of life have been gradually shed to produce the most adaptable creatures.

12. **protocol** (prō'-tə-kôl)—forms of ceremony and etiquette observed by diplomats and heads of states; the first copy of a treaty or document. The Greek roots refer to the first leaf glued to the front of the manuscript and containing the notes of the contents.
    a. Upon his arrival, Ambassador Lefton presented his credentials to the monarch, as *protocol* demanded.
    b. "Forget about *protocol,*" said the hostess, urging us to take any seat.

13. **quatrain** (kwôt'-rān)—a stanza or poem of four lines, usually with alternate rhymes.
    a. "The Rubaiyat of Omar Khayyam" is the famous Fitzgerald translation of a group of *quatrains* by a Persian poet.
    b. The Shakespearean sonnet is composed of three *quatrains* followed by a couplet that summarizes or epitomizes the major point.

14. **quintessence** (kwin-tes'-ns)—the most perfect embodiment of something; the purest or most typical instance. In ancient philosophy, the fifth and highest essence *quinta essentia* ("ether") was supposed to be the constituent matter of the heavenly bodies, the others being earth, air, fire, and water.
    a. Prejudice is the *quintessence* of falsehood.
    b. The *quintessential* characteristic of Shakespeare is his profound understanding of human nature.

15. untrammeled (un-tram'l'd)—unhampered; unrestrained. The fishermen of the Middle Ages made a three-layered net *(tres macula)* of varying degrees of coarseness so that the fish would be entangled in one or more of the meshes.
a. It was Bobby's ardent desire to feel *untrammeled* in his choice of a career.
b. Chicago was said to be *untrammeled* by the financial woes that have plagued major cities.

EXERCISES

I. Which Word Comes to Mind?

In each of the following, read the statement, then circle the word that comes to mind.

1. Negotiations to settle a strike are broken off

   (atonement, dichotomy, double-think)

2. A young lady practices curtsying for hours in preparation for meeting royalty

   (quatrain, ambiguous, protocol)

3. A Golden Age is just around the corner

   (quintessence, millennium, bicameral)

4. A baseball game's eighth inning

   (penultimate, decimate, untrammeled)

5. The radicals' weapons were terrorism, rioting, and subversion

   (primeval, nihilism, Decalogue)

6. A chemical company has to make payments to victims of pollution

   (protocol, atonement, quatrain)

7. Locusts will destroy most of the crop

   (decimate, penultimate, primeval)

8. God and Moses

   (bicameral, nihilism, Decalogue)

9. The model was described by many as being a symbol of pure beauty

   (quintessence, double-think, ambiguous)

10. A meeting of Senate and House leaders

    (untrammeled, bicameral, quatrain)

II. True or False?

In the space provided, indicate whether each statement is true or false.

_____ 1. *Double-think* suggests a careful analysis of both sides of a problem.
_____ 2. Shakespeare's sonnets contain three *quatrains.*
_____ 3. The *Decalogue* is a play with ten speaking parts.
_____ 4. A prisoner being released from jail feels *untrammeled.*
_____ 5. *Dichotomy* and *bicameral* have prefixes with the same meaning.
_____ 6. As part of the Germans' *atonement,* they had to pay reparations to the state of Israel.
_____ 7. The Black Plague severely *decimated* Europe's population.
_____ 8. Our complete agreement pointed up the remaining *dichotomy* between us.
_____ 9. Many cities planned celebrations for the *millennium.*
_____ 10. The real estate developer's *nihilism* led him to a successful career as a builder.

III. Fill in the Blank

Insert one of the new words in the proper space in each sentence below.

1. Observing the proper _____ , Mrs. Berman curtsied before the monarch.
2. In an act of _____ , the former criminal contributed a million dollars to the family he had swindled.
3. Scientists fear that a new virus could _____ much of Europe's population.
4. Abandoning his youthful adherence to _____ Ned became a constructive thinker and responsible citizen.
5. Numerous _____ species are being destroyed each year as mankind continues to pollute the forests and the waterways.
6. Our _____ of opinions on euthanasia will be addressed in a debate.
7. The candidate's hoped-for image is that he is the _____ of honesty.
8. After dessert as the _____ course, the meal ended with coffee.
9. Some previous dictatorships have given way to constitutional _____ legislative bodies.
10. When the entire class scored 100% on the spelling test, my teacher exclaimed, "The _____ has arrived!"

IV. What's the Antonym?

Which of the new words is most nearly *opposite* in meaning to the one provided?

1. restrained   _____
2. modern   _____
3. final   _____
4. togetherness   _____
5. governance   _____
6. lack of regret   _____
7. add to   _____
8. clear   _____
9. rudeness   _____
10. dictatorial   _____

V. Matching

Match the word in column A with its correct definition in column B by writing the letter of that definition in the space provided.

A

_____ 1. ambiguous
_____ 2. atonement
_____ 3. bicameral
_____ 4. Decalogue
_____ 5. decimate
_____ 6. dichotomy
_____ 7. double-think
_____ 8. millennium
_____ 9. nihilism
_____ 10. penultimate
_____ 11. primeval
_____ 12. protocol
_____ 13. quatrain
_____ 14. quintessence
_____ 15. untrammeled

B

a. Mosaic Code
b. annihilate
c. proper behavior
d. next to last
e. perfection
f. belief in contradictory ideas
g. indefinite
h. rejection of any purpose in existence
i. a thousand years
j. congressional, composed of two houses
k. the act of making amends
l. division of opinion
m. earliest
n. four-line stanza
o. freed

Legal Language (I)

Is a *tort* a kind of pastry?

Does an *intestate* person require the services of a physician?

Are three judges necessary to form a *tribunal?*

Can a case be started in an *appellate* court?

What do you do to a body when you *exhume* it?

---

adjudicate
appellate
collusion
deposition
equity
exhume
incommunicado
intestate
ipso facto
lien
litigation
perjury
pettifogger
tort
tribunal

1. **adjudicate** (ə-jōō-də-kāt)—to hear and settle a case by judicial procedure. As a transitive verb, *adjudicate* means to settle the rights of the parties in a court case. As an intransitive verb, it means simply to act as a judge.
   a. The court *adjudicated* the case for months before deciding on the offshore drilling rights of the states.
   b. It takes patience and common sense to *adjudicate* in a dispute between friends and reach a fair decision.

2. **appellate** (ə-pel'-it)—having the power to hear appeals and to reverse lower court decisions. An *appellant* is the one who appeals from a judicial decision or decree. An *appellee* is one against whom an appeal is taken.
   a. The *appellate* court upheld the verdict of the lower court in the celebrated trial involving the student who received a diploma without learning to read.
   b. An *appellate* decision by the state court can be overturned by the Supreme Court.

3. **collusion** (kə-lōō'-zhən)—a secret agreement for a deceitful or fraudulent purpose; conspiracy. Though the word has a serious connotation today, it is derived from the Latin *ludere* ("to play"), and *ludus* ("game"). A *collusion* often implies an attempt to defraud a person of his rights by the forms of law.
   a. The captain of the Zaire forces defending Mutshatsha was accused of acting in *collusion* with the enemy in the surrender of the city.
   b. The senator felt that there was *collusion* on the part of this committee to deny him the chairmanship.

4. **deposition** (dep'-ə-zish'ən)—testimony under oath, especially a written statement by a witness for use in court in his or her absence. In ordinary usage, *deposition* refers to the act of depriving of authority, or the placing or laying down, as of sediment or precipitation.
   a. In the *deposition* made to the police at the scene of the crime, the accused dope smuggler appeared vindictive and unrepentant.
   b. The forcible *deposition* of the president by his own army was intended to bring an end to almost two years of civil war.

5. **equity** (ek'-wə-tē)—something that is just, impartial, and fair; the value of a business or property in excess of any claim against it; justice applied in circumstances not covered by law.
   a. *Equity* demands that the solution to the energy crisis does not bring undue hardship to one group and windfall profits to another.
   b. The family *equity* in the estate after all obligations had been paid amounted to ten thousand dollars.

6. **exhume** (iks-hyōōm')—to dig out of the earth; disinter; reveal. From the Latin *humus* ("ground").
   a. The district attorney, suspecting foul play, got a court order to *exhume* the body.
   b. It took ten years of digging in the library to *exhume* the material that she needed for her exposé of corruption.

7. **incommunicado** (in-kə-myōō'-nə-kä-dō)—without the means or right of communication with others, as one held in solitary confinement.
   a. In order to avoid offending voters, it is sometimes expedient for a political candidate to be *incommunicado* on sensitive issues.
   b. The banker was advised by her lawyers to remain *incommunicado* until the charges against her were made public.

8. **intestate** (in-tes'-tāt)—having made no valid will; one who dies without a legal will.
   a. The media at first reported that the millionaire had died *intestate*.
   b. The administration of property left by an *intestate* is a complicated matter that usually ends with the government receiving the lion's share.

9. **ipso facto** (ip'-sō fak'-tō)—by the fact itself; by that very fact.
   a. Though an alien, *ipso facto,* has no right to a U.S. passport, the administration does not plan to press charges against the eight million who entered the country illegally.
   b. Training in speech is *ipso facto* training in personality.

10. **lien** (lēn)—the right to take and hold or sell the property of a debtor as security or payment for a debt; mortgage. The word is related to the Latin *ligare* ("to bind"), indicating that certain possessions are bound or tied to the payment of a debt.
    a. A *lien* was placed against the Russian vessel that had violated the newly-declared U.S. fishing territorial waters.
    b. Before you purchase that house, check to see if it is free of any *liens* against the present owner.

11. **litigation** (lit-ə-gā'-shən)—legal action or process. A person who will sue at the drop of a hat is said to be *litigious.*
    a. The *litigation* over the closing of the child care centers dragged on for months.
    b. After years of *litigation,* only the lawyers made any money from the case.

12. **perjury** (pur'-jer-ē)—the deliberate, wilful giving of false, misleading, or incomplete testimony by a witness under oath in a criminal proceeding.
    a. Shakespeare tells us, "At lovers' *perjuries,* Jove laughs."
    b. As the guest left, he thanked the hostess with as much enthusiasm as he could muster without actually *perjuring* himself.

13. **pettifogger** (pet'-ē-fäg-ər)—a petty, quibbling, unscrupulous lawyer; a shyster. *Shyster* comes from the American lawyer Scheuster, who in 1840 was rebuked in court for his objectionable practices. *Pettifogger,* similarly, is derived from the pettiness of the Fuggers, a sixteenth-century German family of financiers and merchants.
    a. The attorney's underhanded and disreputable methods earned him a reputation as a *pettifogger*.
    b. The editorial attacked the cautious *pettifoggers,* who could only agree on what could not be done in dealing with the energy crisis.

14. **tort** (tôrt)—any wrongful act not involving breach of contract for which a civil suit can be brought. The Latin *tortum* ("twisted"), is related to *torque,* a twisting force, and *torture.*
    a. The lawyer claimed the injury done to his client was willful and subject to the laws of *tort.*
    b. It was difficult to prove the defendant guilty of a *tort* as his intentions could not be clearly established.

15. **tribunal** (tri-byōō'-nəl)—a seat or court of justice. The tribune was the Roman official chosen by the plebeians (commoners) to protect their rights against the patricians (wealthy class).
    a. The Supreme Court, the highest *tribunal* of our nation, refused to review the convictions of the Watergate defendants.
    b. An honest man is answerable to no *tribunal* but his own judgment.

EXERCISES

I. Which Word Comes to Mind?

In each of the following, read the statement, then circle the word that comes to mind.

1. No evidence of a will was found

    (equity, intestate, litigation)

2. Any statement made now can be held against you

    (deposition, tort, ipso facto)

3. If we do not get satisfaction here, we will take this case to a higher court

    (collusion, tribunal, appellate)

4. The witness has told only half the story in court

    (adjudicate, perjury, exhume)

5. Lie low till the furor subsides

    (incommunicado, pettifogger, lien)

6. The basketball players all agreed to lose the game

    (equity, collusion, perjury)

7. Fido's remains were dug up and buried elsewhere

    (exhume, ipso facto, adjudicate)

8. Debts had to be paid before we could acquire the house

    (lien, incommunicado, tribunal)

9. He conspired to get me fired

    (exhume, appellate, tort)

10. In and out of court regularly

    (collusion, litigation, equity)

II. True or False?

In the space provided, indicate whether each statement is true or false.

_____ 1. A *collusion* is an intellectual clash between two strong lawyers.

_____ 2. An *adjudicated* settlement is one made out of court.

_____ 3. *Torts* involve an injury or damage done without breach of contract.

_____ 4. A *pettifogger* is overly concerned with trifles.

_____ 5. *Ipso facto* refers to facts, like axioms, that are universally accepted.

_____ 6. We turned to the *appellate* division to get justice.

_____ 7. A *deposition* is related to a proposition.

_____ 8. The government's witness was held *incommunicado.*

_____ 9. Because he died *intestate,* no surgery was required.

_____ 10. Different American Indian families belong to special *tribunals.*

III. Fill in the Blank

Insert one of the new words in the proper space in each sentence below.

1. It would take a Solomon to _____ the difficult child custody case.

2. There were contradictions between David's recent testimony and his earlier _____ .

3. We were greatly relieved when the court lifted the _____ against the sale of our home.

4. Some people sue at the drop of a hat but most prefer to avoid _____ .

5. When both stores offered the exact sale prices, we began to suspect _____ between the managements.

6. I am searching for _____ , not an unfair advantage.

7. The suspected spy was held _____ for 48 hours.

8. As an eighteenth-century revolutionary _____ , the French nobleman was found guilty.

9. Although he was cautioned about committing _____ , the witness continued to lie.

10. Since my uncle died _____ , the family has spent a fortune trying to get its hands on the bulk of his estate.

IV. What's the Antonym?

Which of the new words is most nearly *opposite* in meaning to the one provided?

1. bury   _____

2. truth   _____

3. partiality   _____

4. accessible   _____

5. legal act   _____

V. Matching

Match the word in column A with its correct definition in column B by writing the letter of that definition in the space provided.

	A		B
_____	1. adjudicate	a.	testimony under oath
_____	2. appellate	b.	claim against property
_____	3. collusion	c.	a wrongful act
_____	4. deposition	d.	act as a judge
_____	5. equity	e.	one harping on insignificant matters
_____	6. exhume	f.	court of law
_____	7. incommunicado	g.	by that very fact
_____	8. intestate	h.	dig out of the earth
_____	9. ipso facto	i.	conspiracy
_____	10. lien	j.	impartiality
_____	11. litigation	k.	able to uphold or reverse previous decisions
_____	12. perjury	l.	isolated
_____	13. pettifogger	m.	lying under oath
_____	14. tort	n.	not having a will
_____	15. tribunal	o.	legal action

Deposition

Appearances and Attitudes (II)

What is the relationship of *florid* to Florida?

Why might you send a *flaccid* person to a body-building spa?

Would a bald person object to being called *glabrous?*

Do we expect judges to behave in a *dispassionate* manner?

Why must a spy be *circumspect?*

---

circumspect
demure
dispassionate
dolorous
edacious
effete
feisty
flaccid
flippant
florid
glabrous
imperious
ingenious
intractable
intransigent

1. **circumspect** (sur'-kəm-spekt)—careful; cautious; prudent. The original meaning of this word was "to look about." A person who "looks about" is cautious—hence, *circumspect.*
   a. The killer was *circumspect* about leaving any clues that would tie him to the victim.
   b. We complimented the lawyer for his *circumspect* handling of the embarrassing matter.

2. **demure** (di-myo͞or')—modest; shy. It comes from a Latin word that means "mature" or "proper."
   a. Shakespeare's advice to a *demure* young maiden is: "Say nay but take it."
   b. Even when she was in her thirties, the actress was still being cast as a *demure* high school girl.

3. **dispassionate** (dis-pash'-ən-it)—fair; impartial; calm.
   a. As a *dispassionate* observer, I agreed to settle the dispute.
   b. It's easy to be *dispassionate* about international problems that do not appear to affect us directly.

4. **dolorous** (dō'-lər-əs)—painful; mournful.
   a. Merchants whose stores had been looted during the blackout wore *dolorous* expressions.
   b. Nearing the funeral, we were greeted by a *dolorous* chant from the church choir.

5. **edacious** (i-dā'-shəs)—devouring; consuming. It comes from the Latin *edere* ("to eat").
   a. The *edacious* forest fire destroyed everything in its path.
   b. Betty Ann enjoys buffet luncheons because she has an *edacious* appetite.

6. **effete** (e-fēt')—worn out; spent and sterile. The Latin word *effetus* means "that which has brought forth offspring."
   a. After years of intermarriage, the royal family line was *effete* and exhausted.
   b. Long service in the coal mines left Hal Fletcher *effete* and tubercular.

7. feisty (fīs'-tē)—touchy; excitable; quarrelsome.
   a. The *feisty* boxer was sensitive about his height and ready to fight with any taller person.
   b. It took an hour to settle Sara's *feisty* boyfriend down after he thought he had been insulted.

8. flaccid (flak'-sid)—weak; feeble; flabby.
   a. Because she had been confined to her bed for three weeks after surgery, Mrs. Leslie's muscles were *flaccid.*
   b. Senator Dwyer's *flaccid* response to the accusations was highlighted by the media.

9. flippant (flip'-ənt)—disrespectful; saucy, impertinent.
   a. A sure way to get under Mr. Tarranto's skin is to give *flippant* answers to his serious questions.
   b. Marjorie's *flippant* attitude toward her grandmother's illness led to a bitter family argument.

10. florid (flôr'-id)—ruddy; rosy; ornate. Florid also means "highly-colored," which reveals its connection with the Latin word for flower, *floris.*
   a. After living outdoors all summer, Myra had a *florid* glow in her cheeks.
   b. Our mayor is fond of using *florid,* overblown language in his campaign speeches.

11. glabrous (glā'-brəs)—bald; smooth.
   a. The comic's *glabrous* scalp was his trademark in show business.
   b. As I meditate, I find it restful to run my fingertips over the surface of a *glabrous* stone.

12. imperious (im-pir'-ē-əs)—overbearing; arrogant; domineering. It is easy to see the relationship of this word to *emperor.*
   a. We were turned off by the official's *imperious* manner.
   b. In an *imperious* tone, my grandfather ordered the sheriff off his property.

13. ingenious (in-jēn'-yəs)—clever, original; inventive; resourceful.
   a. Rube Goldberg, the cartoonist, was famous for his wildly *ingenious* mechanical devices.
   b. The *ingenious* solution to the city's transportation problems was to cut the fares in half.

14. intractable (in-trak'-tə-b'l)—hard to manage; unruly; stubborn.
   a. The union chief was willing to compromise on wages but he was *intractable* when it came to working conditions.
   b. Mrs. Finkel usually sent her *intractable* pupils directly to the principal's office.

15. intransigent (in-tran'-si-jənt)—uncompromising; refusing to come to an agreement.
   a. Owners of baseball teams used to hire top-notch lawyers to bring *intransigent* players to terms.
   b. The actor took an *intransigent* position when he refused to star in any more cowboy movies.

EXERCISES

I. Which Word Comes to Mind?

In each of the following, read the statement, then circle the word that comes to mind.

1. A married man takes his secretary to a dark restaurant

   (florid, circumspect, intransigent)

2. My father is the absolute boss in our house

   (dispassionate, glabrous, imperious)

3. An argument is in progress; neither side wants to give in

   (intractable, flaccid, edacious)

4. The night club comedian upset his conservative audience

   (flippant, dolorous, effete)

5. A blush stole over the teenager's cheek

   (feisty, ingenious, demure)

6. Our pit bull is hard to handle

   (feisty, circumspect, flippant)

7. The inventor devised a gadget that can work miracles

   (glabrous, florid, ingenious)

8. She cried at the sad organ music

   (effete, edacious, dolorous)

9. Not much hair for the barber to cut

   (flaccid, glabrous, demure)

10. We'll never give in

    (intransigent, dispassionate, edacious)

II. True or False?

In the space provided, indicate whether each statement is true or false.

_____ 1. *Intransigent* people are definitely *intractable.*

_____ 2. A *glabrous* person is usually vain about his attractive hair.

_____ 3. The winner's headquarters was filled with *dolorous* sounds when the victory was announced.

_____ 4. Julius Caesar's *imperious* manner befitted his position as a dictator.

_____ 5. Clark Kent's *effete* appearance was a way of disguising his true identity as Superman.

_____ 6. Shut away from sunlight for two years, Vanya's face had a *florid* glow.

_____ 7. After strenuous gym workouts, my cousin's muscles are no longer *flaccid.*

_____ 8. Quentin's *flippant* responses caused him to be suspended from school.

_____ 9. The English actor impressed us with his *circumspect* behavior and reserved manners.

_____ 10. *Dolorous* music tends to liven up any party.

III. Fill in the Blank

Insert one of the new words in the proper space in each sentence below.

1. Surprisingly, it was a teenager who devised an _____ solution to the scheduling problem.

2. The _____ baseball manager was ejected after pushing the umpire.

3. Several irate customers complained about the _____ attitudes of our salespeople.

4. When the private detective was hired, he was reminded of the need to be _____ .

5. Private Williams had to do fifty push-ups because of his _____ answers to Sergeant Doyle.

6. Our pleas were in vain because Ernesto had adopted an _____ position.

7. The transition from hard-bitten cynic to a _____ young thing was unrealistic.

8. As we approached the funeral parlor, _____ music greeted our ears.

9. Baseball umpires are expected to be _____ in rendering their decisions.

10. Governor Walsh's pompous acceptance speech was filled with _____ language.

IV. What's the Antonym?

Which of the new words is most nearly *opposite* in meaning to the one provided?

1. careless   _____

2. virile   _____

3. hairy   _____

4. flexible   _____

5. pale   _____

6. opinionated   _____

7. arrogant   _____

8. dull   _____

9. respectful   _____

10. calm   _____

V. Matching

Match the word in column A with its correct definition in column B by writing the letter of that definition in the space provided.

	A		*B*
_____	1. circumspect	a.	modest
_____	2. demure	b.	arrogant
_____	3. dispassionate	c.	worn out
_____	4. dolorous	d.	mournful
_____	5. edacious	e.	quarrelsome
_____	6. effete	f.	cautious
_____	7. feisty	g.	clever
_____	8. flaccid	h.	disrespectful
_____	9. flippant	i.	stubborn
_____	10. florid	j.	rosy
_____	11. glabrous	k.	consuming
_____	12. imperious	l.	uncompromising
_____	13. ingenious	m.	bald
_____	14. intractable	n.	flabby
_____	15. intransigent	o.	impartial

Unit 2
(Lessons 11–15)
Mini Review

I. Antonyms

Circle the word that most nearly expresses the *opposite* meaning of the word in capital letters.
1. DOLOROUS: (a) exhausted (b) transparent (c) fiery (d) happy
2. COMATOSE: (a) conscious (b) flexible (c) stubborn (d) resentful
3. PRIMEVAL: (a) constructive (b) modern (c) firsthand (d) cultured
4. EXHUME: (a) bury (b) introduce (c) reject (d) analyze
5. DEMURE: (a) deferential (b) brazen (c) intolerant (d) rigid

II. Synonyms

Circle the word that most nearly expresses the *same* meaning as the word printed in capital letters.
1. INTRACTABLE: (a) worn out (b) mournful (c) uncompromising (d) complex
2. CIRCUMSPECT: (a) comprehensive (b) cautious (c) roundabout (d) arrogant
3. DICHOTOMY: (a) essay (b) agreement (c) clarification (d) division
4. SIMIAN: (a) parallel (b) stunted (c) treacherous (d) apelike
5. BENIGN: (a) gratuity (b) consideration (c) replacement (d) mild

III. Sentence Completions

Select those words from the group below that best fill the blanks.

biopsy   deposition   litigation   quintessence
carcinogen   equine   millennium   saurian
collusion   flippant

1. I developed a new interest in lizards after viewing the _____ exhibit at the Museum of Natural History.
2. We entered into _____ because we felt that an injustice had been done.
3. Accused of _____ in the planning of the robbery, the defendant faced a long jail term.
4. Lab reports revealed that it was a _____ in the water supply that led to the increase in cancer cases in our neighborhood.
5. "When the _____ comes," Aunt Jean remarked, "Buddy will clean up his room."

Mystery and the Occult

Do you have to join a spa to *exorcise?*

Is *alchemy* a respected branch of chemistry?

Should Julius Caesar have heeded the *soothsayer?*

What happens if you fail your *polygraph* test?

Can a crossword puzzle be called a *conundrum?*

---

alchemy
arcane
conundrum
demonology
exorcise
illusion
inscrutable
pallor
polygraph
purloin
ritual
shamus
soothsayer
thaumaturgy
warlock

1. **alchemy** (al'-kə-mē)—a method of miraculous change of one thing into another. In the Middle Ages, the chief aim of honest and dishonest experimenters was to change base metals into gold and to discover the elixir of eternal youth.
   a. Even though the charlatan was practicing fifteenth-century *alchemy,* some fools believed him.
   b. Through some incredible *alchemy,* the ugly frog was changed into a handsome prince.

2. **arcane** (är-kān')—beyond comprehension; mysterious; secret. The Latin word *arcanus* means "shut up" or "hidden."
   a. I find much modern poetry to be *arcane,* totally beyond my grasp.
   b. Teddy offered an *arcane* explanation for his whereabouts that confused us even further.

3. **conundrum** (kə-nun'-drəm)—a riddle; any puzzling question or problem.
   a. The most famous literary *conundrum* can be found in Sophocles' play, *Oedipus Rex.*
   b. Anyone who could solve the *conundrum* of the three caskets would win the hand of the beautiful Portia.

4. **demonology** (dē-mə-näl'-ə-jē)—the study of demons or of beliefs about them.
   a. Seeing the books on *demonology* in their apartment confirmed Rosemary's suspicions about her neighbors.
   b. Before making the movie about witches, the director steeped himself in the lore of *demonology.*

5. **exorcise** (ek'-sôr-sīz)—to drive away an evil spirit by charms or incantations.
   a. The distraught parents asked the Vatican to help *exorcise* the spirit that they believed was tormenting their child.
   b. In the stage play, the priest used a crucifix and a Bible to *exorcise* the demons.

6. **illusion** (ĭ-lōō'-zhən)—a mistaken perception of reality.
   a. What I thought was a ferocious tiger turned out to be an *illusion.*
   b. I hated to destory the *illusion,* but I had no choice.

7. inscrutable (in-skrōō'-tə-b'l)—mysterious; completely obscure; unfathomable.
   a.   Since many Chinese are expert at keeping a straight face, we have developed the cliché about the "*inscrutable* Orientals."
   b.   The detective kept the suspects in the dark with his *inscrutable* expression.

8. pallor (pal'-ər)—lack of color; unnatural paleness.
   a.   Having remained indoors for years, Aunt Sabina had an unhealthy *pallor.*
   b.   When we saw Miriam exit from the haunted house we were frightened by her *pallor.*

9. polygraph (päl'-i-graf)—an instrument that records changes in blood pressure, respiration, pulse rate, etc; a lie detector.
   a.   *The Reader's Digest* ran a feature story on the *polygraph* test administered to the murderer of Martin Luther King.
   b.   In the hands of a specialist, the *polygraph* is almost infallible in getting at the truth.

10. purloin (pur-loin')—to steal.
   a.   To profit from his insurance, Chris arranged to *purloin* his own jewelry.
   b.   Edgar Allan Poe's story, "The *Purloined* Letter," is an international classic.

11. ritual (rich'-ōō-wal)—a system of rites, religious or otherwise; a prescribed form or procedure; ceremony.
   a.   Dr. Lister went through an involved *ritual* of cleansing his hands before every operation.
   b.   The devil worshippers opened every meeting with the *ritual* of their eerie chant.

12. shamus (shā'-mis)—private detective. The caretaker of a synagogue is also called a *shamus* (shä'mis).
   a.   In all the detective stories I have read, the *shamus* was a hard drinking woman-chaser.
   b.   The famous sleuth preferred the title of Private Investigator to *shamus.*

13. soothsayer (sōōth'-sā-ər)—one who predicts the future. *Sooth* is an Anglo-Saxon word meaning "true"; hence, a *soothsayer* is a "sayer of truth."
   a.   The emperor was warned by the *soothsayer* not to go to the temple.
   b.   No *soothsayer* could have predicted the bizarre ending of this real-life mystery.

14. thaumaturgy (thô'-mə-tur-jē)—magic; the supposed working of miracles.
   a.   Through an act of sheer *thaumaturgy* the elephant was made to disappear in front of our eyes.
   b.   In the time of King Arthur, Merlin was the acknowledged master of *thaumaturgy.*

15. warlock (wôr'-läk)—sorcerer; conjurer; male witch. From the Anglo-Saxon word for traitor or liar. A *warlock* was supposed to be able to cast a magic spell because of a compact he made with the Devil.
   a.   Witches and *warlocks* are expected to "do their thing" on October 31st.
   b.   The Salem Puritans suspected many people of being *warlocks,* in cahoots with Lucifer.

EXERCISES

I. Which Word Comes to Mind?

In each of the following, read the statement, then circle the word that comes to mind.

1. The last page of the murder mystery, with all the guests in the living room

    (thaumaturgy, demonology, shamus)

2. "As I gaze into my crystal ball . . ."

    (warlock, soothsayer, arcane)

3. "Man, your face is as white as a ghost's"

    (pallor, conundrum, inscrutable)

4. A pickpocket's nimble fingers

    (purloin, alchemy, ritual)

5. "Would you be willing to take a test to prove your innocence?"

    (exorcise, illusion, polygraph)

6. A good poker player's face

    (alchemy, inscrutable, thaumaturgy)

7. With the I.Q. of a genius, Luz can solve any mathematical puzzle

    (conundrum, warlock, ritual)

8. An alien warship was reported to have flown over Seattle

    (illusion, demonology, shamus)

9. We recite the Pledge of Allegiance each morning

    (exorcise, soothsayer, ritual)

10. At the museum we needed an expert to explain the meaning of the strange painting

    (arcane, purloin, alchemy)

II. True or False?

In the space provided, indicate whether each statement is true or false.

_____ 1. A *warlock* has military responsibilities.

_____ 2. To wear your heart on your sleeve is to have an *inscrutable* expression.

_____ 3. A cattle rustler is one who would *purloin* a sirloin.

_____ 4. When we say, "It's Greek to me," we are referring to something that is *arcane*.

_____ 5. Abracadabra is the start of a familiar *ritual*.

_____ 6. My father's stockbroker practiced *alchemy* by converting our assets into debits.

_____ 7. I was shocked by the shut-in's *pallor*.

_____ 8. After months of *exorcise,* Tonio was in great shape.

_____ 9. Accused of theft, the bank teller offered to submit to a *polygraph.*

_____ 10. Macbeth's witches are a subject for *demonology.*

III. Fill in the Blank

Insert one of the new words in the proper space in each sentence below.

1. Harry Houdini, the celebrated magician, was a master of _____ .

2. As part of his morning _____ , Andre shined his shoes, pressed his trousers, and put a flower in his buttonhole.

3. Many employers would like their workers to take _____ tests, but the unions oppose that procedure.

4. Helen may know several _____ languages, but that hasn't helped her to earn a living in today's society.

5. A famous mathematical _____ , which has stumped the experts for a century, recently was solved with the aid of a microcomputer.

6. Through some amazing _____ , the shy reporter became Superman.

7. The Edison Hotel hired a _____ to deal with recent thefts.

8. A waxen _____ had come over Audra's usually florid face.

9. Colonel Snyder's mission was to _____ the enemy's atomic documents.

10. Awaiting the announcement of the Academy Awards, the composed actor maintained an _____ expression.

IV. Extra Letters

In each of the vocabulary words below there is an extra letter. Put all of the extra letters together and you will be able to spell out a word taught in a previous lesson. Its meaning is "a minor official."

purbloin	arcaned
shameus	allchemy
thaumataurgy	riteual

V. Matching

Match the word in column A with its correct definition in column B by writing the letter of that definition in the space provided.

	A		*B*
____	1. alchemy	a.	beyond comprehension
____	2. arcane	b.	ceremony
____	3. conundrum	c.	sorcerer
____	4. demonology	d.	riddle
____	5. exorcise	e.	to steal
____	6. illusion	f.	the study of demons
____	7. inscrutable	g.	changing one thing into another
____	8. pallor	h.	to drive away an evil spirit
____	9. polygraph	i.	lack of color
____	10. purloin	j.	private eye
____	11. ritual	k.	unfathomable
____	12. shamus	l.	one who predicts the future
____	13. soothsayer	m.	mistaken belief
____	14. thaumaturgy	n.	supposed working of miracles
____	15. warlock	o.	lie detector

Warlock—80 miles to the gallon

Size and Shape (I)

Can *infinitesimal* units be measured?

Who discovered *Lilliput?*

Is *megalopolis* a disease?

Does *palatial* refer to a place or to a part of the body?

How would you feel if someone referred to your *peccadillos?*

amplitude
awry
elfin
infinitesimal
Lilliputian
megalopolis
minimize
minutiae
palatial
peccadillo
picayune
soupçon
teeming
titanic
vista

1. **amplitude** (am'-plə-tōōd)—greatness of size; fullness; breadth of range. The nature of this word has made it extremely useful in specialized fields such as physics, electronics, astronomy, and mathematics. All the technical definitions, however, are related to the idea of a maximum size.
    a. The *amplitude* of the professor's knowledge amazed the audience.
    b. It takes a heart of wisdom to appreciate the *amplitude* of our blessings even in difficult times.

2. **awry** (ə-rī')—twisted toward one side.
    a. When his plans went awry, Ken cursed his fate.
    b. With her clothing awry, Adelaide was humiliated.

3. **elfin** (el'-fin)—fairylike; delicate; small and charmingly merry or mischievous. In folklore, an elf was a tiny, often prankish fairy who lived in the woods and possessed magical powers, like Shakespeare's Puck.
    a. The *elfin* world of the poet's imagination was peopled by gnomes and leprechauns and other creatures of fantasy.
    b. Despite Perry's appearance of innocence, his *elfin* smile tells me I had better beware.

4. **infinitesimal** (in-fin-ə-tes'-ə-m'l)—too small to be measured. Mathematicians, philosophers, and photographers are accustomed to dealing in concepts that range from the infinite (too large to be measured) to the *infinitesimal.*
    a. Messages are carried to the brain through the *infinitesimal* vessels of the nervous system.
    b. Martin may boast a lot, but his contribution to the team effort is *infinitesimal.*

5. **Lilliputian** (lil-ə-pyōō'-shən)—very small; tiny, narrow-minded; petty. In Swift's *Gulliver's Travels,* the hero was shipwrecked on the island of Lilliput, the inhabitants of which stood six inches tall.
    a. No wonder we can't solve our problems if our outlook remains *Lilliputian.*
    b. Standing next to the basketball team's center at the athletic awards assembly, I felt like a *Lilliputian.*

6. megalopolis (meg'-ə-läp'-ə-lis)—an extensive, heavily populated, continuously urban area, including any number of cities. This is larger than a metropolis since it includes an inner city, suburbia, exurbia, and any adjacent towns.
   a.   The area from Baltimore to Washington is so densely populated that the entire stretch can be considered one *megalopolis.*
   b.   If the population explosion continues unchecked, the entire country will gradually be transformed into one gigantic *megalopolis* after another, separated only by farms, rivers, or mountains.

7. minimize (min'-ə-mīz)—to reduce to a minimum; decrease to the least possible amount or degree; belittle. Again we meet a synonym for "small," *minim,* this time combined with the suffix *ize,* "to make," and denoting as in the definition for infinitesimal, making something appear to be of the least possible amount, value, or importance.
   a.   After the accident, Mr. Jenkins tried in vain to *minimize* the effect that the liquor had on his driving.
   b.   By careful attention to our inventory and orders, we can *minimize* our losses and maximize our profits.

8. minutiae (mi-noō'-shē-ē)—small or trivial details; trifling matters. The word is not restricted in meaning to unimportant details since a seemingly minor point can prove to be of major significance.
   a.   The defense attorney pored over the *minutiae* of the case, looking for a crack in the prosecution's argument.
   b.   A thorough knowledge of the *minutiae* of his craft earned the artist an international reputation.

9. palatial (pa-lā'-shəl)—like a palace; large and ornate. A closely related word derived from the same Latin root *palatine* ("palace"), refers to royal privileges, a high official, a Roman soldier as well as to the chief of the seven hills upon which Rome was built.
   a.   The duchess fell upon hard times and had to open her *palatial* estate to tourists.
   b.   The *palatial* tapestry on display at the Cloisters was the highlight of our visit.

10. peccadillo (pek-ə-dil'-ō)—a small sin or fault. We admire the person who dresses impeccably, "without fault"; perhaps are tolerant to the *peccadillos* of our friends; and probably forgive the person who offers his *peccavi* ("confessions," or literally "I have sinned").
   a.   What human being, no matter how upright, has not committed some *peccadillo?*
   b.   We can overlook Melanie's *peccadillos* but not her brazen impudence.

11. picayune (pik-ə-yūn')—of little value or account; petty or prejudiced. Originally, this meant a coin of small value. Inevitably, the meaning was transferred to a person of low esteem because of his or her criticism or bias.
   a.   George remained silent after the beating the team suffered, not wishing to seem *picayune* by criticizing anyone.
   b.   Bentley is notorious for raising the most *picayune* objections.

12. soupçon (soōp-sōn')—suspicion; a slight trace or flavor; a very small amount. The first definition, derived from the French, is the original meaning. The others are extensions of the same idea, a common phenomenon of language development.
   a.   There was merely a *soupçon* of tartar sauce in the delicate concoction.
   b.   Ned spoke with a *soupçon* of arrogance that did not go unnoticed by the interviewer and cost him the job.

13. teeming (tē'-miŋ)—swarming; prolific or fertile. The Old English word *teman* meant "to produce offspring." Indeed, an obsolete meaning of teeming was "to become pregnant to produce offspring." What is perhaps more interesting is that our word *team* also comes from the Old English *team,* which meant "childbearing" or "brood."
   a.   The poem by Emma Lazarus, inscribed on the base of the Statue of Liberty, welcomes the *teeming* masses, yearning to be free.
   b.   Doris' mind is always *teeming* with a thousand projects.

14. **titanic** (tī-tan'-ik)—of enormous size, strength, or power. In classical mythology the *Titans* were a race of giants who ruled the world before the gods and goddesses. Cronus, perhaps the most famous (think of our word *chronology*), swallowed all his children in an attempt to avert a prophecy of doom, but one son, Jupiter (Zeus), survived and eventually overthrew his father.
   a. The quarterback led his team in a *titanic* effort to erase the six-point lead caused by his unfortunate fumble.
   b. The airport was constructed in *titanic* proportions to allow for the anticipated expansion of the city

15. **vista** (vis'-tə)—a far-reaching intellectual view; a view or prospect, especially one seen through a long, narrow avenue or passage; a mental view extending over a long period of time or embracing many remembrances or experiences.
   a. Before us stretches an infinite *vista* of human improvement.
   b. The *vistas* of one's youth are often recalled with pleasure and nostalgia.

EXERCISES

I. Which Word Comes to Mind?

In each of the following, read the statement, then circle the word that comes to mind.

1. The myriad molecules on the head of a pin

   (infinitesimal, vista, picayune)

2. The two cities have grown so quickly you can hardly tell where one ends and the other begins

   (megalopolis, Lilliputian, palatial)

3. Most of their points were scored when our best man was in the penalty box

   (amplitude, elfin, minimize)

4. Mac stumbled once over his lines but otherwise his performance was perfect

   (minutiae, peccadillo, awry)

5. This is the biggest rocket in our arsenal

   (soupçon, titanic, teeming)

6. The seven dwarfs of Disney

   (Lilliputian, palatial, vista)

7. I was bogged down in petty details

   (megalopolis, minutiae, titanic)

8. We took a guided tour of Buckingham Palace

(teeming, palatial, soupçon)

9. The defense kept objecting to every minor point that was raised in court

(picayune, elfin, peccadillo)

10. After climbing to the top of the mountain, we looked out on a marvelous landscape

(minimize, teeming, vista)

II. True or False?

In the space provided, indicate whether each statement is true or false.

_____ 1. An *elfin* creature is huge and lumbering.
_____ 2. *Soupçon* is the call to dinner.
_____ 3. You should feel complimented if your mental powers are called *Lilliputian*.
_____ 4. *Vista* galleries are so called because they attract many visitors.
_____ 5. A *teeming* street is dilapidated and deserted.
_____ 6. It took a *titanic* effort to open the car door under water.
_____ 7. The *amplitude* of the harvest gratified the farmers.
_____ 8. In summers, we seek to trade our *megalopolis* for the country air.
_____ 9. Don't *minimize* Fermi's contributions to the development of the atomic bomb.
_____ 10. My parents are willing to overlook an occasional *peccadillo*.

III. Synonyms and Antonyms

Find and circle two words on each line which are either synonyms or antonyms.

1. infinitesimal	titanic	pompous	hopeful
2. swarming	cooperative	teeming	moderate
3. economy	amplitude	pettiness	range
4. picayune	searching	serviceable	unbiased
5. exaggerate	imitate	minimize	assemble

IV. Matching

Match the word in column A with its correct definition in column B by writing the letter of that definition in the space provided.

A	B
_____ 1. amplitude	a. turned toward one side
_____ 2. awry	b. make less
_____ 3. elfln	c. fullness
_____ 4. infinitesimal	d. unimportant details
_____ 5. Lilliputian	e. trace
_____ 6. megalopolis	f. narrow-minded
_____ 7. minimize	g. fertile
_____ 8. minutiae	h. enormous
_____ 9. palatial	i. delicate
_____ 10. peccadillo	j. extended city
_____ 11. picayune	k. ornate
_____ 12. soupçon	l. petty
_____ 13. teeming	m. minor sin
_____ 14. titanic	n. extended view
_____ 15. vista	o. immeasurably small

Words with Tales Attached

Why would prisoners welcome *gossamer* bars for their cells?

Technically, why is an open-air *conclave* a paradox?

Does *junket* make you think of a trip, scrap metal, or a Chinese ship?

Would you prefer *draconian* or *epicurean* treatment?

Is a *juggernaut* something to fear, to drink, or to wear?

---

accolade
conclave
dirge
draconian
epicurean
gossamer
immolate
juggernaut
junket
ostracism
proletariat
rigmarole
rubric
Socratic
sycophant

1. **accolade** (ak'-ə-lād)—praise or approval; an embrace of greeting or salutation. When French generals kiss the cheeks of the men being honored, they are continuing a custom of the early French kings who placed their arms around the neck (Latin *ad* "to" and *colum* "neck") of the new knight in order to kiss him. William the Conqueror used his fist to confer knighthood. Later a gentle stroke with the flat of the sword on the side of the neck became the accepted method.
   a. In their lavish *accolades,* the critics have compared this play with the finest dramas ever written.
   b. *"Accolades,"* observed Mr. Raritan, "are reserved not merely for good intentions but for superior performances."

2. **conclave** (kän'-klāv)—a private or secret meeting; an assembly or gathering, especially one with authority, power, and influence. When a pope is to be elected, the College of Cardinals meets in a room locked on the inside and outside. No one is permitted to leave until a new pope has been chosen. From Latin, then, a *conclave* is a meeting in a room locked with *(con)* a key *(clavis).* You can recognize the same root in *clef, clavicle,* and *conclude.*
   a. At the annual *conclave,* the delegates proposed a sweeping revision of the charter.
   b. A *conclave* of political leaders was held to name the next mayor.

3. **dirge** (durj)—a funeral hymn; a slow, sad song, poem, or musical composition; a lament. *Dirge* is a contraction of the first word of a Latin funeral service that begins, "Dirige, Domine...." ("O Lord, direct my way in Thy sight"). This in turn is based on the words of a Psalm (" . . . Make Thy way straight before my face").
   a. The widow, moved by the solemn music of the *dirge,* broke into uncontrollable sobs.
   b. The autumn wind sang the *dirge* of summer.

4. **draconian** (drā-kō'-nē-ən)—harsh or vigorous; a law or code of extreme severity. Draco was an Athenian lawgiver whose code or laws, established in 621 B.C., called for the most severe penalties for the smallest offense.
   a. The student editorial labeled the new security system a *draconian* measure that violated individual rights.
   b. To balance the budget, the mayor was forced to adopt *draconian* regulations that further reduced services to the city residents.

5. epicurean (ep-ə-kyoor'-ē-ən)—devoted to the pursuit of pleasure; fond of good food, comfort, and ease. The followers of Epicurus are associated with the pursuit of pleasure, so that *epicureanism* has become synonymous with luxurious living. The early *Epicureans* were contrasted with the Stoics, followers of Zeno, who taught that the wise man should be free from passion and submissive to natural law. The Stoic today is one who endures the hardships of life without complaint.
a   The banquet tables were laden with *epicurean* delicacies that we had never seen before
b.   The *epicurean* way of life holds little attraction to the person who is committed to the nobler ideals of improving society.

6. gossamer (gos'-ə-mer)—soft, sheer, gauzy fabric; fine film of cobwebs seen in autumn; anything delicate, light or insubstantial. Lexicographers theorize that this word, derived from Middle English *goose* and *somer,* was first used as a name for Indian summer, when geese were in season.
a.   The *gossamer*-thin wire was part of the electronic gear transmitting secret information from the foreign embassy.
b.   The merry company, the sparkling conversation, the *gossamer* trees conspired to make Sharon feel heady and romantic.

7. immolate (im'-ə-lāt)—to kill, as a sacrifice; to destroy or renounce for the sake of something else. Ground grain or meal (Latin *mola*) was sprinkled by the Roman priest on the head of an animal before it was sacrificed. Later, this preparatory act of sprinkling, *immolation,* came to mean the sacrifice itself.
a.   As a protest against universal indifference to human suffering, the bearded stranger tried to *immolate* himself on the U.N. plaza.
b.   We value each life too highly to risk the *immolation* of so many young men for the sake of maintaining a puppet dictator in power.

8. juggernaut (jug'-ər-nôt)—anything that exacts blind devotion or terrible sacrifice; any terrible, irresistible force. *Juggernaut* is the Hindu god whose idol is dragged in a religious procession on an enormous cart. Devotees are sometimes crushed under the wheels of the advancing cart. The word today is applied to any large, overpowering, destructive force or object such as war, a giant battleship or a powerful football team.
a.   The Nazi *juggernaut* rolled over the Maginot Line and quickly subdued Western Europe at the outset of World War II.
b.   The formidable Alabama *juggernaut* pushed the defending champions down the field until a fumble, a long pass, and a field goal turned the tide.

9. junket (jun'-kit)—a party, banquet, or outing; a trip taken by an official and paid for with public funds. *Junket* began as a Latin word *juncus* ("a twig"), and referred to a basket made of rushes and twigs. Soon the word was applied to delicacies, especially cream and cheese preparations, served in these baskets. Finally, it became the feast served out of doors, a picnic. The political slant to *junket* probably stems from the clambakes or beer-and-pretzels feasts once offered by political clubs to their followers. After moving into the political sphere, the word acquired its modern meaning of an official trip underwritten by the taxpayer—a long way from the twigs and cheese.
a.   The editor received many letters critical of the congressional *junkets* to the Far East.
b.   The opening gun of the campaign was a *junket* attended by every aspiring politico in the district.

10. ostracism (äs'-trə-siz'm)—a rejection or exclusion from a group or society by general consent. In ancient Athens, if the assembly decided a person was endangering the public welfare or liberty, a vote was taken to send the guilty one into exile. A potsherd or oyster shell (from the Greek *ostra*) on which was written the name of the person to be *ostracized* was dropped into an urn. The modern blackballing of members from organizations closely follows this method.
a.   I called attention to Carol's unselfishness and loyalty and urged the group not to *ostracize* her for one small slip of the tongue.
b.   Roger's attempt to win the game all by himself led to his *ostracism*.

11. proletariat (prō-lə-tar'-ē-ət)—the working class; the unpropertied class. *Proles,* a Latin word for "offspring," is the source of *proletariat* or the poor class, who, because they were prolific, served the state only by producing offspring.
   a.   Over the years, the *proletariat* has made tremendous strides in improving the conditions of life for those formerly deprived.
   b.   In a democratic society, the line between the *proletariat* and the landowners is not so rigid, for people move freely from one to the other.

12. rigmarole (rig'-mə-rōl)—confused, incoherent, foolish talk; a complicated and petty procedure. *Rigmarole* is an alteration of *ragman roll,* a series of documents in which the Scottish noblemen acknowledged their allegiance to Edward I of England.
   a.   Mr. Sykes hated to go through the *rigmarole* of a formal dinner.
   b.   In order to join the fraternity, Bob found he had to go through the *rigmarole* of secret hand-shakes, greetings, and passwords.

13. rubric (rōō'-brik)—a title, heading, or direction in a book, written or printed in red or otherwise distinguished from the rest of the text; an established custom or rule of procedure; a short commentary or explanation covering a broad subject. In the monasteries, the monks who copied the works of the ancient authors often adorned their manuscripts with beautiful decorations. For headings, they followed the Roman practice of using red ink (Latin, *ruber*). Thus *rubric* came to mean not only the initial ornamental letters but also the directive or rule of conduct that was often part of the heading.
   a.   Professor Morand ended his lecture with a *rubric* designed to summarize his principal ideas.
   b.   Following the *rubric* regarding the election of a president, each state continues to send its representatives to the Electoral College.

14. Socratic (sō-krat'-ik)—pertaining to Socrates or his philosophical method of repeated questioning to elicit truths implicit in all rational beings. Socrates, a Greek philosopher and the chief speaker in Plato's *Dialogues,* developed his ideas by constantly asking questions or forcing admissions from his opponents. Condemned to death for irreverence to the gods and corrupting the youth, Socrates is now remembered as a seeker after truth and a man who taught his disciples how to think.
   a.   The *Socratic* method of inquiry is ideally suited to a discussion of motives in a play or novel.
   b.   "There is no need," said Mr. Holmes, "to enter into all this *Socratic* dialogue when the case is so elementary."

15. sycophant (sik'-ə-fənt)—a self-seeking, servile flatterer; fawning parasite; one who attempts to win favor or advance himself by flattering persons of influence. Since the Greek roots mean "showing figs," two possible explanations have been offered for the story behind *sycophant.* One is that the gesture of a fig was used to denounce a criminal, making a *sycophant* an informer. The other is more literal. It was unlawful to export figs and one who reported such an act was called a *sycophant,* or fig-shower. The modern meaning derives from the informer's cringing and servile manner.
   a.   Tom's laughing at all the teacher's jokes and volunteering for every task were looked upon as *sycophancy* by his classmates.
   b.   I do not envy the *sycophant* who has advanced himself at the expense of his self-respect.

I. Which Word Comes to Mind?

In each of the following, read the statement, then circle the word that comes to mind.

1. They are the backbone of our industrial power

    (rubric, proletariat, juggernaut)

2. The silent treatment

    (conclave, dirge, ostracism)

3. In some underdeveloped countries, a thief is punished by having his hand cut off

    (Socratic, draconian, junket)

4. Eat, drink, and be merry

    (epicurean, immolate, sycophant)

5. This play deserves the Drama Critics' Award

    (accolade, rigmarole, gossamer)

6. The president and his cabinet deliberated for three hours

    (rubric, conclave, dirge)

7. Screen stars are often surrounded by flatterers

    (sychophant, immolate, proletariat)

8. Detective Brady went through the lengthy process of reading the prisoner his rights

    (juggernaut, accolade, rigmarole)

9. Belonging to the library board allowed me to take many expense-free trips to conventions

    (sycophant, dirge, junket)

10. The wailing of the widow could be heard over the sound of the organ at the funeral

    (dirge, ostracism, draconian)

II. True or False?

In the space provided, indicate whether each statement is true or false.

_____   1. A *sycophant* speaks with sincerity.

_____   2. A *dirge* would be inappropriate at a wedding.

_____   3. A *rigmarole* is a tall-masted sailing ship.

_____   4. A *rubric* has to be written in red.

_____   5. A model sailing ship in a bottle is a good example of a *juggernaut.*

_____   6. Professor Smith lectured the entire period in true *Socratic* fashion.

_____   7. With *accolades* still ringing in his ears, the star thanked the audience.

_____   8. The warden resorted to *draconian* measures to get the truth out of the felon.

_____   9. His alibi, lacking in substance, was as light as *gossamer.*

_____ 10. Harold organized a taxpayer's protest against congressional *junkets.*

III. Synonyms and Antonyms

Indicate whether the following pairs of words are the same, opposite, or unrelated in meaning by writing S, O, or U in the space provided.

_____   1. ostracism—acceptance

_____   2. accolade—encomium

_____   3. immolate—soften

_____   4. rigmarole—fabrication

_____   5. epicurean—pleasure-bound

IV. Fill in the Blank

Insert one of the new words in the proper space in each sentence below.

1. After their leader's death, the government radio station began to broadcast a _____ .

2. We felt that the new rules were _____ , but our protests were unheeded.

3. The first victims of AIDS were subject to _____ by people who were generally ignorant of the disease.

4. In order to get a loan, you have to go through a tremendous _____ at the local bank.

5. The famous movie producer was surrounded by _____ .

6. The Chicago Bulls' _____ rolled over their opponents with startling ease.

7. In addition to the loud _____ , each star received a floral tribute.

8. The revolution's leaders sought to win the support of the _____ .

9. At an all-night _____ , the angry reporters decided to resign.

10. With his _____ tastes, Vincenzo found it easy to mingle with the sybarites.

V. Matching

Match the word in column A with its correct definition in column B by writing the letter of that definition in the space provided.

	A		B
____	1. accolade	a.	peasantry
____	2. conclave	b.	lament
____	3. dirge	c.	cabal
____	4. draconian	d.	established procedure
____	5. epicurean	e.	rigorous and severe
____	6. gossamer	f.	foolish talk
____	7. immolate	g.	overwhelming force
____	8. juggernaut	h.	excursion
____	9. junket	i.	sensualist
____	10. ostracism	j.	blackballing
____	11. proletariat	k.	delicate
____	12. rigmarole	l.	in the manner of questions and answers
____	13. rubric	m.	obsequious flatterer
____	14. Socratic	n.	commendation, praise
____	15. sycophant	o.	kill for sacrifice

Words with tails attached

Of Loves and Fears and Hates

What does a *philatelist* collect?

Does *hydrophobia* have anything to do with water?

Would a person who thinks he is Napoleon be considered a *paranoid* or a *Francophile?*

Is *claustrophobia* a condition that is best handled by a beautician, a psychologist or a banker?

Where is the most fearful place for a *Russophobe?*

abhor
acrophobia
anathema
bibliophile
claustrophobia
Francophile
hydrophobia
misanthropy
misogyny
paranoid
philately
Philistine
Russophobia
triskaideka-
    phobia
xenophobia

1. **abhor** (ab-hôr')—to shrink from; to consider with horror and disgust.
    a. "I *abhor* violence," the candidate announced.
    b. It was amusing to hear the senator say that he *abhorred* politics.

2. **acrophobia** (ak-rə-fō'-bē-ə)—abnormally intense fear of being in high places.
    a. Standing on the swaying bridge high above the swirling waters was enough to give me a case of *acrophobia* for quite a time.
    b. In his speech accepting the medal for bravery, the veteran fireman told how he was almost disqualified as a trainee because of his *acrophobia*.

3. **anathema** (ə-nath'ə-mə)—something that is cursed or damned; an accursed thing.
    a. Any talk of dieting is *anathema* to Jennifer.
    b. She was good in social studies, but math was *anathema* to Monica.

4. **bibliophile** (bib'-lē-ō-fīl)—one who loves books; a book collector. The opposite is a *bibliophobe.*
    a. The *bibiliophile's* eyes were aglow with his new acquisition, a rare edition of Shakespeare's *The Tempest.*
    b. The discovery of hundreds of library books in Mr. Gerard's home led police to conclude that he was a biblioklept as well as a *bibliophile.*

5. **claustrophobia** (klôs-trə-fō'-bē-ə)—an abnormal dread of being in closed or narrow spaces. One who has a fear of open spaces suffers from *agoraphobia.*
    a. The patient displayed *claustrophobic* tendencies in his insistence that his door remain open at all times.
    b. In pioneer days, *claustrophobia,* if it existed at all, was an individual's problem; in modern times, it is societal.

6. **Francophile** (fraŋ'-kə-fīl)—an admirer of France, its people, and its customs. It may also be used as an adjective.
    a. As with other vogues and fads, the day of the *Francophile* has come to an end.
    b. When Bob began to call himself Rober, accenting the first syllable and rolling the *r*'s in a guttural sound, we knew he was entering the *Francophile* stage of his hallucinations.

7. **hydrophobia** (hī-drə-fō'-bē-ə)—fear of water; rabies. One of the symptoms of the disease caused by the bite of a rabid animal is an inability to swallow; hence, the name *hydrophobia* for the disease itself.
   a. Fearing the child might develop *hydrophobia* from the dog bite, the anguished parents broadcast an appeal to locate the animal and have it tested for rabies.
   b. Little Alex's difficulty in swallowing after his tonsillectomy brought on a spell of *hydrophobia.*

8. **misanthropy** (mis-an'-thrō-pē)—hatred of or distrust of mankind. The *misanthropist* has his opposite in the *philanthropist,* that is, one who loves mankind—and has the means to support worthy causes.
   a. Moral corruption, so rampant in our society, has turned some people into *misanthropes,* others into reformers.
   b. Silas Marner, the classic example of the *misanthrope,* was brought out of the darkness of his existence by the love of a little child.

9. **misogyny** (mis-äj'-ə-nē)—hatred of women.
   a. The portrait of Lucy Manette balances Dickens' *misogynic* representation of women like Madame DeFarge.
   b. In a society where polygamy was practiced, the *misogynist* would be out of place.

10. **paranoid** (par'-ə-noid)—showing unreasonable distrust, suspicion, or an exaggerated sense of one's own importance. Paranoia is usually a chronic condition characterized by delusions of persecution or of grandeur that the afflicted strenuously defends with apparent logic and reason.
   a. Stanley became *paranoid* on the subject of his accident, claiming that the police and the witnesses were conspiring against him.
   b. Our civilization can ill afford the luxury of a *paranoid* attitude toward nuclear proliferation, for even a small misstep could spell doomsday.

11. **philately** (fi-lat'-ə-lē)—the collection and study of postage stamps, postmarks, and related materials. The derivation, from the Greek *philo* ("loving"), and *ateles* ("without charge"), reminds us that the original stamp indicated a tax-free shipment.
   a. The *philatelic* public was delighted by the early announcement of commemorative stamps for the twenty-first century.
   b. Though there is much information and pleasure to be gained from *philately,* the primary motive for some collectors is cash value.

12. **Philistine** (fi-lis'-tīn, -tēn; fil'-i-stēn)—a smug, ignorant, especially middleclass person who is held to be indifferent or antagonistic to artistic and cultural values; boorish or barbarous; an ignoramus or outsider.
   a. Oscar Wlide said; "It is only the *Philistine* who seeks to estimate a personality by the vulgar test of production."
   b. Cynics often act the part of the misunderstood genius at war with *Philistine* society.

13. **Russophobia** (rus-ə-fō'-bē-ə)—dislike or fear of Russia or its policies.
   a. Harry was an ardent *Russophobe* until he took a trip to Moscow.
   b. *Russophobia,* as indeed the fear of anything, can best be dealt with by knowledge and strength.

14. **triskaidekaphobia** (tris-kī-dek-ə-fō'-bē-ə)—fear of the number 13. Though the word is long, the arithmetic etymology from Greek is simple: *treis* ("three"), *kai* ("and"), and *deka* ("ten").
   a. *Triskaidekaphobia* has been carried to ridiculous extremes as in the case of hotels that do not have a floor numbered 13.
   b. Among the Jewish people, *triskaidekaphobia* has not made any headway for a family joyfully celebrates the thirteenth birthday of a young man as he assumes his religious duties and obligations.

15. xenophobia (zen-ə-fō'-bē-ə)—an unusual fear or contempt of strangers or foreigners, especially as reflected in one's political or cultural views.
   a. Insecurity may often lead an American traveling abroad to exhibit *xenophobic* tendencies.
   b. The "One World" philosophy, aided by the advances in mass media, will one day make *xenophobia* extinct.

EXERCISES

I. Which Word Comes to Mind?

In each of the following, read the statement, then circle the word that comes to mind.

1. Bats and beavers are prone to this

   (claustrophobia, hydrophobia, xenophobia)

2. No member of the famous trapeze artists, The Flying Valencias, ever had this

   (Francophilism, misanthropy, acrophobia)

3. Jack the Ripper must have been one

   (misogynist, philatelist, paranoid)

4. Beware of Friday the 13th

   (bibliophile, triskaidekaphobia, Philistine)

5. Many U.S. citizens like anything that is American and detest everything else

   (xenophobe, Russophobe, paranoid)

6. In an elevator, invariably I grow nervous

   (Francophile, claustrophobia, triskaidekaphobia)

7. My uncle spends every vacation in Paris

   (Francophile, xenophobia, bibliophile)

8. Our neighbors trust nobody, absolutely nobody!

   (acrophobia, Philistine, paranoid)

9. Franklin D. Roosevelt was a noted stamp collector

   (philately, misanthropy, anathema)

10. At the start of *A Christmas Carol*, Scrooge hates everybody

   (bibliophile, misanthropy, triskaidekaphobia)

II. True or False?

In the space provided, indicate whether each statement is true or false.

____ 1. A *bibliophile* is a file clerk in a library.
____ 2. A *Francophile* would feel quite at home in Philadelphia.
____ 3. You can assume that a hermit is a *misanthrope*.
____ 4. Some men dream of having a harem, but not the *misogynist*.
____ 5. A *Philistine* would be a frequent visitor to the museums.
____ 6. Scholars who specialize in *philately* are likely to be expert musicians.
____ 7. His *xenophobia* led him to retire from the world.
____ 8. Helen's *acrophobia* prevented her from enjoying the view from atop the Empire State Building.
____ 9. One might say that sardines in a can are suggestive of *claustrophobia*.
____ 10. Suffering from *triskaidekaphobia,* Mario is extremely cautious every Friday the thirteenth.

III. Creating New Words

Using the following roots and affixes from this lesson, form a new word for each definition given.

phil, phila   xeno   acro   biblio
anthropo   triskaideka   phobia

1. love of strangers _____
2. love of mankind _____
3. fear of book _____
4. love of heights _____
5. love of 13 Frenchmen _____

IV. Finding Roots

Find and circle the four roots in the box below that can be combined with—*phobia* or —*phile* to form words from the lesson.

L	O	I	L	B	I	B
O	R	D	Y	H	N	B
N	C	O	S	W	G	D
E	A	P	T	F	M	J
X	M	V	Z	L	P	H

V. Matching

Match the word in column A with its correct definition in column B by writing the letter of that definition in the space provided.

A	B
_____ 1. abhor	a. lover of Gallic customs
_____ 2. acrophobia	b. hate
_____ 3. anathema	c. rabies
_____ 4. bibliophile	d. materialist
_____ 5. claustrophobia	e. lover of books
_____ 6. Francophile	f. fear of the number 13
_____ 7. hydrophobia	g. distrust of everyone
_____ 8. misanthropy	h. distrust of women
_____ 9. misogyny	i. an accursed thing
_____ 10. paranoid	j. fear of high places
_____ 11. philately	k. fear of foreigners
_____ 12. Philistine	l. stamp-collecting
_____ 13. Russophobia	m. dislike of the USSR
_____ 14. triskaidekaphobia	n. one with delusions of grandeur
_____ 15. xenophobia	o. fear of being shut in

Hydrophobia

Science—"Ology" Words

Does *oncology* deal with tumors or rumors?

Does *tautology* have something to do with repetition?

Which is the study of women's diseases: *gynecology* or *endocrinology*?

If a psychologist treats psychoses, does a *neurologist* treat neuroses?

Does *ecology* involve medical research, linguistics, or neither?

---

archaeology
cardiology
ecology
endocrinology
gerontology
gynecology
necrology
neurology
oncology
paleontology
pathology
seismology
tautology
terminology
toxicology

1. **archaeology** (är-kē-äl'-ə-jē)—the systematic recovery by scientific methods of material evidence remaining from man's life and culture in past ages, and the detailed study of this evidence.
   a. *Archaeological* discoveries of potsherds near Tel Aviv, Israel, have shed light on the origins of our written alphabet.
   b. *Archaeology* has attracted many young enthusiasts who see in the patient digging and sorting of artifacts an exciting adventure that combines history, science, and detective work.

2. **cardiology** (kär-dē-äl'-ə-jē)—the medical study of the diseases and functioning of the heart. Emphasis on prevention and treatment of heart disease has made most people familiar with cardiographs, the curve that traces the mechanical movements of the heart.
   a. Many young doctors, inspired by the desire to eradicate heart disease, the nation's number one killer, are entering the field of *cardiology*.
   b. *Cardiology* has made giant strides with open-heart surgery and nuclear-powered pacemakers, but heart transplants remain stymied by the tendency of the body to reject foreign tissue.

3. **ecology** (i-käl'-ə-jē)—the science of the relationships between organisms and their environments. This field is also called bionomics.
   a. *Ecology*-minded groups are a new element in society, acting as a brake to the ruthless exploitation and contamination of the world's natural resources.
   b. A compromise is being sought between the indiscriminate development of new energy sources and *ecological* safeguards to protect the world from disasters.

4. **endocrinology** (en-dō-kri-näl'-ə-jē, -krī-näl'-ə-jē)—the physiology of the ductless glands, such as the thyroid or adrenal, whose secretions pass directly into the blood stream from the cells of the gland.
   a. Tim's abnormal growth pattern was investigated by the *endocrinologist* as a possible dysfunction of the thyroid glands.
   b. *Endocrinology* is a vast field encompassing the complex interrelationship of basic body functions such as renal activity, reproduction, smooth muscle contraction, and normal growth and development.

5. **gerontology** (jer-ən-täl'-ə-jē)—the scientific study of the physiological and pathological phenomena associated with aging. The Greek stem *geront* ("old"), explains the source of the names of such popular medicines as Geritol.
   a. The conquest and control of many diseases in modern times has led to the prolongation of life and opened the new field of *gerontology* to the medical and business world.
   b. *Gerontologists* insist that old age should not be a period of life filled with fear, misery, and loneliness.

6. **gynecology** (gī-nə-käl'-ə-jē)—a branch of medicine that deals with women, their diseases, hygiene, and medical care.
   a. Many doctors specialize in both *gynecology* and obstetrics.
   b. The ovarian infection required *gynecological* surgery.

7. **necrology** (nə-kräl'-ə-jē)—a list or record of people who have died, especially in the recent past.
   a. The publication carried a *necrology* of contributors who had died during the past year.
   b. During our visit to the newspaper plant, we were surprised to learn that the *necrology* of most famous living people had already been prepared and was constantly being updated.

8. **neurology** (noo-räl'-ə-jē, nyoo-)—the medical science of the nervous system and its disorders.
   a. A *neurological* examination suggested the root of the patient's problem was nothing more than excessive fatigue resulting from overwork.
   b. Despite exhaustive interviews and tests, the *neurologist* was unable to determine the cause of Ernie's paralysis and recommended psychological investigation.

9. **oncology** (on-kol'-ə-jē)—the medical study of tumors.
   a. Great work in fighting cancer is being done at *oncology* centers throughout the United States.
   b. In medical school, Paul decided to specialize in *oncology*.

10. **paleontology** (pāl-ē-ən-täl'-ə-jē)—the study of fossils and ancient life forms. *Paleo* is a combining form indicating "ancient" or "prehistoric."
    a. The findings of *paleontology* shed light on the evolution and relationships of modern animals and plants as well as on the chronology of the history of the earth.
    b. *Paleontological* discoveries tend to place the origins of our earth farther back in time than had been hitherto believed.

11. **pathology** (pə-thäl'-ə-jē)—the scientific study of the nature of disease, its causes, processes, development, and consequences; the anatomic or functional manifestations of disease.
    a. The stories Jane concocted were so bizarre we suspected she had become a *pathological* liar.
    b. No symptom was ignored, no detail overlooked as Philadelphia mobilized its scientific resources to track the *pathology* of the strange disease that had mysteriously killed 27 people.

12. **seismology** (sīz-mäl'-ə-jē, sīs-)—the geophysical science of earthquakes and of the mechanical properties of the earth.
    a. *Seismologists,* like meteorologists, can merely predict or measure great natural disturbances but they can do little to prevent them.
    b. The recent earthquake reported by *seismologists* in the Peking area measured an intensity of 8 on the Richter scale.

13. **tautology** (tô-tol'-ə-jē)—needless repetition of the same sense in different words.
    a. Our professor of logic is fond of *tautologies*.
    b. Either it will rain tonight or it won't rain tonight is a well-known *tautology*.

14. **terminology** (tûr-mə-nol'-ə-jē)—technical vocabulary.
    a. Dr. Grill overwhelmed us with his medical *terminology*.
    b. My sister loves baseball, but she doesn't understand the technical *terminology* of the game.

15. toxicology (täk-si-käl'-ə-jē)—the study of the nature, effects, and detection of poisons and the treatment of poisoning.

    a.   Early *toxicologists* used a mixture of toxin and its antitoxin as a vaccine against diphtheria.

    b.   *Toxicology* must deal not only with the effect of poisons on living organisms but with those substances otherwise harmless that prove toxic under peculiar conditions, and with the industrial or legal ramifications of this.

EXERCISES

I. Which Word Comes to Mind?

In each of the following, read the statement, then circle the word that comes to mind.

  1. Fears that the Alaskan pipeline will destroy the delicate balance of animal life in the region

          (neurology, archaeology, ecology)

  2. A special panel on diseases of the aged

          (endocrinology, gerontology, tautology)

  3. The honored list of soldiers who made the supreme sacfifice

          (necrology, gynecology, toxicology)

  4. The monster left an impression of his footprint in the rock

          (paleontology, toxicology, seismology)

  5. The heart specialist sent me for an X-ray

          (cardiology, necrology, pathology)

  6. The medical examiner checked for poison in the corpse.

          (endocrinology, toxicology, archaeology)

  7. With permission from the Egyptian government, we began our dig

          (archaeology, endocrinology, ecology)

  8. We were stunned when the young basketball player succumbed to a heart attack

          (ecology, gerontology, cardiology)

  9. Some California cities have endured dozens of serious earthquakes

          (necrology, paleontology, seismology)

 10. The cadaver's appearance suggested that he might have been poisoned

          (gynecology, toxicology, neurology)

II. True or False?

In the space provided, indicate whether each statement is true or false.

_____ 1. *Archaeology* and *paleontology* could be dealing with the same material.

_____ 2. Mr. Rohas opened the door to the *gynecologist's* office, gulped, and realized he was in the wrong place.

_____ 3. Every *cardiologist* must have a repertoire to demonstrate his dexterity with a deck of cards.

_____ 4. *Morphology* is concerned with finding pain killers.

_____ 5. *Pathologists* work closely with engineers to construct safe, durable roadways.

_____ 6. In a study of the area's *ecology,* we determined the extent of pollution.

_____ 7. When visiting Grandma in her health-related facility, I discussed her case with the *gerontologist* on duty.

_____ 8. The linguist confused everyone with his technical *terminology.*

_____ 9. Edith studied *neurology* to discover how to cure the numbness in her feet.

_____ 10. Our town maintains a *necrology* of those citizens who died in our country's wars.

III. Putting the Scientists in the Proper Place

For each of the following pairs indicate *yes* in the space provided if the scientist is correctly paired with the "tools of his/her trade" and *no* if not.

_____ 1. archaeologist—arches

_____ 2. gerontologist—aged people

_____ 3. gynecologist—athletics

_____ 4. seismologist—Richter scale

_____ 5. pathologist—charts and maps

_____ 6. paleontologist—fossils

_____ 7. neurologist—caves

_____ 8. toxicologist—serums

_____ 9. oncologist—zoo animals

_____ 10. necrologist—old coins

IV. Find the Words

Somewhere in this box of letters, reading up, down, across, or diagonally, the roots of six vocabulary words that were taught in this lesson are hidden. As you locate each one, draw a circle around it.

E	N	N	C	E	T
O	D	E	R	N	O
S	E	C	O	B	X
N	A	R	P	H	I
N	E	U	R	R	C
G	Y	N	E	C	D

V. Matching

Match the word in column A with its correct definition in column B by writing the letter of that definition in the space provided.

A	B
_____ 1. archaeology	a. environmentalism
_____ 2. cardiology	b. obituary
_____ 3. ecology	c. study of antiquities
_____ 4. endocrinology	d. study of afflictions of the nervous system
_____ 5. gerontology	e. something abnormal
_____ 6. gynecology	f. study of diseases of the heart
_____ 7. necrology	g. study of earthquakes
_____ 8. neurology	h. study of aging
_____ 9. oncology	i. study of tumors
_____ 10. paleontology	j. pathology of ductless glands
_____ 11. pathology	k. technical vocabulary
_____ 12. seismology	l. study of prehistoric fossils
_____ 13. terminology	m. study of women's diseases
_____ 14. tautology	n. study of poisons
_____ 15. toxicology	o. needless repetition

Studying scientists

Review

A. The Out-of-Place Word

In each of the following groups, find and circle the one vocabulary word that is out of place. You should be able to explain what the other three words have in common.

1. pettifogger, quatrain, litigation, deposition
2. mastectomy, biopsy, vasectomy, equity
3. philately, alchemy, bibliophile, xenophobia
4. draconian, Lilliputian, Socratic, bovine
5. warlock, demonology, exorcise, etiology
6. cardiology, toxicology, gynecology, tautology
7. titanic, picayune, vulpine, infinitesimal
8. vixen, purloin, bovine, leonine
9. amplitude, Decalogue, quintessence, dichotomy
10. equine, feline, ursine, elfin

B. Rearranging Words

Rearrange the following groups of words using the first letter of each word to spell out one of the new words taught in this unit.

1. cardiology, cadaver, ostracism, neurology, endocrinology, litigation, abscess, vixen

   _____

2. ursine, Lilliputian, imperious, paleontology, exorcise, nihilism

   _____

3. thaumaturgy, collusion, millennium, etiology, aphasia, shamus, ostracism, oncology

   _____

4. conundrum, tort, tribunal, ingenious, immolate, acrophobia, necrology

   _____

5. dirge, claustrophobia, minimize, epicurean, inscrutable, equine, atonement, triskaidekaphobia

   _____

C. On Location

What would you expect to find in the following places? Circle the correct answer.

1. The morgue

   (collusion, cadaver, ritual, aphasia)

2. A courtroom

   (equity, rubric, dichotomy, nihilism)

3. A gypsy tea room

   (shamus, warlock, soothsayer, pettifogger)

4. The library

   (bibliophile, Philistine, sycophant, proletariat)

5. A medical supply house

   (conundrum, prosthesis, tort, Decalogue)

6. A Russophobe

   (bacchanal, catharsis, misanthropist, extrovert)

7. A zoo

   (simian, quatrain, pettifogger, shamus)

8. Opera house

   (xenophobe, taurine, accolade, Decalogue)

9. Skyscrapers

   (tribunal, alchemist, megalopolis, Philistine)

10. Bullfight

    (vulpine, tort, aficionado, protocol)

D. Making Pairs

From the group below, find the pairs of words that have something in common and record them in the spaces provided. You should be able to find ten such pairs and list them numerically, using the same number for each pair.

circumspect_____	Lilliputian _____	decimate_____	amplitude ____
peccadillo _____	titanic _____	Russophobe _____	adjudicate ____
intractable _____	Decalogue _____	misanthropist _____	effete _____
tort _____	tribunal _____	demure _____	flaccid _____
picayune _____	litigation _____	intransigent_____	infinitesimal __

E. Cliché Time

Which of the words from this unit fit into the following familiar expressions? Choose the correct word from the choices given and record it in the space provided.

1. The sick man had a ghostly _____ .

   (dirge, pallor, lien, vista)

2. Charlie Chan was called an _____ Oriental.

   (intractable, intestate, inscrutable, epicurean)

3. The prisoner was held _____ .

   (incommunicado, comatose, glabrous, immolate)

4. A _____ mass of humanity.

   (demure, saurian, draconian, teeming)

5. A congressional _____ .

   (Philistine, junket, peccadillo, protocol)

Appearances and Attitudes (III)

Is there any merit in being *meretricious?*

What is the relationship between *mutable* and mutation?

Why did Shakespeare call Romeo's *mercurial* friend Mercutio?

Does one need a license to be *licentious?*

How should you feel if your creative writing is described as *jejune?*

dilettante
jejune
libidinous
licentious
mercurial
meretricious
minatory
mutable
nonchalant
noxious
obdurate
obtuse
officious
omniscient
pusillanimous

1. **dilettante** (dil-i-tänt')—an amateur; lover of fine arts.
    a. Josef pretended to know a great deal about classical music, but in reality he was a *dilettante*.
    b. His limited knowledge exposed him as a *dilettante* in the field of fine art.

2. **jejune** (ji-jōōn')—barren; flat; dull. The Latin word *jejunus* means "empty."
    a. Sad to say, he took an exciting theme and turned it into a *jejune* story that put us all to sleep.
    b. Blanche was raised on a *jejune* diet of soap operas that did nothing to develop her mind.

3. **libidinous** (li-bid'-nəs)—characterized by lust; lewd; lascivious. In psychoanalytic theory, the *libido* is the driving force behind all human action.
    a. The comic's *libidinous* patter was censored by the cautious sponsor before it ever got on the air.
    b. Much material of a *libidinous* nature is available only in certain areas of the city.

4. **licentious** (li-sen'-shəs)—morally unrestrained; lascivious. This is derived from an Old French word that meant "license" and referred to an abuse of liberty or undisciplined freedom.
    a. The Broadway play was picketed by a civic group on the grounds that it was *licentious*.
    b. Having spent the preceding twenty years of his life in a *licentious* manner, Clive decided to join a monastery.

5. **mercurial** (mər-kyoor'-ē-əl)—changeable; volatile. These adjectives are characteristic of the heavy, silver-white metallic element mercury. In Roman mythology the swift messenger of the gods, Mercury, was volatile, quick-witted, eloquent, and manually skillful.
    a. Since my boss is a man of *mercurial* moods, we never know what to expect from him.
    b. Shakespeare's Mercutio in *Romeo and Juliet* was aptly named because he had a *mercurial* temperament.

6. **meretricious** (mer'-ə-trish'-əs)—flashy; tawdry; falsely alluring. It is from the Latin word *meretricius* ("prostitute").
   a. The young woman projects a *meretricious* quality that often distresses her parents
   b. The clever defense lawyer changed his client's garb from *meretricious* to prim.

7. **minatory** (min'-ə-tôr-ē)—menacing; threatening.
   a. Our flight attendant assured the obnoxious passenger that he could be arrested for his *minatory* remarks.
   b. The Secretary of State said that he would never knuckle under to *minatory* gestures from foreign leaders.

8. **mutable** (myo͞ot'-ə-b'l)—inconstant; fickle; tending to frequent change. In biology, a *mutation* is a change in some inheritable characteristic.
   a. She swore by the moon but her lover pointed out how *mutable* that was.
   b. As politicians often find out, the electorate can be most *mutable*.

9. **nonchalant** (nän-shə-länt,'-lənt)—cool; indifferent; without warmth or animation. It comes from a French root, *chaloir* ("to care for").
   a. Julio's seemingly *nonchalant* manner is actually a cover-up for his nervousness.
   b. Detective Gates sauntered toward the suspect in a *nonchalant* way, trying not to arouse his suspicions.

10. **noxious** (näk'-shəs)—unwholesome; harmful to health. The Latin *nocere* means "to hurt."
    a. The firemen began to gasp as they got a whiff of the *noxious* gas.
    b. Automobile manufacturers have been given a deadline for eliminating most of their cars' *noxious* fumes.

11. **obdurate** (äb'-door-ət, -dyoor)—hardhearted; inflexible; not easily moved to pity.
    a. Despite many pleas from his supporters, the general remained *obdurate* in his refusal to run for the presidency.
    b. Judge Lenihan had an undeserved reputation for being obstinate and *obdurate*.

12. **obtuse** (əb-to͞os')—slow to understand; dull.
    a. Her husband's *obtuse* behavior proved a constant embarrassment to Lillian.
    b. "How can one person be so *obtuse!*" Nurse Stevens shouted as she prepared to explain the treatment to her new aide for the fifth time that morning.

13. **officious** (ə-fish'-əs)—meddlesome; offering unnecessary and unwanted advice.
    a. The room was filled with *officious* bureaucrats who were doing their best to frustrate the public.
    b. I don't mind working for a competent supervisor but I hate to get involved with an *officious* foreman.

14. **omniscient** (äm-nish'-ənt)—having infinite knowledge; knowing all things.
    a. When we are young we pester our parents with questions because we believe they are *omniscient*.
    b. Judy went into the exam with an *omniscient* attitude but came out feeling like a moron.

15. **pusillanimous** (pū-s'l-an'-ə-məs)—cowardly; fainthearted In Latin, "tiny mind."
    a. General Patton could not tolerate *pusillanimous* performance in battle.
    b. The Danish patriots warned their government against *pusillanimous* arrangements with the Nazis in 1940.

EXERCISES

I. Which Word Comes to Mind?

In each of the following, read the statement, then circle the word that comes to mind.

1. A Chinese fortune cookie accurately predicts your future

    (jejune, omniscient, licentious)

2. Eight poker players puffing on cigars in your living room

    (noxious, officious, mercurial)

3. You receive an anonymous letter hinting at violence

    (libidinous, minatory, nonchalant)

4. Your father absolutely refuses to let you borrow his car

    (meretricious, obtuse, obdurate)

5. The Lion in *The Wizard of Oz*

    (pusillanimous, mercurial, mutable)

6. It doesn't take much to upset James to the point of exasperation

    (mutable, mercurial, noxious)

7. Maxine can't make up her mind about which dress to wear

    (jejune, meretricious, mutable)

8. Jose had abandoned five wives, but he was ready to try again

    (licentious, pusillanimous, meretricious)

9. Malcolm blames everyone but himself for his failures

    (obtuse, licentious, nonchalant)

10. Nothing seems to excite him

    (officious, nonchalant, minatory)

II. True or False?

In the space provided, indicate whether each statement is true or false.

_____ 1. The conservative congregation was quite pleased with the minister's *libidinous* position.

_____ 2. One of our most coveted military awards, the Purple Heart, is given to those who have distinguished themselves by *pusillanimous* actions in combat.

_____ 3. An *officious* bank manager can make his tellers uneasy.

_____ 4. Professor Hardy modestly called himself a *dilettante* in the field in which he had a distinguished record.

_____ 5. Interior decorators generally abhor *meretricious* furniture.

_____ 6. Clara spoke in a *jejune* tone that attracted everyone's attention.

_____ 7. Being of a *mercurial* temperament, Tom could not restrain his delight.

_____ 8. A *noxious* element in human relations inclines people to be forgiving.

_____ 9. Becoming *omniscient* is unattainable even for the greatest among us.

_____ 10. Anxious to achieve a quick success, the president dispatched his most *obtuse* negotiator.

III. Fill in the Blank

Insert one of the new words in the proper space in each sentence below.

1. The _____ nature of the negotiators made it likely they would come to blows.

2. The professor's _____ attitude about any subject led us to regard him with awe and discomfort.

3. Being human is equivalent to being _____ for, as Heracleitus said, change is the only permanence we can count on.

4. Twenty years of _____ living had taken its complete toll of Mr. Bodack.

5. The marriage proposal was made in such a(n) _____ manner that Gloria doubted its sincerity.

6. The fumes from the gigantic fire were judged to be so _____ that the authorities issued a general evacuation order for nearby homes.

7. Alvin's generous offer to call the bout a draw was mistakenly regarded as a(n) _____ act.

8. When Iris learned that the role of Roxanne required her to wear _____ garb, she opted to turn down the offer.

9. Elizabeth's _____ interference did not endear her to the people in her office.

10. Only after Bob had spent an exciting, eye-opening year in the Peace Corps did he realize the _____ monotony of his previous life.

IV. What's the Antonym?

Which of the new words is most nearly *opposite* in meaning to the one provided?

1. friendly   _____

2. exciting   _____

3. harmless   _____

4. stouthearted   _____

5. yielding   _____

6. acute   _____

7. ignorant   _____

8. zealous   _____

9. subdued   _____

10. chaste   _____

V. Matching

Match the word in column A with its correct definition in column B by writing the letter of that definition in the space provided.

	A		B
____	1. dilettante	a.	morally unrestrained
____	2. jejeune	b.	threatening
____	3. libidinous	c.	volatile
____	4. licentious	d.	unwholesome
____	5. mercurial	e.	indifferent
____	6. meretricious	f.	cowardly
____	7. minatory	g.	uninteresting, dull
____	8. mutable	h.	amateur
____	9. nonchalant	i.	slow to understand
____	10. noxious	j.	hardhearted
____	11. obdurate	k.	flashy; cheap
____	12. obtuse	l.	meddlesome
____	13. officious	m.	knowing all things
____	14. omniscient	n.	inconstant
____	15. pusillanimous	o.	lewd

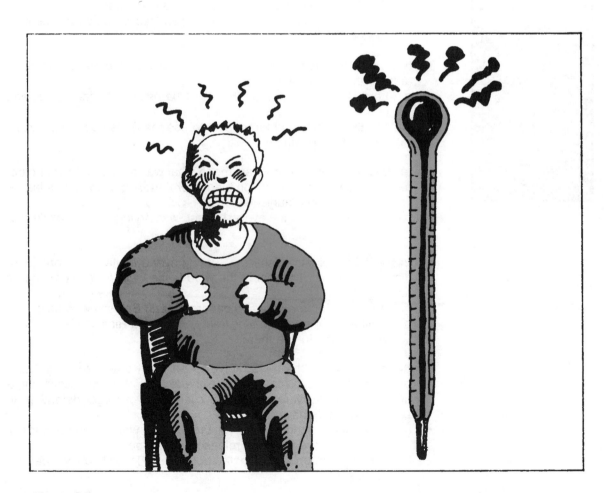

Mercurial

Legal Language (II)

Why do prison reformers advocate *indeterminate* sentences?

What does a lawyer mean when he labels a question as *immaterial?*

Should our *extradition* treaties with other countries be of interest to a criminal?

Why is a *litigious* person likely to be found in court?

When is a lawyer a *barrister?*

---

amicus curiae
arson
barrister
embezzle
extradition
habeas corpus
immaterial
incarcerate
indeterminate
larceny
litigious
miscreant
perpetrator
plagiarism
probation

1. **amicus curiae** (ə-mī'-kəs-kyoor'-ī-ē)—a friend of the court; a lawyer or layman who advises the court on a legal matter.
    a. Our law professor is frequently called to serve as *amicus curiae* on difficult cases.
    b. I offered my help as *amicus curiae* in the family squabble but both sides rejected it.

2. **arson** (är'-s'n)—the crime of setting fire to property in order to collect insurance.
    a. The Fire Marshall characterized the case as *arson.*
    b. A pyromaniac has a compulsion to start fires; an *arsonist* does it for money.

3. **barrister** (bar'-is-tər, ber'-)—lawyer in England. A *barrister* practices at the bar, or court of justice.
    a. Lord Dorset called upon the finest *barrister* in London to defend him.
    b. It's always amusing for tourists to see the British *barristers* wearing their court wigs.

4. **embezzle** (im-bez'l)—to steal money that was entrusted to your care.
    a. The treasurer of our union tried to *embezzle* pension funds but he was caught and punished.
    b. Aunt Anna thought every banker was trying to *embezzle* her savings.

5. **extradition** (eks-trə-dish'-ən)—turning over a fugitive from one jurisdiction to another. The root of the word is the Latin *trachtio* ("the act of handing over").
    a. Armed with the *extradition* papers, Sheriff Bates flew to Italy.
    b. Until we sign an *extradition* treaty with Costa Rica, some criminals will continue to flee there.

6. **habeas corpus** (hā-bi-əs kôr'-pəs)—a court order requiring that a prisoner be produced to determine the legality of his imprisonment; a procedure that lawyers use to get clients out of illegal detention. In Latin it means "to have the body."
    a. When the defendant's lawyer produced a writ of *habeas corpus,* the police were forced to release their suspect.
    b. Captain Gordon was demoted because he failed to obey a *habeas corpus* order.

7. **immaterial** (im̃-ə-tir'-ē-əl)—without substance; unimportant.
   a. Lawyers are fond of calling a question *"immaterial,* irrelevant, and inconsequential."
   b. What seemed to be serious charges turned out to be quite *immaterial.*

8. **incarcerate** (in-kär'-sə-rāt)—to jail; confine.
   a. Judge Miller threatened to *incarcerate* anyone who disturbed his court.
   b. King Edward *incarcerated* his brother, Clarence, in the Tower of London.

9. **indeterminate** (in-di-tur'-mi-nit)—having inexact limits; indefinite.
   a. If prisoners are given an *indeterminate* sentence of 2–20 years, they can be freed early if they behave well in jail.
   b. "Scarface" Kelly had to serve the full fifteen years of his *indeterminate* sentence because of his numerous attempts to escape.

10. **larceny** (lär'-sə-nē)—theft. *Grand larceny* involves theft in excess of a fixed sum, whereas *petty larceny* refers to a less consequential theft.
    a. Since this is George's fourth conviction for grand *larceny,* he will go to jail for life.
    b. My partner was promoted to detective after making an important *larceny* arrest.

11. **litigious** (li-tij'-əs)—quarrelsome; given to carrying on lawsuits.
    a. Uncle Charlie, our *litigious* relative, is currently involved in three cases.
    b. A litigant is a *litigious* person engaged in a litigation.

12. **miscreant** (mis'-kri-ənt)—villain; criminal; evil person. The original meaning was "unbeliever" or "heretic." From there it was an easy jump to "villain."
    a. The *miscreant's* tears had no effect on Judge Safian.
    b. We were not taken in by the *miscreant's* vow to turn over a new leaf.

13. **perpetrator** (pur'-pə-trā-tər)—a person who commits an offense.
    a. Police officers are careful to use the term "alleged *perpetrator*" when describing a suspect.
    b. Although Roy was the *perpetrator* of the cruel hoax, he escaped serious punishment.

14. **plagiarism** (plā'-jə-riz'm)—passing off someone else's writings or ideas as your own. The Latin word for kidnapper is *plagiarius.*
    a. We were saddened to learn that Henry was found guilty of *plagiarism* in the poetry contest.
    b. My English teacher tolerates almost any mistake but she detests *plagiarism.*

15. **probation** (prō-bā-'shən)—a period of testing or trial. This refers to a suspension of sentence on the condition that the convicted person demonstrates good behavior in order to stay out of jail.
    a. After his release from prison, Vincent was required to report to his *probation* officer every month.
    b. Before getting permanent status, the young police officer had to undergo a six-month period of *probation.*

EXERCISES

I. Which Word Comes to Mind?

In each of the following, read the statement, then circle the word that comes to mind.

1. A prominent psychiatrist offers to help out in a court case

    (perpetrator, larceny, amicus curiae)

2. The fire marshal suspects foul play

    (probation, arson, immaterial)

3. Detectives fly across the border to bring back a suspect

    (indeterminate, extradition, habeas corpus)

4. A scholar suggests that Shakespeare was not especially original

    (plagiarism, incarcerate, miscreant)

5. The crooked bank manager fears the day when his books will be audited

    (litigious, embezzle, barrister)

6. Sal was sentenced to five to ten years in jail

    (probation, indeterminate, larceny)

7. The teacher quickly recognized that Gary's report was beyond his capacity

    (larceny, immaterial, plagiarism)

8. The jury found the defendant guilty as charged

    (barrister, litigious, miscreant)

9. The bank officer suddenly acquired unexplainable wealth

    (litigious, embezzle, incarcerate)

10. Enid made a proposal that had no connection to the problem

    (immaterial, probation, extradition)

II. True or False?

In the space provided, indicate whether each statement is true or false.

_____ 1. Burning down a building is an act of *larceny.*
_____ 2. *Litigious* people provide a good income for lawyers.
_____ 3. An alert lawyer can use a writ of *habeas corpus* to keep his client out of jail before charges are brought against him.
_____ 4. When you *embezzle* funds you misuse money that has been entrusted to you.
_____ 5. That which is *immaterial* is usually critical in any court case.

_____ 6. A *miscreant* is likely to be involved in grand *larceny*.
_____ 7. *Probation* is an investigative procedure to determine if a crime has been committed.
_____ 8. A *perpetrator* is someone who betrays his country.
_____ 9. A *barrister* would likely be familiar with court procedure.
_____ 10. A person guilty of *arson* could sometimes be charged with murder.

III. Fill in the Blank

Insert one of the new words in the proper space in each sentence below.

1. Anyone who believes "there is a little _____ in everyone's heart" is merely trying to rationalize his own failing.

2. The rigorous _____ period was intended to discourage unsuitable applicants.

3. Murder was added to the _____ charge when the firemen discovered a body in the burned out structure.

4. The terrorist sought refuge in a country where he believed he would be free from _____ .

5. _____ may not be punishable by a prison sentence but it can cost a pretty penny and ruin a reputation.

6. The unexpected appearance of a(n) _____ gave the prosecution the impetus to follow through to a guilty verdict.

7. The British _____ may sound more sophisticated but he is in reality the same as a U.S. lawyer.

8. Paul, ever the romantic, told Peggy she was guilty of _____ for she had stolen his heart.

9. It was hard to believe that the club treasurer would _____ the money entrusted to him.

10. The police collared the _____ but lacked witnesses or evidence to get an indictment.

IV. What's the Antonym?

Which of the new words is most nearly *opposite* in meaning to the one provided?

1. important   _____
2. release   _____
3. forgiving   _____
4. precise   _____
5. paragon   _____
6. reimburse   _____
7. benefactor   _____
8. easy-going   _____
9. definite   _____
10. liberate   _____

V. Matching

Match the word in column A with its correct definition in column B by writing the letter of that definition in the space provided.

	A		B
_____	1. amicus curiae	a.	court order for a prisoner's appearance
_____	2. arson	b.	misappropriate money
_____	3. barrister	c.	unimportant
_____	4. embezzle	d.	villain
_____	5. extradition	e.	friend of the court
_____	6. habeas corpus	f.	one who commits an offense
_____	7. immaterial	g.	quarrelsome
_____	8. incarcerate	h.	British lawyer
_____	9. indeterminate	i.	false claim of authorship
_____	10. larceny	j.	indefinite
_____	11. litigious	k.	period of testing
_____	12. miscreant	l.	transfer of a fugitive
_____	13. perpetrator	m.	place in jail
_____	14. plagiarism	n.	crime of setting fire
_____	15. probation	o.	theft

Foreign Terms (I)

Is a *junta* a tasty dessert?

What foreign expression means "end of the century"?

What does a firing squad have to do with *coup de grâce?*

How does *laissez-faire* differ from *savior faire?*

Why does Emily Post frown upon behavior that is *gauche?*

---

avant-garde
bête noire
bon mot
coup de grâce
cul-de-sac
deus ex
 machina
fait accompli
fin de siècle
gauche
junta
laissez-faire
mot juste
non compos
mentis
non sequitur
sine qua non

1. **avant-garde** (ä-vänt-gärd')—the leaders of a movement; vanguard. *Avant-garde* people are generally regarded as reformers, people with new ideas who are somewhat ahead of their time.
   a. Lord Keynes was an *avant-garde* economist in the period before World War I.
   b. The painter once belonged to an *avant-garde* movement but is considered a conservative today.

2. **bête noire** (bāt nwär')—someone or something that is feared or disliked. In French, the two words mean "black beast." A black sheep was an eyesore in the flock—its wool was less valuable. If something is your *bête noire,* you do your best to avoid it; it is a thorn in your side.
   a. Although I was good in math, geometry proved to be my *bête noire.*
   b. The regional primaries were later seen as the incumbent's *bête noire.*

3. **bon mot** (bōn' mō')—a bright saying; witticism. In French, *bon* means "good," and *mot* means "word." A clever remark or ad lib is often labeled a *bon mot.*
   a. Groucho Marx was applauded for his *bon mot* on the talk show.
   b. I tried all evening to come up with a sparkling *bon mot* but my wit had deserted me.

4. **coup de grâce** (kōō-də-gräs')—the shot or blow that brings death; the finishing stroke. The actual French meaning is "blow of mercy." The officer in charge of a firing squad administers the *coup de grace* by firing a bullet into the victim's head after his men have shot.
   a. Tom's foul shot in the last second of the game was the *coup de grâce* for our opponents.
   b. After the prisoner confessed, his torturers administered the *croup de grâce.*

5. **cul-de-sac** (kul'-də-sak')—a passage or street with only one outlet; a situation from which there is no escape; an argument that leads nowhere. In French it means "bottom of the sack."
   a. We chose to build in a *cul-de-sac* because there would be little traffic on our block.
   b. Although we disagree on busing, that topic always proves to be a *cul-de-sac* in our family.

6. **deus ex machina** (dē'-əs eks mak'-i-nə)—someone who intervenes unexpectedly to solve a dilemma. The literal Latin meaning is "god out of the machine." In the ancient theater the first few acts laid out the problems facing the characters and when no solution was apparent, a "god" was lowered onto the stage and helped to resolve the issues.
   a. When things were mighty bleak, Jerry's rich uncle arrived from Canada and turned out to be the family's *deus ex machina*.
   b. His plays often end with a *deus ex machina* that the critics call a far-fetched coincidence.

7. **fait accompli** (fe'-tä-kōn-plē')—something that is already done so that there is no use in debating it. In French, "an accomplished fact."
   a. Dad brought home a Buick, and that *fait accompli* put an end to our discussion as to what kind of car we should buy.
   b. There was nothing democratic about the general's way of running the army because he relied upon the technique of *fait accompli*.

8. **fin de siècle** (fan-də-sye'-kl)—referring to the last years of the nineteenth century; decadent. The French meaning is "end of the century."
   a. The art gallery staged a showing of *fin de siècle* paintings.
   b. We accused our grandfather of having *fin de siècle* ideas.

9. **gauche** (gōsh)—awkward; lacking grace; without tact. It is French for "left-handed." Lefties were thought to be clumsy (*sinister* in Latin). Another French meaning is "warped."
   a. Following his *gauche* behavior, Arthur was ordered to leave the room.
   b. Harriet's *gauche* remark was unforgivable, and she deserved to have egg on her face.

10. **junta** (hoon'-tə, jun'-)—a political group that seeks to control a government; a faction or cabal. In Spanish this word originally meant "to join." In Spain, a *junta* was a legislative assembly; the word was corrupted to *junto,* which meant "clique" or "faction." Today, we use the original word with its changed meaning.
   a. The air force *junta* was arrested before it could overthrow the dictator.
   b. After seizing power, the three-man *junta* held a press conference.

11. **laissez-faire** (les-ā-fer')—hands-off policy; letting business operate without government interference. There was a mid-eighteenth century school of French economists whose motto was *laissez-faire, laissez-passer* ("let us alone, let us have free passage for our goods").
   a. My parents were very progressive, and followed a *laissez-faire* policy in bringing us up.
   b. The South American government adopted a *laissez-faire* attitude in order to attract foreign investment.

12. **mot juste** (mō zhüst')—the right word; exact phrase.
   a. You can always rely upon Shakespeare to come up with the *mot juste*.
   b. I was searching for the *mot juste* but my mind was a blank.

13. **non compos mentis** (nän-käm'-pəs-men'-tis)—incapable of handling one's own affairs; insane. In Latin, "not of sound mind." This could be said of someone who has lost his memory and understanding by reason of disease or accident.
   a. The judge declared Mrs. Elkins *non compos mentis* and appointed a lawyer to handle her estate.
   b. After three martinis, the drunkard was definitely *non compos mentis*.

14. **non sequitur** (nän' sek'-wi-ter)—in logic this is a conclusion that does not follow from the evidence; a remark that seems out of place. The Latin meaning is "it does not follow."
   a. When she does not pay attention to our conversation, Betty comes up with one *non sequitur* after another.
   b. I said that Albert is near-sighted, and Phyllis, with a typical *non sequitur,* said, "Yes, he's hard of hearing."

15. **sine qua non** (sin'-ā kwä nōn')—an essential condition; that which is indispensable. The Latin meaning is "without which not."
   a. Money is the *sine qua non* in our society.
   b. The *sine qua non* for admission to our club is a sense of humor.

EXERCISES

I. Which Word Comes to Mind?

In each of the following, read the statement, then circle the word that comes to mind.

1. A murderer who pleads temporary insanity

    (laissez-faire, non compos mentis, cul-de-sac)

2. An ailing horse is being put out of his misery

    (coup de grâce, mot juste, gauche)

3. Several schemers plan a take-over

    (fait accompli, junta, sine qua non)

4. You ask for her age and she says, "I'm five feet tall"

    (bête noire, fin de siècle, non sequitur)

5. Alban Berg was a composer who experimented with atonalities

    (avant-garde, bon mot, deus ex machina)

6. The discussion centered around how history would characterize the last years of the twentieth century

    (non sequitur, avant-garde, fin de siècle)

7. Loss of trust in a do-nothing leadership

    (fait accompli, laissez-faire, junta)

8. The right word at the right time

    (bon mot, gauche, non compos mentis)

9. It's a pity but there was no alternative

    (non sequitur, non compos mentis, sine qua non)

10. A weak spot

    (bête noir, cul-de-sac, mot juste)

II. True or False?

In the space provided, indicate whether each statement is true or false.

_____ 1. Being born in this country is a *sine qua non* for anyone running for the presidency.

_____ 2. If you are in the *avant-garde,* you are inclined to conservatism.

_____ 3. Someone who always seems to get the better of you is your *bête noire.*

_____ 4. It is considered *gauche* to sip your coffee from the saucer.

_____ 5. "Open sesame" was the *mot juste.*

_____ 6. *Non sequitur* refers to a leader who has no following.

_____ 7. A *fait accompli* is a done deed.

_____ 8. *Laissez-faire* invites people to do their own thing with few restrictions.

_____ 9. A creative writer will not find it necessary to resort to *deus ex machina*.

_____ 10. The fleeing criminal was lucky to find a *cul-de-sac*.

III. Fill in the Blank

Insert one of the new words in the proper space in each sentence below.

1. The accused hoped his _____ responses would corroborate his insanity plea.

2. The revelation that all the hero's adventures were really a dream is the kind of _____ that suggests a lack of originality by the author.

3. The thief was cornered when the police chased his car into a _____ .

4. The military _____ promised to hold democratic elections as soon as the turmoil subsided.

5. As we go deeper into the twenty-first century, I wonder if we will regard our _____ as decadent as the previous one.

6. According to some pundits, the _____ that is threatening the senator's reelection bid is his own wife.

7. Isn't it strange that the _____ you searched for at the party escaped you till you got home?

8. The discussion of abortion inevitably ends in a(n) _____ .

9. The _____ for success in business is a wealthy father-in-law.

10. We laughed at Perry's interest in a political career because his outstanding trait is his _____ way of expressing himself.

IV. What's the Antonym?

Which of the new words is most nearly *opposite* in meaning to the one provided?

1. superfluous   _____

2. dexterous   _____

3. competent   _____

4. conservative   _____

5. beginning   _____

6. perfectly logical _____

7. strictness   _____

8. just getting started _____

9. guardian angel   _____

10. graceful   _____

V. Matching

Match the word in column A with its correct definition in column B by writing the letter of that definition in the space provided.

A

_____ 1. avant-garde
_____ 2. bête noire
_____ 3. bon mot
_____ 4. coup de grâce
_____ 5. cul-de-sac
_____ 6. deus ex machina
_____ 7. fait accompli
_____ 8. fin de siècle
_____ 9. gauche
_____ 10. junta
_____ 11. laissez-faire
_____ 12. mot juste
_____ 13. non compos mentis
_____ 14. non sequitur
_____ 15. sine qua non

B

a. one who changes the course of events
b. end of the century
c. clumsy
d. political faction
e. something hateful
f. hands off
g. insane
h. bright saying
i. out of place remark
j. absolute requirement
k. blind alley
l. vanguard
m. right word
n. completed deed
o. finishing stroke

En Français

Where would you go if you took a *tour de force?*

Could the operator of a penny lemonade stand be called an *entrepreneur?*

Why does the word *impasse* often occur in labor-management relations?

Is an *éclat* likely to be found in a pastry shop?

Would you like to be complimented for your *repartee?*

---

au courant
coiffure
denouement
de rigueur
éclat
élan
entrepreneur
impasse
ingenue
malaise
repartee
sangfroid
tête-à-tête
tour de force
vignette

1. **au courant** (ō-kōō-rän')—up-to-date; modern.
   a. Listening to radio news will keep you *au courant* on world affairs.
   b. Sid apologized for not being *au courant* on the bond issue.

2. **coiffure** (kwä-fyoor')—a style of hair arrangement.
   a. Mrs. Dupont's elegant *coiffure* was admired by all the ladies.
   b. The dampness in the air ruined the model's expensive *coiffure.*

3. **denouement** (dă-nōō-män)—the final outcome of the intricacies of a plot. The French meaning is "the untying of a knot."
   a. The *denouement* of the play was so unrealistic that the audience booed loudly.
   b. At the time of the lengthy opera's *denouement,* we were fast asleep.

4. **de rigueur** (də–rē-goer')—required; necessary.
   a. Formal clothing was *de rigueur* at the wedding.
   b. Attendance at the daily briefing was *de rigueur.*

5. **éclat** (ā-klä')—acclaim; brilliant success. The French word *éclater* means "to burst out."
   a. The novelist's *éclat* brought him a host of relatives seeking loans and gifts.
   b. The great diva feared that her *éclat* would vanish with the onset of old age.

6. **élan** (ā-län')—enthusiasm; ardor; vigor. Its original meaning was "to throw a lance."
   a. Actor Bob Hope, who died at the age of 100, was admired for his *élan* to the very end of his life.
   b. With uncharacteristic *élan,* Cynthia devoted herself to making a success of her third marriage.

7. **entrepreneur** (än-trə-prə-nur')—one who organizes and manages a business undertaking.
   a. Sol Hurok, the great *entrepreneur,* first brought the Russian Bolshoi Theatre to this country.
   b. A shrewd *entrepreneur* made a fortune in sponsoring teenage beauty contests throughout the United States.

8. **impasse** (im'-pas)—difficulty without a solution; stalemate; blind alley.
   a. When both sides reached an *impasse,* a mediator was called to settle the dispute.
   b. After struggling for 24 hours, the exhausted chess players acknowledged the *impasse* and adjourned the game.

9. **ingenue** (an-zhə-nōō')—actress playing an innocent, inexperienced young woman.
   a. Sheila told the producer that she was sick of playing *ingenue* roles.
   b. It was ridiculous for the 50-year-old actress to undertake the part of the *ingenue.*

10. **malaise** (ma-lāz')—a feeling of discomfort or uneasiness. In French, *mal* means "bad" and *aise* means "ease."
    a. I had a sense of *malaise* about the investment and should have paid attention to my intuition.
    b. The heart attack started with a mild *malaise* and then graduated to severe chest pains.

11. **repartee** (rep-ər-tē')—quick, witty reply; wit. The French meaning is "the quick return of a thrust or blow."
    a. The riotous comedian was noted for his brilliant *repartee.*
    b. We expected sparkling *repartee* at our party, but it turned out to be a dull evening.

12. **sangfroid** (saŋ-frwä')—composure; equanimity. In French it means "cold blood."
    a. To be "cool" today means to be possessed of *sangfroid.*
    b. Ellis was suspicious of Irene's *sangfroid* because she was normally quite emotional.

13. **tête-à-tête** (tāt'-ə-tāt')—intimate conversation between two people. The literal meaning is "head-to-head."
    a. At the rear of the restaurant, Lorraine and Jules were engaged in a romantic *tête-à-tête.*
    b. After a brief *tête-à-tête,* Leslie saw it my way.

14. **tour de force** (toor-də-fôrs')—a feat of strength or skill.
    a. The Chicago Bulls' seventy victories in one season was indeed a rare *tour de force.*
    b. Mark Spitz's *tour de force* of winning seven gold medals in the 1972 Olympics has not been duplicated.

15. **vignette** (vin-yet')—an anecdote; a brief literary composition.
    a. Television reporters fanned out on the convention floor in search of *vignettes* with human interest.
    b. Blossom sent a humorous *vignette* about her kindergarten class to the *Reader's Digest,* and they published it.

EXERCISES

I. Which Word Comes to Mind?

In each of the following, read the statement, then circle the word that comes to mind.

1. A cold-blooded killer

   (vignette, sangfroid, ingenue)

2. There is loud applause for the star of *Hamlet*

   (tour de force, au courant, malaise)

3. You get together with your brother for a serious conversation

   (denouement, entrepreneur, tête-à-tête)

4. Two rival hostesses emerge abashed after some sharp word play

(repartee, coiffure, éclat)

5. A producer advertises his search for a 14-year-old Juliet

(élan, impasse, ingenue)

6. The surprise ending was a stroke of genius

(de rigueur, éclat, denouement)

7. The non-stop 12-hour session failed to produce an agreement

(élan, impasse, vignette)

8. A feeling that things are going wrong

(sangfroid, malaise, au courant)

9. A humorous anecdote

(malaise, vignette, élan)

10. Beauty parlor

(sangfroid, coiffure, éclat)

II. True or False?

In the space provided, indicate whether each statement is true or false.

_____ 1. The *denouement* of a mystery story should satisfy every one of the readers' questions.
_____ 2. In order for success in most projects, a certain degree of *élan* is required.
_____ 3. The bargainers reached an *impasse,* and everyone went home satisfied with the way the strike had been concluded.
_____ 4. A man with *sangfroid* could stare a gunman in the eye and not show his fear.
_____ 5. Madame de Pompadour was noted for her *coiffure.*
_____ 6. The *entrepreneur* attributed his success to his long years of experience.
_____ 7. The suffering country was in the grip of a *malaise.*
_____ 8. The starring role of the *ingenue* was played with éclat by the young actress.
_____ 9. The *vignette* caught our attention but its inordinate length eventually put us to sleep.
_____ 10. *Repartee* may be compared to a duel without swords.

III. Fill in the Blank

Insert one of the new words in the proper space in each sentence below.

1. The _____ between Terry and Marsha cleared the air.

2. The octogenarian _____ had only a fifth grade education, but he had outsmarted the most savvy competitors.

3. Mischa, not blessed with the gift of _____ , could only answer the insult with an embarrassed stammer.

4. We were all enraptured with the _____ about the little girl and the red baboon.

5. With her wide blue eyes and diffident smile, Carol was a natural for the _____ role.

6. The peace talks reached a(n) _____ when neither side would budge an inch since their last confrontation.

7. I can vouch for his _____ but not for his honesty.

8. The actor's _____ in his first film was followed by a disappointing series of failures.

9. Marie Antoinette set the pattern for women's _____ throughout the realm.

10. President Carter's declaration that the feeling in the country was one of _____ was a faux pas that may have cost him a second term.

IV. What's the Antonym?

Which of the new words is most nearly *opposite* in meaning to the one provided?

1. failure   _____

2. settlement   _____

3. agitation   _____

4. saga   _____

5. well-being   _____

6. boredom   _____

7. a flop in business   _____

8. building events in a story to a climax   _____

9. a veteran actress who has seen better days   _____

10. a relatively unimpressive act   _____

V. Matching

Match the word in column A with its correct definition in column B by writing the letter of that definition in the space provided.

<table>
<tr><td colspan="2" align="center">*A*</td><td colspan="2" align="center">*B*</td></tr>
<tr><td>_____</td><td>1. au courant</td><td>a.</td><td>organizer and manager</td></tr>
<tr><td>_____</td><td>2. coiffure</td><td>b.</td><td>outcome of a story</td></tr>
<tr><td>_____</td><td>3. denouement</td><td>c.</td><td>feeling of uneasiness</td></tr>
<tr><td>_____</td><td>4. de rigueur</td><td>d.</td><td>deadlock, stalemate</td></tr>
<tr><td>_____</td><td>5. éclat</td><td>e.</td><td>composure</td></tr>
<tr><td>_____</td><td>6. élan</td><td>f.</td><td>actress playing unsophisticated roles</td></tr>
<tr><td>_____</td><td>7. entrepreneur</td><td>g.</td><td>conversation for two</td></tr>
<tr><td>_____</td><td>8. impasse</td><td>h.</td><td>up-to-date</td></tr>
<tr><td>_____</td><td>9. ingenue</td><td>i.</td><td>skillful performance</td></tr>
<tr><td>_____</td><td>10. malaise</td><td>j.</td><td>brilliant success</td></tr>
<tr><td>_____</td><td>11. repartee</td><td>k.</td><td>vigor</td></tr>
<tr><td>_____</td><td>12. sangfroid</td><td>l.</td><td>colorful anecdote</td></tr>
<tr><td>_____</td><td>13. tête-à-tête</td><td>m.</td><td>necessary</td></tr>
<tr><td>_____</td><td>14. tour de force</td><td>n.</td><td>hairdo</td></tr>
<tr><td>_____</td><td>15. vignette</td><td>o.</td><td>wit</td></tr>
</table>

Tête-à-tête?

Crossword Puzzle Words

Was Bernard Shaw's play called "*Alms* and the Man"?

What would you see if you spied a *bevy* of chorines?

Which of the vocabulary words below might be used to describe a tycoon?

Why might a "peeping Tom" be near an *aperture?*

What does *careen* tell you about the control of a moving vehicle?

---

acrid
addle
ado
alms
amulet
aperture
askew
bauble
bevy
bilk
blithe
careen
chary
nabob
onus

1. **acrid** (ak'-rid)—bitter; sharp; irritating to taste or smell.
   a. *Acrid* smoke arising from the burning couch awakened the family dog.
   b. Visitors are always amused by the *acrid* level of debate in Parliament.

2. **addle** (ad'-l)—to muddle; confuse. This word is often used in compounds such as *addlebrained.*
   a. The rookie became *addled* when he had to reassemble the many parts of the machine gun.
   b. One government report indicated that you can *addle* your brain through excessive use of marijuana.

3. **ado** (ə-doo')—fuss; trouble; bother.
   a. When all the excitement died down, we could see that it had been much *ado* over nothing.
   b. In order to spare his parents any further *ado,* Daniel packed his bags and left town.

4. **alms** (ämz)—money, food, or clothing given to poor people. Note the connection with *eleemosynary* which means "charitable."
   a. Each morning the Buddhist monks go into Bangkok seeking *alms.*
   b. "Call it the dole, welfare, *alms*—I'm in favor of helping people who cannot help themselves."

5. **amulet** (am'-yə-lit)—something worn around the neck as a protection against bad luck; a charm.
   a. The most precious object found in the tomb was a golden *amulet* that had been worn by the Egyptian princess.
   b. Lester treasured his *amulet*—a family heirloom that brought him good luck.

6. **aperture** (ap'-ər-chər)—opening; hole; gap.
   a. Rodents had a field day, leaping through the *aperture* in our kitchen wall.
   b. By staring into the cave's dark *aperture,* we could see the dim light of the miner's helmet.

7. **askew** (ə-skyoo')—on one side; crooked.
   a. The emcee's tie was *askew* but he straightened it just before the show went on the air.
   b. Every picture in my apartment is *askew* when the cleaning woman leaves.

8. bauble (bô'-b'l)—trinket; toy; showy but worthless thing. The Old French word *baubel* meant "toy."
   a. My little niece is fascinated by *baubles,* bangles, and beads.
   b. "Just a little *bauble* for your birthday," said Mr. Astor, proudly displaying the emerald bracelet.

9. bevy (bev'-ē)—group; flock. *Bevy* comes from an Old French word that meant "drinking group."
   a. The hunters' guns were poised as everyone waited for the *bevy* of quail to be flushed out of the tall grass.
   b. As the *bevy* of cheerleaders swept by, Timmy shouted, "Give me a J!"

10. bilk (bilk)—deceive; swindle; cheat. This word may be a corruption of *balk,* a term used in the card game of cribbage.
   a. The real estate agent protested that he never intended to *bilk* us out of our investment.
   b. Many students who did not pay back their government loans have, in effect, *bilked* the tax-payers.

11. blithe (blīth)—light-hearted; joyful; cheerful. The Anglo-Saxon word *blithia* was used to describe a bright sky.
   a. Because Eloise was always so cheerful in the mornings, her husband called her his "*blithe* spirit."
   b. Noel had a *blithe* way of treating the most depressing facts.

12. careen (kə-rēn')—to cause to lean sideways; to lurch or toss from side to side. The Latin word *carina* means "side of a ship."
   a. We watched the tiny sailboat *careen* wildly during the electrical storm.
   b. The drunk *careened* down Broadway, bumping into shoppers and lamp posts.

13. chary (cher'-ē, char'-)—careful; cautious; shy. The Anglo-Saxon word *cearig* meant "sorrowful."
   a. Having once been burned by a get-rich-quick scheme, Gil was *chary* about investing his money.
   b. We taught Bertha to be *chary* about accepting auto rides from strangers.

14. nabob (nā'-bäb)—a very rich or influential man. A *nabob* was a native district ruler or a European who became very wealthy in India.
   a. All of the union *nabobs* gathered in Miami Beach to plan for industry negotiations.
   b. Mr. Onassis, the Greek shipping *nabob,* owned dozens of private planes.

15. onus (ō'-nəs)—task; burden; responsibility.
   a. For the rest of his life, Mr. Chillingworth bore the *onus* of his sin.
   b. The fiery manager of the soccer team accepted the *onus* for their long losing streak.

EXERCISES

I. Which Word Comes to Mind?

In each of the following, read the statement, then circle the word that comes to mind.

1. An arm covered with costume jewelry

   (addle, bauble, nabob)

2. Walking through the cemetery at night

   (amulet, bilk, chary)

3. Peering into the camera lens

   (onus, blithe, aperture)

4. A beggar on the streets of Calcutta

(alms, bevy, askew)

5. An angry crowd gathers to protest

(ado, careen, acrid)

6. A man abandons his family

(bilk, onus, careen)

7. A person of means

(nabob, amulet, chary)

8. Mutual recriminations

(chary, acrid, blithe)

9. Completely nonplussed

(addled, careen, askew)

10. A bauble fit for a king

(bevy, amulet, aperture)

II. True or False?

In the space provided, indicate whether each statement is true or false.

_____ 1. An expensive *amulet* is a *bauble.*
_____ 2. It's easy to be *blithe* when everything is going wrong.
_____ 3. *Addle*-pated individuals are clear thinkers.
_____ 4. People are likely to seek favors and money from *nabobs.*
_____ 5. Saying good-by to poverty is bidding a "farewell to *alms.*"
_____ 6. A *blithe*-spirited person would tend to be optimistic.
_____ 7. Being *bilked* is usually a pleasant experience.
_____ 8. A *bevy* of thoughts dwell in the mind of a thinking person.
_____ 9. A *careening* car is probably out of control.
_____ 10. Collecting *alms* for the rich is hard to justify.

III. Find the Words

Somewhere in this box of letters, reading up, down, across, or diagonally, eleven vocabulary words that were taught in this lesson are hidden. As you locate each one, draw a circle around it.

S	T	E	L	D	D	A	G
N	W	H	O	B	M	C	E
A	G	A	E	U	O	R	H
B	D	V	L	P	N	I	T
O	Y	E	H	M	U	D	I
B	T	W	E	K	S	A	L
F	K	L	I	B	R	O	B

IV. Anagrams

In each of the following, add or subtract the indicated number of letters from the word, then rearrange the letters to form the new word whose meaning is given.

1. aperture – 3 letters = candle _____
2. bilk – 1 letter = sort, kind _____
3. chary – 2 letters = meal for horses _____
4. nabob – 2 letters = restriction _____
5. onus + letter = extra money _____

V. Matching

Match the word in column A with its correct definition in column B by writing the letter of that definition in the space provided.

A

_____ 1. acrid
_____ 2. addle
_____ 3. ado
_____ 4. alms
_____ 5. amulet
_____ 6. aperture
_____ 7. askew
_____ 8. bauble
_____ 9. bevy
_____ 10. bilk
_____ 11. blithe
_____ 12. careen
_____ 13. chary
_____ 14. nabob
_____ 15. onus

B

a. group
b. confuse
c. cautious
d. cheerful
e. trouble
f. responsibility
g. assistance given to the poor
h. to cheat
i. opening; gap
j. rich man
k. trinket
l. crooked
m. toss from side to side
n. a charm
o. sharp; irritating

Unit III
(Lessons 21–25)

Mini Review

I. Antonyms

Circle the word that most nearly expresses the *opposite* meaning of the word in capital letters.
1. OBTUSE: (a) flagrant (b) bulky (c) imaginative (d) candid
2. MISCREANT: (a) ignoramus (b) coward (c) trifler (d) paragon
3. BON MOT: (a) faux pas (b) exclamation (c) malediction (d) distortion
4. INGENUE: (a) amateur (b) sophisticate (c) devotee (d) connoisseur
5. CHARY: (a) picayune (b) pious (c) reckless (d) ruddy

II. Synonyms

Circle the word that most nearly expresses the *same* meaning as the word printed in capital letters.
1. OFFICIOUS: (a) insulting (b) coarse (c) interfering (d) intricate
2. IMMATERIAL: (a) eternal (b) objective (c) vanished (d) inconsequential
3. BÊTE NOIRE: (a) bias (b) abomination (c) curse (d) fetish
4. ONUS: (a) image (b) brawl (c) jumble (d) burden
5. CAREEN: (a) pitch (b) tilt (c) dawdle (d) fling

III. Sentence Completions

Select those words from the group below that best fill the blanks.

addle   bevy   blithe   chary   entrepreneur   epicurean   habeas corpus   minimize

1. Underneath Henry's _____ exterior lurked an uneasy feeling that he was about to be fired.

2. Rather than _____ the children, Mr. Simmons quietly explained that he did not know how their supplies had disappeared, but that there were enough emergency rations for everyone.

3. The _____ brought many talented musicians to Carnegie Hall.

4. The lawyer hurried to get a(n) _____ so his client would not have to remain in prison.

5. Once on board, she was greeted by the sounds of a _____ of boisterous sailors.

Mythology (II)

Why would you hear hisses from a *gorgon?*

What were the *Argonauts* seeking?

Why would a *Cyclops* tend to turn his head more than a normal being?

Were the *Harpies* vicious creatures or lovers of refined music?

Is a *paean* a peasant, a song, or a serious injury?

---

argonaut
calliope
cyclopean
gorgon
harpy
homeric
myrmidon
oracular
paean
Promethean
siren
stygian
tantalize
terpsichorean
thespian

1. **argonaut** (är'-gə-nôt)—adventurer; one who sailed with Jason on the Argo in search of the Golden Fleece. Specifically, the word refers to a participant in the California Gold Rush of 1849.
    a. The *Argonauts* included many famous Greek heroes like Hercules, Theseus, and Orpheus.
    b. Most of the *argonauts* in the California Gold Rush had little to show for their adventure.

2. **calliope** (kə-lī'-ə-pē, kal'-ē-ōp)—a musical instrument fitted with steam whistles, played from a keyboard, and usually heard at carnivals and circuses. It is named after Calliope, the Greek Muse of epic poetry.
    a. The music of the *calliope* has become an integral part of the merry-go-round ride.
    b. The sneezing of the diners, caused by the overdose of pepper in the food, sounded like an off-key *calliope.*

3. **cyclopean** (sī-klə-pē'-ən)—vast, massive and rough; suggestive of the Cyclops, the race of one-eyed giants, descended from the Titans. One of the most exciting tales in the *Odyssey* recounts the blinding of the one-eyed Polyphemus, who had confined Odysseus' crew in his cave and promised to "reward" Odysseus by eating him last.
    a. The mountain climbers found shelter from the avalanche in a *cyclopean* cave, surprisingly vast in its interior.
    b. The eye of the cyclone, like that of some suddenly aroused *cyclopean* bird, moved ominously closer to the terrified city.

4. **gorgon** (gôr'-gən)—a repulsively ugly or terrifying woman. In Greek mythology, the Gorgon sisters included the mortal Medusa, who had snakes for hair, and eyes that, if looked into, turned the beholder into stone.
    a. Ted returned home early, claiming his blind date could have doubled for a *gorgon.*
    b. Perseus managed to slay the *Gorgon* Medusa by viewing only her reflection in his bright shield.

5. **harpy** (här'pē)—a shrewish woman; a predatory person. The name is derived from the Harpies, one of several loathsome, voracious monsters, having a woman's head and trunk, and a bird's tail, wings and talons.
    a. The mistrustful bachelor looked upon every new female acquaintance as a potential *harpy* who wanted to get her claws into him.
    b. The bars were crowded by day as well as by night with screaming *harpies.*

6. **homeric** (hō-mer'-ik)—suggestive of Homer or his poetry; of heroic dimensions; grand; imposing.
   a.   Pulitzer prizes are awarded annually for *homeric* feats of reporting.
   b.   Landing on the moon was an achievement of *homeric* proportions.

7. **myrmidon** (mur'-mə-dän, -dən)—a faithful follower who carries out orders without question. The Myrmidons were the legendary Greek warriors of ancient Thessaly who followed their king Achilles on the expedition against Troy.
   a.   The Mafia chieftain assigned one of his *myrmidons* the task of removing the threat to his leadership.
   b.   A new spirit has swept across the youth of today and they no longer follow like *myrmidons* the wills of their parents or mentors.

8. **oracular** (ô-rak'-yə-lər)—uttered or delivered as if divinely inspired or infallible; ambiguous or obscure; portentous; ominous. Priests or priestesses in the shrines of ancient Greece would give ambiguous answers as the response of a god to an inquiry. One famous shrine was the oracle of Apollo at Delphi.
   a.   Some modern poetry is a jumble of *oracular* statements.
   b.   Exposing witches by *oracular* means smacks of witchcraft itself.

9. **paean** (pē'-ən)—any song of praise, joy or triumph. In classical mythology, a Paean was a god serving as a physician to the Olympian gods, later identified with Apollo.
   a.   The bicentennial celebration was a great *paean* to liberty.
   b.   With the appearance of the celebrity, a great cheer rose in a wild *paean* of frenzy.

10. **Promethean** (prō-mē'-thē-ən)—creative and boldly original. Prometheus was a Titan who taught mankind various arts and confined all its troubles in the box that Zeus treacherously gave to Epimetheus as the dowry of Pandora. For having stolen fire from Olympus and given it to mankind in defiance of Zeus, Prometheus was chained to a rock where an eagle daily tore at his liver, until he was finally released by Hercules.
    a.   There will always be nonconformists, rebels, *Promethean* pioneers.
    b.   Do not confuse an ornery or contrary attitude with the true *Promethean* spirit.

11. **siren** (sī'-rən)—a seductive woman. In Greek mythology, the Sirens lured seamen to their destruction on the rocks.
    a.   The sexy blonde played a *siren* in many "B" movies.
    b.   He paid no attention to the *siren* song of Wall Street.

12. **stygian** (stij'-ē-ən, stij'-ən)—gloomy and dark; hellish; infernal; inviolable (safe from profanation). The river Styx was one of the rivers of Hades, across which Charon ferried the souls of the dead.
    a.   Wordsworth describes the kiss of death as follows: "Upon those roseate lips a *stygian* hue."
    b.   Mr. Stone took a *stygian* oath never to reveal his secret pact with the devil.

13. **tantalize** (tan'-tə-līz)—tease. Tantalus stole the food of the gods and gave it to mortals. He was condemned to suffer eternal hunger and thirst in the presence of food and drink that was just beyond his reach.
    a.   Vernon was *tantalized* by the attractive offer, but he finally refused it.
    b.   Cynthia found that doubling her salary was a *tantalizing* illusion.

14. **terpsichorean** (turp-si-kə-rē'-ən)—pertaining to dancing. Terpsichore was the Muse of dancing and choral singing.
    a.   Anna's *terpsichorean* talents earned her the leading role in the musical.
    b.   Two stars of the *terpsichorean* art, Gene Kelly and Fred Astaire, teamed up to produce a nostalgic movie.

15. **thespian** (thes'-pē-ən)—dramatic (adj.); an actor or actress (noun). Thespis was the Greek poet of the sixth century B.C. who was the reputed originator of tragic drama.
    a.   The director got excellent *thespian* cooperation.
    b.   Gregory Peck was a *thespian* of great renown.

EXERCISES

I. Which Word Comes to Mind?

In each of the following, read the statement, then circle the word that comes to mind.

1. Music like a hundred steam whistles

   (harpy, calliope, siren)

2. I would do anything you ask

   (myrmidon, homeric, paean)

3. Not recommended to give exact directions

   (gorgon, argonaut, oracular)

4. He is an outstanding dramatic actor

   (terpsichorean, thespian, tantalize)

5. Beneficial to mankind

   (cyclopean, stygian, Promethean)

6. An inviting offer led to ultimate disappointment

   (stygian, thespian, siren)

7. A sweeping, best-selling novel

   (cyclopean, homeric, paean)

8. A song of victory

   (paean, argonaut, gorgon)

9. A trip to the underworld

   (harpy, stygian, thespian)

10. Dancing feet

   (cyclopean, thespian, terpsichorean)

II. True or False?

In the space provided, indicate whether each statement is true or false.

_____ 1. *Stygian* has some association with gloom.
_____ 2. A *terpsichorean* would be ideal for a comic role.
_____ 3. She played the role of a soap opera *siren*.
_____ 4. *Homeric* laughter refers to the humorous passages in the *Iliad* and the *Odyssey*.
_____ 5. A *calliope* is a means of conveyance.
_____ 6. The first astronauts to the moon may be called *argonauts*.
_____ 7. *Harpy* and *gorgon* refer specifically to women.
_____ 8. *Myrmidons* were faithful to their leader.
_____ 9. Both *stygian* and *promethean* are related to the Titans.
_____ 10. *Cyclopean* and *promethean* are connected to giants in Greek mythology.

III. Synonyms and Antonyms

Find and circle the two words in each line that are either synonyms or antonyms.

1. harpy	musical	calliope	termagant
2. gorgon	oracular	obdurate	stubborn
3. myrmidon	paean	anguish	servant
4. loquacious	awkward	oracular	terpsichorean
5. puny	homeric	infallible	graceful

IV. Missing Letters

Each word below has a missing letter. Fill in these missing letters and then rearrange them to form a word meaning "hymn of praise."

1. thespia
2. tersichorean
3. stygin
4. cyclopan
5. orcular

V. Matching

Match the word in column A with its correct definition in column B by writing the letter of that definition in the space provided.

A	*B*
_____ 1. argonaut	a. a scolding, bad-tempered woman
_____ 2. calliope	b. ugly woman
_____ 3. cyclopean	c. grand
_____ 4. gorgon	d. seductive woman
_____ 5. harpy	e. slavish follower
_____ 6. homeric	f. tease
_____ 7. myrmidon	g. huge and rough
_____ 8. oracular	h. original
_____ 9. paean	i. gloomy and dark
_____ 10. Promethean	j. having to do with dancing
_____ 11. siren	k. adventurer
_____ 12. stygian	l. an actor
_____ 13. tantalize	m. ambiguous
_____ 14. terpsichorean	n. musical instrument
_____ 15. thespian	o. exultant outburst

Look on a Gorgon — turn to stone.

Appearances and Attitudes (IV)

Is the Pontiff (Pope) *pontifical* in his prose?

Even if you didn't know the meaning of *sleazy,* why wouldn't you buy a *sleazy* suit?

Supercilious comes from "raised eyebrows." Does that give you a clue to its meaning?

Can you tell a *ribald* story in mixed company without raising someone's eyebrows?

Why is a *pedantic* person likely to be *prolix?*

---

pedantic
pertinacious
pontifical
pretentious
prolix
puerile
quiescent
recalcitrant
restive
ribald
sardonic
sedulous
sleazy
supercilious
voluptuous

1. **pedantic** (pi-dan'-tik)—stressing trivial points of learning; lacking a sense of proportion in scholarship. A *pedant* is a narrow-minded teacher who insists on rigid adherence to a set of arbitrary rules.
    a. Professor Valentine knows how to communicate with his students; and although he is brilliant, he is never *pedantic.*
    b. Janie's father turned her off with his *pedantic* lectures about diet, drugs, and dating.

2. **pertinacious** (pur-tə-nā'-shəs)—stubborn; unyielding; holding firmly to some belief.
    a. I had a *pertinacious* fever that hung on for weeks despite all the medicines I had been given.
    b. Because both management and labor took *pertinacious* positions, we expected a long strike.

3. **pontifical** (pän-tif'-i-k'l)—ornate; stiff; having the pomp and dignity of a high priest or Pope.
    a. Nothing puts an audience to sleep more quickly than an orator with a *pontifical* style.
    b. By substituting simple expressions for the author's *pontifical* ones, the editor was able to improve the book dramatically.

4. **pretentious** (pri-ten'-shəs)—making claims to some distinctions; showy. *Pretentious* people put on airs, try to appear more important than they are.
    a. Don't encourage Anita's *pretentious* pose of being related to Danish royalty.
    b. That which is *pretentious* in art has little chance of permanent success.

5. **prolix** (prō-liks', prō'-liks)—wordy; long-winded.
    a. The *prolix* senator was accused of being intellectually constipated.
    b. It's amazing how *prolix* an advertiser can get in a 60-second television commercial.

6. **puerile** (pyoo'-ər-əl, pyoor'-əl)—childish; silly; young. In Latin it means "boy."
   a. When Joshua was four, we found him amusing; now that he is fourteen, we regard him as *puerile* and immature.
   b. Dropping water-filled bags from the dormitory window is as criminal as it is *puerile.*

7. **quiescent** (kwī-es'-nt)—inactive; in repose; latent.
   a. The sea monster, *quiescent* for centuries, was awakened by the earthquake.
   b. Although the composer has been *quiescent* for some years, he is preparing a new musical for Broadway.

8. **recalcitrant** (ri-kal'-si-trənt)—unruly; refusing to obey authority. In Latin it meant "to kick one's heels *(calx)* in defiance."
   a. Our principal can handle the most *recalcitrant* pupil.
   b. The *recalcitrant* young man refused to shave off his beard.

9. **restive** (res'-tiv)—hard to control; restless; contrary.
   a. On the eve of the big fight, the champ remained *restive* and impatient.
   b. Dr. Mitchell prescribed a strong sedative for his *restive* patient.

10. **ribald** (rib'-əld)—coarse; vulgar in language; irreverent.
    a. Eddie's *ribald* humor was better suited to the saloon than it was to our party.
    b. Some people who enjoy a *ribald* story told by a man will object to hearing it from a woman.

11. **sardonic** (sär-dän'-ik)—sarcastic; bitterly sneering. It is believed that this word can be traced back to a Sardinian plant whose bitter taste caused facial distortion.
    a. The movie cameras recorded the actor's *sardonic* smile as he squeezed the trigger.
    b. Harold's laugh was loud but I was frightened by its *sardonic* quality.

12. **sedulous** (sej'-oo-ləs)—busy; working hard; diligent.
    a. Through *sedulous* study, Joan was able to get her degree in three years.
    b. The beehive was the hub of *sedulous* activity by hundreds of bustling drones.

13. **sleazy** (slē'-zē)—flimsy or thin in texture or substance; of poor quality. This word can be traced back to cloth made in Silesia, Germany.
    a. Once Mr. Mansfield lived in a mansion but today his home is in a *sleazy* slum neighborhood.
    b. The glib storekeeper was trying to get a high price for his *sleazy* merchandise.

14. **supercilious** (soo-pər-sil'-ē-əs)—naughty; arrogant; contemptuous.
    a. The saleslady with the *supercilious* manner made Emma tongue-tied.
    b. Most of the prisoners were friendly but Count Palozzi maintained a *supercilious* attitude.

15. **voluptuous** (və-lup'-choo-əs)—sensuous; full of sensual delights and pleasures.
    a. He fell into a *voluptuous* sleep, buoyed by the clear mountain air.
    b. The oriental delicacies, combined with the subtle flavors of the rare herbs and spices, made the dinner a *voluptuous* experience.

EXERCISES

I. Which Word Comes to Mind?

In each of the following, read the statement, then circle the word that comes to mind.

1. A gangster's cruel smile

    (puerile, sedulous, sardonic)

2. Second-rate fabric that wears poorly

    (quiescent, pertinacious, sleazy)

3. Someone who uses a dozen words when one would do

    (prolix, supercilious, recalcitrant)

4. The natives were nervous before the battle

    (pontifical, restive, pretentious)

5. A night club comic's suggestive monologue

    (pedantic, ribald, voluptuous)

6. A child who refuses to obey his parents and teachers

    (puerile, recalcitrant, sedulous)

7. The actress's beauty rather than her talent was responsible for her popularity

    (ribald, pertinacious, voluptuous)

8. Once Barry forms an opinion, he'll never change his mind

    (pertinacious, pretentious, pontifical)

9. A trait that makes a person a success

    (pedantic, sedulous, supercilious)

10. Someone follows the rules but misses the spirit

    (pontifical, pedantic, quiescent)

II. True or False?

In the space provided, indicate whether each statement is true or false.

_____ 1. Mules and oxen are frequently described as being *pertinacious.*
_____ 2. *Sleazy* products deserve the high price they command.
_____ 3. The actor, famed for using words sparingly, drew compliments for that *prolix* style.
_____ 4. Although we strive to be young, no one wants to be described as *puerile.*
_____ 5. *Quiescent* talent can often be brought to the surface through patient teaching techniques.

_____ 6. *Puerile* behavior is not likely to win you friends.

_____ 7. The defendant was acquitted because of his *sleazy* background.

_____ 8. A *restive* person would appreciate frequent periods of silence.

_____ 9. Being *puerile,* Brenda often does not act her age.

_____ 10. The *voluptuous* figures in the museum attracted the attention of the crowd.

III. Fill in the Blank

Insert one of the new words in the proper space in each sentence below.

1. Joanna, finding it difficult to tolerate the _____ attitude of the salespeople in the exclusive boutique, left without buying anything.

2. The unscrupulous travel agent tried to sell the mystery trip as an adventure that would contain many _____ experiences.

3. Realizing he was losing friends because of his _____ airs, Martin vowed to stop being showy.

4. The _____ character of the two rivals prolonged the argument; neither would budge an inch.

5. Defending his _____ style, Professor Dobbins claimed he had written the book for scholars like himself.

6. The teacher advised the class not to adopt a(n) _____ tone in a letter of application.

7. Jerry actually drove his customers away with his _____ sales pitch.

8. The valedictorian was careful to keep _____ expressions out of her speech.

9. Parents wait for the day when their children will be as _____ in fulfilling their family responsibilities as they are in preparing for a party.

10. There is a time for fun and revelry, but that does not include an overdose of _____ speech.

IV. What's the Antonym?

Which of the new words is most nearly *opposite* in meaning to the one provided?

1. indolent   _____

2. mature   _____

3. terse   _____

4. docile   _____

5. refined   _____

6. dynamic   _____

7. docile   _____

8. unassuming   _____

9. austere   _____

10. concise   _____

V. Matching

Match the word in column A with its correct definition in column B by writing the letter of that definition in the space provided.

A

_____ 1. pedantic
_____ 2. pertinacious
_____ 3. pontifical
_____ 4. pretentious
_____ 5. prolix
_____ 6. puerile
_____ 7. quiescent
_____ 8. recalcitrant
_____ 9. restive
_____ 10. ribald
_____ 11. sardonic
_____ 12. sedulous
_____ 13. sleazy
_____ 14. supercilious
_____ 15. voluptuous

B

a. childish
b. of poor quality
c. haughty
d. unruly
e. sensuous
f. ornate; overdone; high-sounding
g. restless
h. diligent
i. stressing trivial points
j. irreverent
k. in repose
l. sarcastic
m. stubborn
n. wordy
o. showy

Foreign Terms (II)

Would a good golfer know about *par excellence?*

What is meant by *de facto* segregation?

Have you ever been chosen to serve on an *ad hoc* committee?

Why is *a cappella* a challenge for a singer?

How does the public respond to a *nolo contendere* plea in court?

---

a cappella
ad hoc
bon vivant
de facto
gemütlich
leitmotif
nolo contendere
par excellence
parvenu
pièce de
   résistance
postprandial
quid pro quo
qui vive
savoir faire
sub rosa
vis-à-vis

1. **a cappella** (ä kə-pel'e)—without instrumental accompaniment. Usually used to describe choral singing. In Italian, the meaning is "in the chapel style."
    a. When her pianist failed to appear, Helen had to sing *a cappella.*
    b. I have arranged to hire one of the greatest *a cappella* performers alive today.

2. **ad hoc** (ad häk')—for this case only; temporary. The most frequent use of this Latin term is to describe a committee that is organized to deal with a specific issue and will be disbanded later.
    a. I was pleased to be selected for the *ad hoc* committee for the Senior Prom.
    b. When the *ad hoc* fund raising project proved so successful, it was made into a permanent unit of our club.

3. **bon vivant** (bän vi-vänt')—one who enjoys good food and other pleasant things.
    a. Although Charles was quite thin, he was known in restaurant circles as a *bon vivant.*
    b. Yesterday a *bon vivant,* today the unemployment line!

4. **de facto** (di-fak'-tō)—in fact; actual. The law may require one thing *(de jure),* but as a matter of fact *(de facto)* the reality is quite different.
    a. Segregated schools are not lawful, but *de facto* segregation is common in this country.
    b. The former army colonel was the head of his *de facto* government until his assassination.

5. **gemütlich** (ge-müt'-lih)—agreeable; cheerful. This German word is often used to describe a sense of well-being.
    a. Jerry lit the fire, and we settled down to a *gemütlich* evening at home.
    b. Adding colorful tablecloths and flowers gave a *gemütlich* touch to the Princess Pat Tea Room.

6. **leitmotif** (līt'-mō-tēf)—a short musical phrase that recurs and is associated with a given character, situation, or emotion in an opera. This technique was first used by the German composer, Richard Wagner.
    a. Every time the evil sorcerer appeared, the orchestra struck up a chilling *leitmotif.*
    b. We agreed that even though the play would be serious, a *leitmotif* of comic relief was required.

7. **nolo contendere** (nō'-lō-kən-ten'-də-rē)—a defendant's plea declaring that he will not make a defense but not admitting his guilt.
   a. Because Buddy's lawyer did not want to put him on the witness stand, he suggested a *nolo contendere* plea.
   b. Although a *nolo contendere* defense does not admit to guilt, most people are likely to assume that only a guilty person would follow such a course.

8. **par excellence** (pär ek'-sə-läns)—in the greatest degree of excellence. This French term also means "beyond comparison."
   a. In the 1976 Olympiad, the Romanian girl proved to be a gymnast *par excellence.*
   b. Julia Child, the famed TV chef, is a cook *par excellence.*

9. **parvenu** (pär'-və-noō,-nyoō')—one who has suddenly acquired wealth or power; a person who is considered an upstart because he does not conform to the standards of the class into which he has risen. This word has the same "put down" connotation as "nouveau riche."
   a. After winning a million dollars in the lottery, the *parvenu* bought two pink Cadillacs.
   b. At the elegant dinner party, Mr. Fischer was constantly reminded of his status as a *parvenu.*

10. **pièce de résistance** (pyes'-də-rā-zēs'-täns')—the principal dish of a meal; the main item or event in a series.
    a. At the end of the seven-course dinner, our hostess brought out the *pièce de résistance*—a scrumptious strawberry shortcake.
    b. The *pièce de résistance* in the magician's act came when he sawed his assistant in half.

11. **postprandial** (pōst-pran'-dē-əl)—after dinner. In Latin, *prandium* means "noonday meal."
    a. Ben Green's greatest delight was his *postprandial* cigar.
    b. We gathered on the porch for *postprandial* cordials and a discussion of politics.

12. **quid pro quo** (kwid'-prō-kwō')—one thing in return for another.
    a. The mayor helped us but we knew he expected a *quid pro quo.*
    b. In politics, the term for a *quid pro quo* is "log-rolling."

13. **qui vive** (kē-vēv')—to be on the lookout or on the alert is to be on the *qui vive.* The literal French meaning is "who lives?" or "who goes there?" and, as such, was a term used by sentries.
    a. Our firm likes to hire young people who are on the *qui vive.*
    b. Anyone who makes a day-to-day living in the stock market must be on the *qui vive.*

14. **savoir faire** (sav'-wär-fer')—a ready knowledge of what to do or say; tact.
    a. I have always been impressed with Cousin Gloria's *savoir faire.*
    b. Totally lacking in *savoir faire,* Eloise kept saying the wrong things and embarrassing her family.

15. **sub rosa** (sub-rō'-zə)—secretly; confidentially. In Latin, "under the rose." The rose was a symbol of silence or secrecy in ancient times.
    a. Our agreement was made *sub rosa,* and I hoped that it would never be made public.
    b. Donald whispered, "Let's just keep this between the two of us, *sub rosa,* you might say."

16. **vis-à-vis** (vēz-e-vē')—a person or thing that is face to face with another; opposite; in reference to; opposed to.
    a. When she stands *vis-à-vis* her competitors, she will not be so confident.
    b. The mayor's point of view, *vis-à-vis* capital punishment, is well known.

EXERCISES

I. Which Word Comes to Mind?

In each of the following, read the statement, then circle the word that comes to mind.

1. A person who enjoys good food and wine

    (bon vivant, postprandial, pièce de résistance)

2. A group of citizens form a committee to beautify their town

    (a cappella, qui vive, ad hoc)

3. In court, the defendant rises to plead

    (nolo contendere, parvenu, de facto)

4. Every time the camera switches to the cavalry, trumpets are heard

    (par excellence, leitmotif, sub rosa)

5. You are asked to repay a favor

    (savoir faire, quid pro quo, gemütlich)

6. Though the general was not voted in, he was, in fact, the leader of the country

    (bon vivant, de facto, sub rosa)

7. As expected, when the songstress appeared on stage, the strains of her latest hit wafted across the packed theater

    (leitmotif, savoir faire, par excellence)

8. Charles knew just what to say to cover up his slip of the lip

    (qui vive, parvenu, savoir faire)

9. The amateur boxer was quite cheerful after scoring a first round KO

    (gemütlich, postprandial, vis-à-vis)

10. Ronald's deep baritone was so compelling, we did not miss the absence of the musical accompaniment

    (pièce de résistance, a capella, bon vivant)

II. True or False?

In the space provided, indicate whether each statement is true or false.

_____ 1. Publication of a *sub rosa* agreement can prove embarrassing.

_____ 2. An opportunist may be described as one who is on the *qui vive.*

_____ 3. Minority groups are likely to protest about *de facto* segregation.

_____ 4. In her *a cappella* performance, the star criticized her accompanist.

_____ 5. Sophisticated people are expected to possess *savoir faire.*

_____ 6. Being in a *gemütlich* mood, Kate enjoyed the comedian's "bring-down-the-house" monologue.

_____ 7. The weightiest problems are sometimes solved by *ad hoc* committees.

_____ 8. The *pièce de résistance* of the program, the fireworks display, naturally drew the greatest applause.

_____ 9. Henry's *qui vive* was a big factor in his political downfall.

_____ 10. Coping with his status as a *parvenu* was more difficult for Scott than the poverty he endured before striking it rich.

III. Fill in the Blank

Insert one of the new words in the proper space in each sentence below.

1. The lawyer suggested a(n) _____ plea as the most prudent way to deal with the charges against his client.

2. The commissioner's response to the question _____ his exorbitant travel expenses was a flat denial.

3. During the long illness of the leader, the country was in a(n) _____ state of anarchy.

4. One has to admit that singing _____ places a greater strain on the performer.

5. The Medal of Honor is bestowed upon the soldier _____ who has demonstrated consummate bravery.

6. The best way to get things done is to deal with problems on a(n) _____ basis.

7. When a _____ meets a hedonist, you can bet the conversation will center around good food and good times.

8. Gary learned very quickly that _____ was the rule in politics.

9. The dictator claimed he had destroyed all his biological and nuclear weapons, but the _____ situation was quite different.

10. Rose's presence made everyone feel _____ and ready to enjoy the evening with friends.

IV. What's the Antonym?

Which of the new words is most nearly *opposite* in meaning to the one provided?

1. grouch   _____

2. offensive   _____

3. publicly   _____

4. permanent   _____

5. tactlessness   _____

6. blundering   _____

7. inferior   _____

8. severe   _____

9. public   _____

10. trivial   _____

V. Matching

Match the word in column A with its correct definition in column B by writing the letter of that definition in the space provided.

	A		*B*
____	1. a cappella	a.	temporary
____	2. ad hoc	b.	no defense
____	3. bon vivant	c.	actual
____	4. de facto	d.	after dinner
____	5. gemütlich	e.	recurring musical phrase
____	6. leitmotif	f.	something in return for another
____	7. nolo contendere	g.	alert
____	8. par excellence	h.	without instrumental accompaniment
____	9. parvenu	i.	chief dish
____	10. pièce de résistance	j.	secretly
____	11. postprandial	k.	cheerful
____	12. quid pro quo	l.	tact
____	13. qui vive	m.	one who enjoys good food
____	14. savoir faire	n.	outstanding
____	15. sub rosa	o.	upstart; newly rich
____	16. vis-à-vis	p.	in reference to

Appearances and Attitudes (V)

Is there a connection between crochet and *crotchety?*

Would a *dilatory* person win a punctuality award?

What is the relationship between spleen and *splenetic?*

Are the police pleased to get a *loquacious* stool pigeon?

What medicine is appropriate for a *bucolic* condition?

---

ambivalent
bucolic
crotchety
dilatory
disconsolate
dudgeon
froward
genteel
jocund
loquacious
splenetic
tendentious
truculent
vacuous
venal

1. **ambivalent** (am-biv'-ə-lənt)—having conflicting feelings toward a person or thing, such as love and hate.
    a. I've read a great deal on the topic of capital punishment but I'm still *ambivalent* about it.
    b. On the surface, Sloan was loyal to the chemical company but she maintained *ambivalent* feelings about its defense policies.

2. **bucolic** (byōō-käl'-ik)—rural; rustic; pastoral. The Greek word *boukolikos* means "herdsman."
    a. The artist was celebrated for his *bucolic* canvases painted at the Ohio farm.
    b. Two hours out of the big city, our eyes were refreshed by *bucolic* countryside scenes.

3. **crotchety** (kräch'-it-ē)—full of peculiar whims; ill-tempered; eccentric. Crochet work was done with a small, twisted hook; from "twisted" it was an easy jump to "eccentric"—thus the connection between crochet and *crotchety.*
    a. No one took Uncle Sid seriously when he asked for watermelon pudding because he had a reputation for being *crotchety.*
    b. The *crotchety* old millionaire left his fortune to his twelve cats.

4. **dilatory** (dil'-ə-tôr-ē)—slow; late in doing things; inclined to delay; meant to gain time.
    a. The crooked sheriff's *dilatory* tactics prevented Columbo from watching the thieves that night.
    b. Phyllis' *dilatory* habits drove her punctual husband up the wall.

5. **disconsolate** (dis-kän'-sə-lit)—sad; dejected; cheerless.
    a. After the bad news arrived in a telegram from the Secretary of Defense, the new widow was understandably *disconsolate.*
    b. When Zelda Fitzgerald was *disconsolate,* she sought relief through alcohol.

6. **dudgeon** (duj'-ən)—resentment; an angry or offended feeling. It comes from the Anglo-French expression *en digeon,* which meant "the hand on the dagger hilt."
    a. Captain Ralston was in high *dudgeon* after having been demoted.
    b. Filled with *dudgeon,* Edgar sought revenge against his stepbrother, Edmund.

7. **froward** (frō'-erd,-werd)—contrary; not easily controlled; stubbornly willful.
   a. The *froward* colt was led into the ring by three handlers who were careful not to be kicked.
   b. Petruchio displayed one way to deal successfully with a *froward* woman in *The Taming of the Shrew.*

8. **genteel** (jen-tēl')—well-bred; refined; excessively polite.
   a. Mrs. Berman's *genteel* manners were quite out of place in the sailors' bar she operated.
   b. Etiquette and *genteel* behavior were taught by Emily Post and Amy Vanderbilt.

9. **jocund** (jäk-end, jō'-kend)—pleasant; agreeable; genial. Our word *joke* can be traced back to *jocund.*
   a. One of the things that gets me off to a good start each morning is our elevator operator's *jocund* face.
   b. The company's *jocund* mood was shattered by the blackout.

10. **loquacious** (lō-kwā'-shes)—talkative. Some synonyms are *garrulous, voluble, prolix, verbose,* and *prating.*
    a. With a few drinks under his belt, my normally quiet cousin can become quite *loquacious.*
    b. The *loquacious* talk-show host never gave his guests a chance to tell about themselves.

11. **splenetic** (spli-net'-ik)—irritable; bad-tempered; spiteful. The word derives from *spleen,* the abdominal organ that the ancients regarded as the seat of emotions.
    a. Frieda's *splenetic* outburst at the dinner table was in poor taste.
    b. One way to drive Albie into a *splenetic* frenzy is to discuss income taxes with him.

12. **tendentious** (ten-den'-shes)—opinionated; advancing a definite point of view or doctrine.
    a. Although the *Post's* political columns are often *tendentious,* I find them very informative.
    b. Our school board rejected several history texts, objecting to the *tendentious* writing they contained.

13. **truculent** (truk'-yoo-lent)—fierce; cruel; savage.
    a. In a *truculent* editorial, the newspaper's owner ripped the Supreme Court decision to shreds.
    b. Lord Hastings was unprepared for Richard's *truculent* outburst.

14. **vacuous** (vak'-yoo-was)—empty; purposeless; stupid; senseless.
    a. Two years on drugs had changed Roger's alert look to a *vacuous* stare.
    b. The judge dropped the assault charges when he realized how *vacuous* they were.

15. **venal** (vē'-n'l)—readily bribed or corrupted.
    a. Originally there was enough money to cover all expenses but *venal* officials took most of it.
    b. When caught for speeding, George tried to set up a *venal* bargain with the arresting officer.

I. Which Word Comes to Mind?

In each of the following, read the statement, then circle the word that comes to mind.

1. Cows in the meadow, sheep in the corn

   (venal, bucolic, disconsolate)

2. First, I want to go—then I want to stay

   (ambivalent, truculent, dudgeon)

3. "What's your rush? So what if we're late?"

   (jocund, dilatory, genteel)

4. The millionaire asked to be buried in his Rolls Royce

   (crotchety, tendentious, froward)

5. "Were you vaccinated with a phonograph needle?"

   (vacuous, loquacious, splenetic)

6. Jane always has a smile on her face

   (froward, venal, jocund)

7. Firing someone can easily put him/her into this frame of mind

   (dudgeon, tendentious, bucolic)

8. The slightest remark sets Virginia off on a rampage

   (truculent, splenetic, dilatory)

9. I can't make up my mind

   (crotchety, ambivalent, tendentious)

10. A decidedly partisan view of the inaugural address

    (genteel, splenetic, tendentious)

II. True or False?

In the space provided, indicate whether each statement is true or false.

_____ 1. A *jocund* person has a good chance of being hired as a receptionist.
_____ 2. *Splenetic* behavior is always a sign of good breeding.
_____ 3. Truly great bullfighters welcome an animal that is *froward*.
_____ 4. The gangster's company has become synonomous with *venal* arrangements.
_____ 5. Skyscrapers and subways are integral parts of the *bucolic* life.

_____ 6. Greg's *genteel* nature may account for his shyness.

_____ 7. A *truculent* response is guaranteed to win friends.

_____ 8. Feeling *disconsolate* over his loss, Fred briefly considered retiring from baseball.

_____ 9. The student's *vacuous* stare suggested he did not understand the question.

_____ 10. Because of his *loquacious* nature, Carlos had little to say.

III. Fill in the Blank

Insert one of the new words in the proper space in each sentence below.

1. Martha wondered how Gary could hope to convince her with such _____ explanations.

2. The successful politician walks a thin line between appearing too _____ and too wishy-washy.

3. Stephan tried to sort out his _____ feelings of respect and resentment towards his father.

4. After the hectic campaign, the president-elect was refreshed by his _____ retreat.

5 A(n) _____ child perhaps needs more love than a well-adjusted one.

6. The _____ life has its merits, but most people cannot resist the attractions and excitement of the city.

7. A _____ person tends to give others little opportunity to express themselves.

8. The fans were deeply disappointed to learn that their idol had been bitten by the _____ bug.

9. The _____ host easily broke the iciness between two of the guests who had been enemies for years.

10. Because of George's _____ habits, we often referred to him as the late George Owens.

IV. What's the Antonym?

Which of the new words is most nearly *opposite* in meaning to the one provided?

1. punctual   _____

2. gentle   _____

3. even-tempered   _____

4. gross   _____

5. incorruptible   _____

6. agreeable   _____

7. cheerful   _____

8. unequivocal   _____

9. urban   _____

10. intelligent   _____

V. Matching

Match the word in column A with its correct definition in column B by writing the letter of that definition in the space provided.

	A		B
_____	1. ambivalent	a.	resentment
_____	2. bucolic	b.	not easily controlled
_____	3. crotchety	c.	having conflicting feelings
_____	4. dilatory	d.	ill-tempered
_____	5. disconsolate	e.	talkative
_____	6. dudgeon	f.	irritable
_____	7. froward	g.	opinionated
_____	8. genteel	h.	empty
_____	9. jocund	i.	refined
_____	10. loquacious	j.	rural
_____	11. splenetic	k.	inclined to delay
_____	12. tendentious	l.	genial
_____	13. truculent	m.	able to be bribed
_____	14. vacuous	n.	savage
_____	15. venal	o.	dejected

Size and Shape (II)

What is the trouble with a *tenuous* plan?

To which author are we indebted for the word *gargantuan?*

How is an artist likely to feel about his *magnum opus?*

Who would have reason to rely on a *micrometer?*

What traffic sign would you expect to find on a *serpentine* road?

---

1. **amorphous** (ə-môr'-fəs)—without definite form; shapeless.
    a. The science fiction movie featured an *amorphous* monster who preyed on Chicago.
    b. As a result of numerous mergers, the conglomerate presented an *amorphous* picture.

2. **copious** (kō'-pē-əs)—abundant; large.
    a. Everett took *copious* notes in our biology class.
    b. U.S. farmers raised a *copious* crop of corn last year.

3. **gargantuan** (gär-gan'-cho͞o-ən)—huge; gigantic; prodigious. The word comes from Rabelais' sixteenth-century political satire, *Gargantua and Pantagruel.*
    a. After skipping breakfast and lunch, I had a *gargantuan* appetite for dinner.
    b. When the opposing team came on the basketball court, we saw that they had a *gargantuan* center.

4. **iota** (ī-ōt'-ə)—very small quantity; a jot. Iota is the ninth letter of the Greek alphabet.
    a. I don t care one *iota* for your relatives' wishes.
    b. If Larry had an *iota* of sense, he would propose to Vivian.

5. **lissome** (lis'-əm)—supple; limber; flexible.
    a. Ballet dancers are apt to be *lissome.*
    b. The heavyweight champion slimmed down from a ponderous 250 pounds to a *lissome* 210.

6. **macrocosm** (mak'-rə-käz'm)—the great world; the universe. The opposite of this is *microcosm* (see definition 9 below).
    a. My philosophy professor is constantly concerned with the vastness of the *macrocosm.*
    b. Space explorers have unlocked some of the mysteries of the *macrocosm.*

7. **magnitude** (mag'-nə-to͞od)—greatness of size or extent; importance or influence.
    a. District Attorney Hogan unveiled the *magnitude* of the corruption.
    b. After his death, the *magnitude* of the "pauper's" wealth first came to light.

8. magnum opus (mag'-nəm ōpəs)—a great work, especially of art or literature.
    a.   Picasso's *Guernica* is considered by some to be his *magnum opus.*
    b.   When the composer's *magnum opus* was panned by the critics, he left the country.

9. microcosm (mi'-krə-käz'm)—a little world; miniature universe. It is the opposite of *macrocosm.*
    a.   Spencer spent six years developing his unique *microcosm* made out of matchsticks.
    b.   Anything in the *microcosm* I can grasp, but *macrocosmic* concepts are beyond me.

10. micrometer (mī-kräm'-ə-ter)—an instrument for measuring very small distances, angles, diameters. In Latin, *micro* means small and *meter* means to measure.
    a.   With the aid of a surgical *micrometer,* the doctor was able to undertake the difficult operation.
    b.   Since the size of the angle was in dispute, we sent for a *micrometer* to settle the argument.

11. scintilla (sin-til'-ə)—the least trace; a particle. In Latin, *scintilla* means "a spark."
    a.   There is not a *scintilla* of truth in the accusations.
    b.   Unless new evidence is produced, Richie does not have a *scintilla* of a chance to get out of jail.

12. serpentine (sur'-pən-tēn,-tīn)—evilly cunning or subtle; treacherous; coiled; twisting.
    a.   As our bus snaked its way down the narrow, *serpentine* road, all of the passengers prayed silently.
    b.   The extortionist's *serpentine* plot failed because of a careless oversight.

13. sinuous (sin'-yoo-wəs)—bending; wavy. The word *sinus* ("a cavity in the bones of the skull") is related to *sinuous.*
    a.   With *sinuous* movements, the dancer portrayed a venomous snake.
    b.   Driving along the California coast, we took a *sinuous* route.

14. smidgen (smij'-ən)—a small amount; a bit. This word is related to "midge" or midget.
    a.   My mother added just a *smidgen* of paprika to the recipe.
    b.   In the Crimean battle, the British general did not display even a *smidgen* of intelligence.

15. tenuous (ten'-yoo-wəs)—unsubstantial; flimsy; physically thin.
    a.   Our company's plans to move to New Jersey are *tenuous* at this time.
    b.   The rope bridge over the river was so *tenuous* that only one person at a time could use it.

EXERCISES

I. Which Word Comes to Mind?

In each of the following, read the statement, then circle the word that comes to mind.

1. A writer spends ten years preparing his masterpiece

   (macrocosm, magnum opus, micrometer)

2. Cyclops had an enormous appetite

   (scintilla, gargantuan, microcosm)

3. A graceful gymnast

   (lissome, smidgen, iota)

4. An indefinite proposal

   (serpentine, copious, tenuous)

5. The actress adopted a sexy walk

   (amorphous, magnitude, sinuous)

6. A doctor carefully measures the size of the tumor

   (amorphous, micrometer, lissome)

7. The overthrow of the government began with an act of treachery

   (serpentine, magnitude, lissome)

8. An insignificant amount

   (sinuous, scintilla, gargantuan)

9. A jacket with huge pockets to hold candy

   (amorphous, tenuous, copious)

10. A trace of seasoning

    (microcosm, smidgen, magnum opus)

II. True or False?

In the space provided, indicate whether each statement is true or false.

_____ 1. The *microcosm* of man reflects the *macrocosm* of the universe.

_____ 2. The *magnitude* of the Grand Canyon frequently awes travelers.

_____ 3. A *tenuous* idea is often offered hesitantly.

_____ 4. Two words in this lesson that are closely related are *smidgen* and *iota*.

_____ 5. The *amorphous* scheme was spelled out in such detail that it was grasped by all.

_____ 6. The bank robbers got away with a *copious* amount of cash.

_____ 7. The million dollar gift exemplified his *gargantuan* kindness.

_____ 8. The *lissome* ballerina glided through her performance with unparalleled grace.

_____ 9. Fielding's *Joseph Andrews* was his *magnum opus*.

_____ 10. Frank's *tenuous* explanation was hardly enough to justify his outburst.

III. Fill in the Blank

Insert one of the new words in the proper space in each sentence below.

1. Because of the _____ of the offense, the judge set a high bail.

2. Space exploration advances suggest that our civilization has developed in a very limited _____ .

3. Mr. Ludwig would not admit that his business success had been achieved through _____ tactics.

4. The race was so close it would take a(n) _____ to measure who was the winner.

5. Margaret Mitchell's _____ *Gone With the Wind* was her only book.

6. There was not a _____ of truth to the accusation.

7. The team had a(n) _____ hold on first place until a rash of injuries sent them reeling.

8. The commencement speaker told the graduates that the road to success is full of _____ turns.

9. Cleaning up after the parade proved to be a _____ task.

10. The strange creature we found on the beach was so _____ , we could not identify its species.

IV. What's the Antonym?

Which of the new words is most nearly *opposite* in meaning to the one provided?

1. sturdy   _____

2. diminutive   _____

3. slight   _____

4. having form   _____

5. wooden   _____

6. straight   _____

7. inflexible   _____

8. insignificance _____

9. universe   _____

10. amateur attempt _____

V. Matching

Match the word in column A with its correct definition in column B by writing the letter of that definition in the space provided.

	A		*B*
_____	1. amorphous	a.	shapeless
_____	2. copious	b.	bending, wavy
_____	3. gargantuan	c.	greatness of size
_____	4. iota	d.	a very small quantity
_____	5. lissome	e.	supple
_____	6. macrocosm	f.	a great work
_____	7. magnitude	g.	winding
_____	8. magnum opus	h.	precision measuring instrument
_____	9. microcosm	i.	abundant
_____	10. micrometer	j.	a tiny jot
_____	11. scintilla	k.	the least trace
_____	12. serpentine	l.	the universe
_____	13. sinuous	m.	flimsy
_____	14. smidgen	n.	the little world
_____	15. tenuous	o.	huge

Unit III
(Lessons 21–30)

Review

A. The Out-of-Place Word

In each of the following groups, find and circle the one vocabulary word that is out of place. You should be able to explain what the other three words have in common.

1. licentious, pusillanimous, libidinous, ribald
2. lissome, voluptuous, bucolic, sinuous
3. bon mot, mot juste, non sequitur, repartee
4. mercurial, pontifical, argonaut, Promethean
5. quid pro quo, sub rosa, amicus curiae, qui vive
6. minatory, sinuous, bête noire, truculent
7. gauche, savoir faire, sangfroid, nonchalant
8. pertinacious, obdurate, officious, recalcitrant
9. miscreant, oracular, omniscient, tendentious
10. amorphous, mutable, ambivalent, amulet

B. Rearranging Words

Rearrange the following groups of words using the first letter of each word to spell out one of the new words in this unit.

1. barrister, amulet, obdurate, nonchalant, bucolic

    _____

2. noxious, avant-garde, restive, sine qua non, onus

    _____

3. oracular, ambivalent, truculent, impasse

    _____

4. embezzle, vacuous, ad hoc, loquacious, nonchalant

    _____

5. nabob, gargantuan, iota, truculent, tendentious, entrepreneur, extradition, venal

    _____

C. Finding Partners

Which word best describes a person or thing you would need in each of the following situations? Circle the correct answer.

1. You want to pour your heart out

    (parvenu, tête-à-tête, magnum opus, pièce de résistance)

2. You are in a legal jam

    (cul-de-sac, perpetrator, barrister, entrepreneur)

3. You have a million questions

   (deus ex machina, amicus curiae, omniscient, bête noire)

4. You have a yen to dance up a storm

   (scintilla, terpsichorean, junta, amulet)

5. You're a director looking for an actress to play a young innocent

   (ingenue, vignette, miscreant, gorgon)

D. Making Pairs

From the group below, find the pairs of words that have something in common and record them in the spaces provided. You should be able to find ten such pairs. List them numerically, using the same number for each pair.

voluptuous _____	pontifical _____	jocund_____	cul-de-sac ____
impasse _____	embezzle _____	bon mot _____	homeric _____
mercurial_____	perpetrator _____	miscreant _____	Promethean __
bilk _____	libidinous _____	gemütlich _____	mutable _____
iota _____	mot juste_____	oracular _____	scintilla _____

E. Cliché Time

Which of the words from this unit fit into the following familiar expressions? Choose the correct word from the choices given and record it in the space provided.

1. The _____ old miser never knew the joys of companionship.

   (sardonic, chary, tenuous, crotchety)

2. The president appointed an _____ committee to select a band for the next affair.

   (officious, prolix, ad hoc, onus)

3. The opera star's _____ temper was well known to her audiences.

   (mercurial, jejune, avant-garde, indeterminate)

4. There is a little _____ in all of us.

   (myrmidon, leitmotif, larceny, bauble)

5. After a beautiful afternoon spent experiencing the _____ delights of a walk through the woods, the couple dined by candlelight.

   (sedulous, voluptuous, sub rosa, de facto)

Language

Is "granite jaw" an example of a *simile* or *metaphor?*

Is *oxymoron* a paradoxical expression or an act of animal folly?

Is "he saw with his own eyes" an example of *panegyric* or *semantics?*

Is "damning with faint praise" a form of *metaphor* or *bathos?*

---

abstract
alliteration
ambiguous
bathos
epithet
malapropism
metaphor
onomatopoeia
oxymoron
panegyric
paradigm
polyglot
semantics
simile
threnody

1. **abstract** (ab-strakt')—hard to understand; apart from concrete.
   a. We expect some *abstract* thinking from a philosopher.
   b. Sandra's *abstract* ideas confused her friends.

2. **alliteration** (ə-lit'-ə-rā-shən)—two or more words with the same initial sound.
   a. Edgar Allan Poe is noted for his use of *alliteration* in his poetry.
   b. "Sally sells seashells at the seashore" is an example of *alliteration*.

3. **ambiguous** (am-big'-yoo-əs)—open to more than one interpretation.
   a. I was completely confused by Mike's *ambiguous* remarks.
   b. Judge Spencer's rulings were crystal clear, with no evidence of an *ambiguous* decision anywhere. (Do you remember this word from Lesson 13?)

4. **bathos** (bā'-thäs, bā'-thôs)—anticlimax; triteness or triviality in style; sentimentality. *Bathos* is also used to denote an insincere pathos, an evocation of pity or compassion.
   a. In his summation to the jury, the defense attorney stooped to *bathos* to portray his client as a misunderstood and unhappy victim of circumstances.
   b. The drama suffered from *bathos,* the strongest and most telling point having been made in the first act.

5. **epithet** (ep'-ə-thet)—an abusive word or phrase.
   a. The cruel *epithet* was edited out of the newspaper column.
   b. Regina demanded an apology for the *epithet* that Danny used to describe her.

6. **malapropism** (mal'-ə-präp-iz'm)—ridiculous misuse of words, especially by confusion of words that are similar in sound. Mrs. Malaprop, a character in Sheridan's famous Restoration play, *The Rivals,* is noted for her misapplication of words.
   a. One or two unfortunate faux pas established Richard as a master of *malapropism*.
   b. In an obvious *malapropism,* Mrs. Farrell said she was bemused by the exciting circus performance.

7. **metaphor** (met'-ə-fôr, -fər)—the application of a word or phrase to an object or concept that it does not literally denote, in order to suggest a comparison with another object or concept. The use of *metaphors* may help to clarify or ennoble an idea, but one must not mix *metaphors*. This practice results in humorous effects, such as "We must put our noses to the grindstone and push."
   a. "A mighty fortress is our God" is a *metaphor* expressing the permanence, power, and protectiveness of the Deity.
   b. William explained to the police that he was only speaking *metaphorically* when he described the strangers as men from Mars.

8. **onomatopoeia** (än-ə-mät-ə-pē'-ə)—formation of words in imitation of natural sounds; the use of words whose sound suggests the sense. The "bow-wow theory" of language maintains that language originated in imitation of natural sounds. By contrast, the "pooh-pooh theory" says language originated in interjections that gradually acquired meaning.
   a.   *Onomatopoeic* words have a strong appeal to children.
   b.   A study of the poet's frequent use of *onomatopoeia* shows he had an unusual ear for natural sounds, as if he were listening to Nature and letting it speak for itself.

9. **oxymoron** (äk-si-môr'-än)—a figure of speech by which a particular phrasing of words produces an effect by seeming self-contradiction, as in "cruel kindness" or "laborious idleness." The Greek meaning is "pointed foolishness."
   a.   The *oxymoron* "make haste slowly" has been a piece of folk wisdom for centuries.
   b.   To indicate Romeo's shallow feelings for Rosaline as opposed to his deep love for Juliet, Shakespeare has him utter a string of *oxymorons* like "loving hate, heavy lightness, cold fire."

10. **panegyric** (pan-ə-jir'-ik, -jī'-rik)—an oration, discourse, or writing in praise of a person or thing; eulogy.
    a.   Forgetting partisanship, representatives of all parties delivered *panegyrics* at the funeral of the late president.
    b.   The board chairman felt the revolutionary fuel substitute had merit but had not yet earned the *panegyrics* that had been heaped upon it.

11. **paradigm** (par'-ə-dim, -dīm)—example or pattern; a set of forms in grammar all of which contain a particular element, especially the set of all inflected forms based on a single stem (as in verb declensions).
    a.   Some politicians who were supposed to be *paradigms* of honesty proved themselves unscrupulous and deceptive.
    b.   In the past, language was studied by reciting lists of *paradigms;* modern methodology stresses correct usage and conversation.

12. **polyglot** (päl'-i-glät)—knowing many or several languages; containing, composed of, or in several languages; a confusion of languages; a person with a speaking or reading knowledge of a number of languages; a book, especially a Bible, containing the same text in several languages.
    a.   The population of our city ranges from the very rich to the masses of *polyglot* poor.
    b.   His travels around the world have made our neighbor something of a *polyglot.*

13. **semantics** (sə-man'-tiks)—the study of meaning; the study of linguistic development by classifying and examining changes in meaning and form. *Semantics* is also called *significi,* a branch of *semiotics* (signs and symbols) dealing with the relationship between signs and what they denote. *General semantics* is an educational discipline concerning the relationship between symbols and reality and with improving the adjustment of people to each other and to the environment.
    a.   We now find it hard to believe that an entire nation swallowed the racist *semantics* of the fanatical Nazi propaganda.
    b.   The word "soon" has undergone *semantic* change from the Old English meaning of "immediately."

14. **simile** (sim'-ə-lē)—a figure of speech in which two unlike things are explicitly compared using the words "like" or "as," as in "she is like a rose."
    a.   *Similes* are not confined to poetry, for they appear frequently in our daily use, adding spice and wit to the commonplace.
    b.   *Similes* like "as tight as a drum," and "as sweet as sugar," have become clichés and hence lost their effectiveness.

15. **threnody** (thren'-ə-dē)—a poem, speech, or slang of lamentation, especially for the dead; dirge; funeral song.
    a.   William Cullen Bryant's "Thanatopsis" is one of the most famous *threnodies* in our literature.
    b.   A failure is to be deplored but is not cause for a *threnody.*

EXERCISES

I. Which Word Comes to Mind?

In each of the following, read the statement, then circle the word that comes to mind.

1. She was too young to die

   (polyglot, simile, threnody)

2. The allegories on the banks of the Nile

   (malapropism, metaphor, simile)

3. Snap! Crackle! Pop!

   (paradigm, oxymoron, onomatopoeia)

4. Insincere pathos

   (bathos, paradigm, semantics)

5. A moving eulogy

   (metaphor, panegyric, onomatopoeia)

6. Jack answered the insult by saying, "I resemble that remark"

   (bathos, malapropism, oxymoron)

7. Napoleon is credited with saying, "From the sublime to the ridiculous, it is but one step"

   (panegyric, threnody, bathos)

8. He was a lion in battle

   (simile, metaphor, oxymoron)

9. Our guest spoke seven languages

   (paradigm, metaphor, polyglot)

10. Military intelligence has been called this

    (semantics, oxymoron, threnody)

II. True or False?

In the space provided, indicate whether each statement is true or false.

_____ 1. Both *metaphor* and *simile* use forms of comparison.
_____ 2. A *malaprop* is an expert with language.
_____ 3. A *polyglot* is a person with a taste for exotic foods.
_____ 4. *Semantics* is concerned with the syntax of a language.
_____ 5. A *panegyric* is a test devised to determine the linguistic level of a speaker.

_____ 6. *Paradigm* and paragon both refer to an example.

_____ 7. Every *simile* uses the words "like" or "as."

_____ 8. *Onomatopoeia* refers to a group of words beginning with the same consonant.

_____ 9. *Bathos* is the sudden change in style producing a ludicrous effect.

_____ 10. The *threnody* was suitable for the child's funeral.

III. Find the Impostor

Find and circle the one word on each line that is not related to the other three.

1. metaphor	simile	literary	comparative
2. threnody	legacy	elegy	dirge
3. encomium	panegyric	panorama	accolade
4. paradox	paradigm	paragon	touchstone
5. panegyric	threnody	dirge	paradigm

IV. Find the Words

Somewhere in this box of letters, reading up, down, across, or diagonally, five vocabulary words that were taught in this lesson are hidden. As you locate each one, draw a circle around it.

M	E	T	O	N	O	M	Y
G	B	A	T	H	O	S	D
I	P	P	L	N	I	O	O
D	A	E	O	M	O	X	N
A	N	N	I	A	R	Y	E
R	E	L	S	M	O	M	R
A	E	G	Y	R	I	C	H
P	O	L	Y	G	L	O	T

V. Matching

Match the word in column A with its correct definition in column B by writing the letter of that definition in the space provided.

<table>
<tr><td colspan="2" align="center">A</td><td colspan="2">B</td></tr>
<tr><td>_____</td><td>1. abstract</td><td>a.</td><td>commendation</td></tr>
<tr><td>_____</td><td>2. alliteration</td><td>b.</td><td>humorous misapplication of a word</td></tr>
<tr><td>_____</td><td>3. ambiguous</td><td>c.</td><td>open to several interpretations</td></tr>
<tr><td>_____</td><td>4. bathos</td><td>d.</td><td>a buzzword</td></tr>
<tr><td>_____</td><td>5. epithet</td><td>e.</td><td>hard to understand</td></tr>
<tr><td>_____</td><td>6. malapropism</td><td>f.</td><td>study of words as symbols</td></tr>
<tr><td>_____</td><td>7. metaphor</td><td>g.</td><td>echoic sounds</td></tr>
<tr><td>_____</td><td>8. onomatopoeia</td><td>h.</td><td>a resemblance made explicit</td></tr>
<tr><td>_____</td><td>9. oxymoron</td><td>i.</td><td>funeral song</td></tr>
<tr><td>_____</td><td>10. panegyric</td><td>j.</td><td>implied comparison</td></tr>
<tr><td>_____</td><td>11. paradigm</td><td>k.</td><td>multilingual</td></tr>
<tr><td>_____</td><td>12. polyglot</td><td>l.</td><td>paradox; contradiction</td></tr>
<tr><td>_____</td><td>13. semantics</td><td>m.</td><td>anticlimax</td></tr>
<tr><td>_____</td><td>14. simile</td><td>n.</td><td>standard or example</td></tr>
<tr><td>_____</td><td>15. threnody</td><td>o.</td><td>words with the same initial sound</td></tr>
</table>

Speech

Is *harangue* a salty fish, a lemon pit, or a buttonholing tirade?

Which is harder on the ego, being censored or *censured?*

Does a *guttural* sound come from an alcoholic, the abdomen, or the throat?

Would you expect the *argot* of the underworld to be the same as its *jargon?*

Is *gobbledegook* the same as talking turkey?

---

argot
aspersion
badinage
bombast
braggadocio
censure
countermand
gainsay
gobbledegook
guttural
harangue
jargon
mellifluous
resonant
sententious

1. **argot** (är'-gō, -gət)—the specialized vocabulary and idioms of those in the same work or way of life, especially of the underworld. The French origin, meaning "to beg," associates beggary with thievery.
    a. The sociobiologists' *argot* describing juvenile delinquency amounts to a condemnation of a permissive society that fosters its development.
    b. It is hard to keep up with the *argot* of teenagers, which changes almost daily.

2. **aspersion** (ə-spur'-zhən, -shən)—act of defaming; a damaging or disparaging remark; a sprinkling of water, as in baptizing. This final definition, now rare, is based on an archaic meaning of the original Latin word for "sprinkle." The modern definition refers to "sprinkling" a few maliciously chosen words to vilify someone.
    a. The last few days of the campaign were marked by vicious attempts by the candidates to cast *aspersions* on each other.
    b. Such vehement *aspersions* that defame our sacred ideals and institutions cannot be ignored.

3. **badinage** (bad-ən-äzh', bad'-in-ij)—playful, teasing talk; banter.
    a. In one brief moment, the speaker rose from the level of *badinage* to grandiloquence.
    b. Raoul was a master of *badinage* but he could not be relied upon to serve in a position of leadership.

4. **bombast** (bäm'-bast)—originally a soft material used for padding; talk or writing that sounds grand or important but has little meaning; pompous language. *Bombastic* refers to speech or writing that is heavily padded with words; *grandiloquent* suggests grandiose language and an oratorical tone; *euphuistic* writing is characterized by artificiality and a straining for effect; *turgid* suggests the style has obscured the meaning.
    a. Some enjoy the rant and *bombast* of politics while others are more comfortable simply to exercise their voting rights at the polls.
    b. *Bombast* and extravagance are no longer fashionable in the press; instead we follow the dictum of "telling it like it is."

5. **braggadocio** (brag-ə-dō'-shē-ō, -dō'-shō)—a braggart; pretentiousness; vain, noisy, or bragging swaggering manner. The word was coined by Edmund Spenser for his personification of boasting in the "Faerie Queene."
    a. The *braggadocio* of Uganda's Idi Amin became a source of embarrassment to other African leaders.
    b. The boxer's *braggadocio* in claiming to be "the greatest" was a mixture of showmanship, psychology, and conformity to championship style.

6. **censure** (sen'-shər)—strong disapproval; a judgment or resolution condemning a person for misconduct.
   a. To explain the light sentence, the judge said the defendant was more to be pitied than *censured.*
   b. Newspapers were unanimous in their *censure* of the bill raising gasoline taxes as a means of discouraging energy waste.

7. **countermand** (koun'-tər-mand, koun-tər-mand')—to cancel or revoke a command; to call back by a contrary order.
   a. Realizing the futility of continuing the defense of the island, McArthur *countermanded* his original order to fight to the last man.
   b. Business fell sharply when the auto companies *countermanded* the order to reduce prices by six percent.

8. **gainsay** (gān'-sā)—to deny; to speak or act against; contradiction; denial.
   a. Beyond *gainsay,* the picture is a genuine Rembrandt.
   b. Our purpose in supporting the huge military budget is to make certain that no nation can *gainsay* us.

9. **gobbledegook** (gäb'-'l-dē-gook')—wordy and generally unintelligible jargon; specialized language of a group that is usually wordy and complicated and often incomprehensible to an outsider; a meaningless jumble of words.
   a. Laws now require the *gobbledegook* on insurance policies to be changed to understandable language.
   b. College professors claim that the average freshman composition is nothing but *gobbledegook.*

10. **guttural** (gut'-ər-əl)—of the throat; harsh, rasping sound.
    a. Certain *guttural* sounds, like the glottal stop and the *ch* in German *Buch,* do not exist in English.
    b. Part of the evening music of the country is the *guttural* symphony of the frogs.

11. **harangue** (hə-raŋ')—a long, blustering, noisy, or scolding speech; tirade. The original Italian word meant "a site for horse races and public assemblies."
    a. I recall that every poor grade on my report card brought forth a *harangue* on the subject of studying.
    b. The long, tiresome *harangue* by the director was full of bombast and ended with the firing of three actors.

12. **jargon** (jär'-gən)—a language or dialect unknown to one so that it seems incomprehensible; a mixed or hybrid language or dialect, especially pidgin; specialized idioms of those in the same work, profession; speech or writing full of long, unfamiliar, or roundabout words or phrases. The Middle French root means "a chattering of birds." The word is ultimately of echoic origin.
    a. Can you imagine anyone being so ethnocentric as to consider all foreign languages rude *jargons?*
    b. Medical *jargon* conceals from the public facts about diseases and medicines that all are entitled to know.

13. **mellifluous** (me-lif'-loo-wəs)—sounding sweet and smooth; honeyed.
    a. Juanita's mother wondered if her daughter wasn't more attracted by the suitor's *mellifluous* voice than by his character.
    b. Everyone was enraptured by the *mellifluous* tones of the Mozart opera.

14. **resonant** (rez'-ə-nənt)—echoing; reinforced and prolonged by reflection or by sympathetic vibration of other bodies. The word has specialized uses in various fields—chemistry, electricity, medicine, phonetics, physics.
    a. To develop a *resonant* voice, Carlos was willing to practice many hours.
    b. All talking stopped when the *resonant* thundering of cannons reverberated through the dark night.

15. **sententious** (sen-ten'-shəs)—self-righteous.
    a. One type of judge is magisterial; another is *sententious.*
    b. Paul's idea of a valedictory address was a compilation of *sententious* platitudes.

EXERCISES

I. Which Word Comes to Mind?

In each of the following, read the statement, then circle the word that comes to mind.

1. Sports lingo

    (harangue, jargon, resonant)

2. A snide remark

    (countermand, badinage, aspersion)

3. Coughing sound

    (gobbledegook, guttural, censure)

4. Sweet-sounding talk

    (mellifluous, sententious, bombast)

5. A thousand times no!

    (braggadocio, argot, gainsay)

6. How the rejected suitor concealed the sorrow in his heart

    (gainsay, badinage, harangue)

7. The opera star shook the room with his voice

    (resonant, braggadocio, mellifluous)

8. A 180-degree turnaround

    (gobbledegook, argot, countermand)

9. Frank's threats are not as frightening as they sound

    (aspersion, bombast, censure)

10. An incomprehensible language

    (jargon, sententious, guttural)

II. True or False?

In the space provided, indicate whether each statement is true or false.

_____ 1. *Argot* and *jargon* have one meaning in common.

_____ 2. *Bombast* may be a cover for weak content.

_____ 3. *Countermanding* is equivalent to sticking to your guns.

_____ 4. *Sententious* is more concerned with sense than sound.

_____ 5. *Badinage* is a minor vice that indicates immaturity.

_____ 6. A *harangue* is likely to be full of bombast.

_____ 7. *Censure* refers to a firm belief in a theory under discussion.

_____ 8. *Gobbledegook* is a language that attempts to imitate bird sounds.

_____ 9. *Guttural* speech is socially unacceptable.

_____ 10. Observing the size and strength of his opponent, Mark was wise not to *gainsay* his assertions.

III. Missing Letters

Each word below has a missing letter. Fill in these missing letters and then rearrange them to form a word meaning "the speech and idiom of the underworld."

1. bragadocio
2. gutturl
3. countemand
4. sentenious
5. resnant

IV. Synonyms and Antonyms

Find and circle two words on each line that are either synonyms or antonyms.

1. glorification	release	aspersion	dismay
2. mellifluous	ethos	attitudes	soft
3. timidity	paranoid	braggadocio	freedom
4. plebescite	gainsay	votary	deny
5. rhapsodic	peccadillo	falsetto	bombastic

V. Matching

Match the word in column A with its correct definition in column B by writing the letter of that definition in the space provided.

A	B
____ 1. argot	a. damaging remark
____ 2. aspersion	b. tirade
____ 3. badinage	c. pompous language
____ 4. bombast	d. terse
____ 5. braggadocio	e. dialect
____ 6. censure	f. gibberish
____ 7. countermand	g. criticism
____ 8. gainsay	h. harsh; rasping
____ 9. gobbledegook	i. oppose
____ 10. guttural	j. honeyed
____ 11. harangue	k. echoing
____ 12. jargon	l. pretentiousness
____ 13. mellifluous	m. specialized language
____ 14. resonant	n. revoke
____ 15. sententious	o. banter

History and Government (I)

Would you attack an enemy with a *canon?*

Does *renascent* refer to something new, young, or old?

Is a *subversion* a view of a secondary problem?

Is a *regicide* one who always sides with the king?

Is *peonage* a condition of certain laborers, a period of history, or a species of flowers?

canon
hegemony
oligarchy
peonage
plebiscite
plenary
plenipotentiary
proxy
recession
regicide
renascent
reprisal
subversion
surrogate
votary

1. **canon** (kan'-ən)—an ecclesiastical or secular law or code of laws; a basis for judgment; any officially recognized set of books. *Canon* has many specialized meanings in religion and in literature referring to the authoritative list of accepted books.
    a. According to newspaper *canon,* a big story calls for a lot of copy.
    b. There are thirty-seven plays in the Shakespearean *canon.*

2. **hegemony** (hi-jem'-ə-nē; hej'-ə-mō-nē)—leadership; superior influence or authority, especially of a government or state.
    a. Until the rise of rival city-states, the *hegemony* of ancient Greece was in the hands of Athens.
    b. In an uninformed electorate, the *hegemony* of the party passes to the one who promises more than any other contender.

3. **oligarchy** (äl'-ə-gär-kē)—form of government in which the ruling power lies in the hands of a select few.
    a. The founders of the new country set up an *oligarchy* in order to maintain tight control.
    b. There is a wide philosophical gap between those who choose democracy and those who favor *oligarchy.*

4. **peonage** (pē'-ə-nij)—a system by which debtors are bound in servitude to their creditors until debts are paid; the condition of being an unskilled day laborer, especially in Latin America and the southwestern United States. The word *peon* ultimately is traceable to the Latin word for "walker" and therefore also developed a meaning of "foot soldier."
    a. *Peonage* at one time involved convict labor leased to contractors in parts of the southeastern United States.
    b. The fallacy of the *peonage* system lies in the inability of a person in prison to earn the money to repay the debt for which he was sent to prison.

5. **plebiscite** (pleb'-ə-sīt)—a direct vote of the qualified electors of a state in regard to some important public question. The word is derived from the Latin words *plebis scitum* ("the people's decree").
    a. A *plebiscite* was held to determine whether the people of the disputed territory preferred autonomy or unification with their giant neighbor.
    b. *Plebiscites* are the most democratic way of settling political or legislative questions, but they are too cumbersome and costly to be used on every issue.

6. **plenary** (plē'-nə-rē)—full; fully attended.
   a. At a *plenary* session, the governor was attacked by the legislature.
   b. The board of directors had *plenary* control of the budget.

7. **plenipotentiary** (plen-i-pə-ten'-shē-er-ē)—invested with or conferring full power; a diplomatic agent fully authorized to represent his government.
   a. As a *plenipotentiary* of the American government, Mr. Linowitz concluded the Panama Canal Treaty talks.
   b. *Plenipotentiary* powers were not entrusted to the minister as his mission was only of an exploratory nature.

8. **proxy** (präk'-sē)—an agent or substitute; a document giving one authority to act for another.
   a. Legal status has been given to voting or marriage by *proxy.*
   b. Books are not *proxies* for experience.

9. **recession** (rē-sesh'-ən)—the act of withdrawing or going back; a moderate and temporary decline in economic activity that occurs during a period of otherwise increasing prosperity.
   a. Economists for a time could not agree on whether the business decline was a *recession* or a depression.
   b, Climatologists were concerned that a *recession* of the lakes and streams would endanger the water supply.

10. **regicide** (rej'-ə-cīd)—the killing of a king; one who kills or helps to kill a king.
    a. The judges who condemned Charles I to death were guilty of *regicide.*
    b. With the number and power of kings greatly reduced, *regicide* no longer looms as a probability in modern times.

11. **renascent** (ri-nās'-ənt)—coming into being again; showing renewed growth or vigor. The word is related to *Renaissance,* the humanistic revival of classical art, literature and learning that originated in Italy in the fourteenth century and later spread throughout Europe.
    a. In recent years there has been a *renascent* interest in Egyptology.
    b. The new freedom has brought with it a *renascent* individualism that some consider detrimental to society.

12. **reprisal** (rə-prī'-zəl)—the practice of using political or military force without actually resorting to war; retaliation for an injury with the intent of inflicting at least as much injury in return.
    a. *Reprisals* can run the gamut from embargo to military attack.
    b. After he ordered the attack, the general expected a *reprisal.*

13. **subversion** (sub-vur'-zhən)—ruination or complete destruction; corruption; complete overthrow. As the meaning implies, the original Latin word meant "to turn upside down."
    a. Economic assistance, it was felt, would cause the *subversion* of the existing tribal order.
    b. We cannot tolerate schemes of *subversion* when the liberties our country has cherished for two centuries are at stake.

14. **surrogate** (sur'-ə-gāt, sur'-,-git) a substitute; in some states, a judge having jurisdiction over the probate of wills and the settlement of estates. As a verb, the word means "to substitute or to put into the place of another."
    a. Some people regard teachers as parent *surrogates.*
    b. Those who de-emphasize correctness in writing regard it as only a *surrogate* of oral communication.

15. **votary** (vō'-tə-rē)—a person bound by vows to live a life of religious worship and service, as a monk or nun; any person fervently devoted to a religion, activity, leader, or ideal.
    a. Pagan worshippers tried to cultivate the good will of their gods, and so induce them to bestow their benefits on their *votaries.*
    b. In Las Vegas, gaming tables are thronged all night by the *votaries* of chance.

EXERCISES

I. Which Word Comes to Mind?

In each of the following, read the statement, then circle the word that comes to mind.

1. Sharecroppers or migrant workers

    (surrogate, proxy, peonage)

2. A basis for judgment

    (reprisal, renascent, canon)

3. Voice of the people

    (votary, plebiscite, subversion)

4. A man to be reckoned with

    (regicide, canon, plenipotentiary)

5. Times are bad but they could be worse

    (oligarchy, recession, hegemony)

6. Holier than thou

    (surrogate, canon, regicide)

7. Tit for tat

    (proxy, subversion, reprisal)

8. A commitment for life

    (votary, renascent, oligarchy)

9. Who's the boss?

    (peonage, hegemony, surrogate)

10. A second chance

    (proxy, renascent, surrogate)

II. True or False?

In the space provided, indicate whether each statement is true or false.

_____ 1. *Hegemony* refers to the currency in circulation.

_____ 2. A *proxy* and a *surrogate* are similar, both suggesting a substitute.

_____ 3. A *votary* is one who keeps his word.

_____ 4. A *regicide* favors the restoration of a monarchy.

_____ 5. Vengeance is an act of *reprisal.*

_____ 6. In an *oligarchy* everyone has an equal share in the government.

_____ 7. A *plenipotentiary* is a dedicated revolutionary.

_____ 8. *Subversion* is an attempt to change the system that is now in place.

_____ 9. Working under *peonage* is a good way to build a future in government.

_____ 10. In a *plebiscite* the people exercise their right of self-determination.

III. Missing Letters

Each word below has a missing letter. Flil in these missing letters and then rearrange them to form a word meaning "a secret meeting."

1. plenipoteniary

2. oligachy

3. votar

4. surrogae

5. plebicite

IV. Find the Words

Somewhere in this box of letters there are five vocabulary words that were taught in this lesson. By making one turn for each word, you can find four of these words. The letters of the fifth word, meaning "rule by a select group," are scattered throughout the box.

H	I	V	O	O
E	E	E	T	T
G	Y	N	A	C
E	X	O	R	P
M	O	N	Y	L

V. Matching

Match the word in column A with its correct definition in column B by writing the letter of that definition in the space provided.

<table>
<tr><td colspan="2" align="center">A</td><td colspan="2">B</td></tr>
<tr><td>_____</td><td>1. canon</td><td>a.</td><td>legal authorization to act for another</td></tr>
<tr><td>_____</td><td>2. hegemony</td><td>b.</td><td>being reborn</td></tr>
<tr><td>_____</td><td>3. oligarchy</td><td>c.</td><td>undermining</td></tr>
<tr><td>_____</td><td>4. peonage</td><td>d.</td><td>full</td></tr>
<tr><td>_____</td><td>5. plebiscite</td><td>e.</td><td>probate judge</td></tr>
<tr><td>_____</td><td>6. plenary</td><td>f.</td><td>basis for judgment</td></tr>
<tr><td>_____</td><td>7. plenipotentiary</td><td>g.</td><td>believer</td></tr>
<tr><td>_____</td><td>8. proxy</td><td>h.</td><td>economic setback</td></tr>
<tr><td>_____</td><td>9. recession</td><td>i.</td><td>referendum</td></tr>
<tr><td>_____</td><td>10. regicide</td><td>j.</td><td>slayer of kings</td></tr>
<tr><td>_____</td><td>11. renascent</td><td>k.</td><td>control; influence</td></tr>
<tr><td>_____</td><td>12. reprisal</td><td>l.</td><td>repayment</td></tr>
<tr><td>_____</td><td>13. subversion</td><td>m.</td><td>ambassador</td></tr>
<tr><td>_____</td><td>14. surrogate</td><td>n.</td><td>a kind of slavery</td></tr>
<tr><td>_____</td><td>15. votary</td><td>o.</td><td>rule by a few</td></tr>
</table>

Travel

Why is *wanderlust* a travel agent's dream?

What do *transmigrate* and *traverse* have in common?

From the name of Aristotle's followers, *Peripatetics,* what can we deduce about Aristotle's method of teaching?

Is a *safari* a kind of gem or a caravan?

Would people be helped or hindered by working in *tandem?*

---

cartography
concierge
hegira
hustings
landmark
parochial
peripatetic
portmanteau
safari
tandem
transmigrate
traverse
trek
wanderlust
wayfarer

1. **cartography** (kär-täg'-rə-fē)—art or business of drawing or making charts or maps. The original meaning of *chart* was a map for the use of navigators indicating the outline of coasts, position of rocks, sandbanks, and channels.
   a. The exploration of the New World was advanced by the science of *cartography.*
   b. Modern astronauts are guided by the *cartography* of incredibly complex maps drawn with the aid of giant computers.

2. **concierge** (kän-sē-urzh')—doorkeeper; caretaker; custodian; janitor. The *concierge* in French and other European hotels has a more important position than is implied by the title of janitor or custodian.
   a. Travelers quickly learn the importance of getting on the good side of their *concierge.*
   b. A *concierge,* looking as stern as Madame de Farge, guarded the lobby night and day.

3. **hegira** (hi-jī'-rə, hej'-ər-ə)—any flight or journey to a more desirable or congenial place than where one is. *Hegira* was the flight of Muhammad from Mecca to Medina to escape persecution in 622 A.D., a date regarded as the beginning of the Muslim era.
   a. Fashion experts are making their annual *hegira* to Paris.
   b. With the onset of the hot weather, the *hegira* to the beach resorts began in earnest.

4. **hustings** (hus'-tiŋz)—the route followed by a campaigner for political office; an election platform; the proceedings at an election. The original Old English word referred to a lord's household assembly as distinct from a general assembly.
   a. Televised debates have replaced the rough give-and-take of the *hustings.*
   b. Taking to the *hustings* required boundless energy, extraordinary endurance, and an unflagging voice.

5. **landmark** (land'-märk)—any fixed object used to mark the boundary of a piece of land; any prominent feature of the landscape, serving to identify a particular locality; an event or discovery considered as a high point or a turning point in the history or development of something.
   a. The huge oak tree was so prominent in the curve of the road it became a *landmark* to travelers.
   b. Our age has seen a *landmark* shift in morals and values.

6. **parochial** (pə-rō'-kē-əl)—narrowly restricted; provincial.
   a. The sheltered author was criticized for his *parochial* outlook.
   b. Cindy escaped her *parochial* environment by coming to the big city.

7. **peripatetic** (per-i-pə-tet'ik)—moving from place to place; itinerant; of the followers of Aristotle, who walked about the Lyceum while he was teaching.
   a. Donald's *peripatetic* habits during his youth came back to haunt him when he later tried to find a steady job.
   b. As a professional photographer, Mr. Randall managed to stay in one place with his camera, avoiding a *peripatetic* life.

8. **portmanteau** (pôrt-man'-tō, -tō')—a case or bag to carry clothing while traveling, especially a leather trunk or suitcase that opens into two halves. The literal French meaning is "cloak carrier." A more recent use of the word in linguistics is to define a blend, a word made by putting together parts of other words, as *dandle,* made from *dance* and *handle.*
   a. Lewis Carroll, author of *Alice in Wonderland,* made frequent use of *portmanteau* words, as in his combination of *snort* and *chuckle* to form *chortle.*
   b. Sir Oliver was late for the meeting because his *portmanteau* had been placed on the wrong plane.

9. **safari** (sə-fär'-ē)—a journey or hunting expedition, especially in East Africa; the caravan of such an expedition; a long, carefully planned trip, usually with a large entourage.
   a. Roald Amundsen's safari to the Arctic in 1926 won him the title of "Discoverer of the North Pole."
   b. Hemingway wrote of the introspection or confrontation that was a by-product of the *safari.*

10. **tandem** (tan'-dəm)—a two-wheeled carriage drawn by horses harnessed one behind the other; a team of horses harnessed one behind the other; a bicycle with two seats and sets of pedals placed one behind the other; a relationship between two persons or things involving cooperative action and mutual dependence. *Tandem* may be a noun, an adjective, or an adverb.
   a. The president expressed the hope that all parties would function in *tandem* to solve the nation's major problems.
   b. A more persuasive *tandem* could not be found, nor were there two women with more desire to bring peace to the struggling factions in Northern Ireland.

11. **transmigrate** (trans-mī'-grāt)—to move from one habitation or country to another; in religion, to pass into some other body at death (of the soul). Believers in *reincarnation* and *metempsychosis* also feel that the souls of the dead successively return to earth in new forms and bodies.
   a. Some people believe that the soul may *transmigrate* into an animal as well as a person.
   b. Early in the Colonial period, the pioneers *transmigrated* from the Rocky Mountain slopes to the fertile plains.

12. **traverse** (tra'-vurs, trə-vurs')—to pass, move, or extend over or across; oppose; to survey or inspect carefully; to swivel or pivot; to move across a mountain slope in an oblique direction (as in skiing); a zigzagging course.
   a. I accept no precepts that *traverse* my moral freedom.
   b. The new discovery opens a wide area of investigation that must now be *traversed* by historians.

13. **trek** (trek)—to travel by ox wagon; to travel slowly or laboriously. Colloquially, the word means "to go, especially on foot." *Trek* is also used as a noun.
   a. The shortage of new housing led to a consequent *trek* into older apartments.
   b. George Washington Carver's *trek* up from slavery was a harbinger of the civil rights advances made in the latter half of the twentieth century.

14. **wanderlust** (wän'-dər-lust, wôn'-)—an impulse, longing, or urge to travel or wander.
   a. Modern traveling comforts and conveniences have simplified the problems of those who are afflicted with *wanderlust.*
   b. No one could figure out why a *wanderlust* seized the successful businessman and drew him to a life of vagabondage.

15. wayfarer (wā'-fer-ər)—a person who travels, especially from place to place on foot.
   a.   We are all *wayfarers* on the road to eternity.
   b.   Some of the old virtues, like showing kindness to the weary *wayfarer,* have been lost in the hubbub of city life.

EXERCISES

I. Which Word Comes to Mind?

In each of the following, read the statement, then circle the word that comes to mind.

   1. A train makes whistle-stops across the Midwest

   (trek, hustings, hegira)

   2. Smog, brunch, guesstimate

   (peripatetic, concierge, portmanteau)

   3. The Supreme Court decision on school integration

   (cartography, landmark, hegira)

   4. Tracking lions in their native habitat

   (safari, wayfarer, wanderlust)

   5. A bicycle built for two

   (transmigrate, tandem, traverse)

   6. Moving across a mountain

   (traverse, tandem, safari)

   7. The annual trip to a summer residence

   (landmark, safari, hegira)

   8. The "feel the flesh" aspect of electioneering

   (wayfarer, hustings, trek)

   9. Miles to go before I sleep

   (traverse, peripatetic, transmigrate)

   10. Airport luggage

   (tandem, trek, portmanteau)

II. True or False?

In the space provided, indicate whether each statement is true or false.

_____ 1. A *safari* can properly be described as a *trek* through the jungle.

_____ 2. The art of *cartography* has proved to be helpful for navigators.

_____ 3. The early *Peripatetics* were philosophers.

_____ 4. *Transmigration* is a form of ESP.

_____ 5. *Wanderlust* describes the sensuality of the homeless criminal.

_____ 6. Gaining the good will of the *concierge* can prove very helpful for a detective.

_____ 7. When the basketball players worked in *tandem,* they were hard to defeat.

_____ 8. *Transmigration* can refer to movements of the soul as well as of the body.

_____ 9. Broadly speaking, *cartography* includes traveling by wagon, car, train, or plane.

_____ 10. The handshake of the former enemies was considered a *landmark* gesture.

III. Find the Impostor

Find and circle the one word on each line that is not related to the other three.

1. peripatetic	hegira	globe-trotting	travail
2. vagabondage	wayfarer	valediction	nomadism
3. tirade	trek	harangue	diatribe
4. astronaut	travail	navigator	pilgrim
5. anticipate	opposite	different	antithetic

IV. Find the Words

Somewhere in this box of letters, reading up, down, across, or diagonally, four vocabulary words that were taught in this lesson are hidden. As you locate each one, draw a circle around it. Then find one word, meaning "a person who travels," whose letters are scattered throughout the box.

H	K	F	A	R	M
W	E	E	R	E	D
A	R	G	D	P	A
Y	T	N	I	O	L
S	A	F	A	R	I
T	A	N	T	I	A

V. Matching

Match the word in column A with its correct definition in column B by writing the letter of that definition in the space provided.

A	B
____ 1. cartography	a. map-making
____ 2. concierge	b. two-seated carriage
____ 3. hegira	c. traveler
____ 4. hustings	d. itinerant
____ 5. landmark	e. journey from one place to another
____ 6. parochial	f. luggage
____ 7. peripatetic	g. hunting expedition
____ 8. portmanteau	h. addiction to traveling
____ 9. safari	i. provincial
____ 10. tandem	j. travel with difficulty
____ 11. transmigrate	k. event marking the turning point
____ 12. traverse	l. flight
____ 13. trek	m. oppose
____ 14. wanderlust	n. election platform
____ 15. wayfarer	o. caretaker

Foods and Taste

Is *cuisine* a traditional family recipe?

Which would be served at a *refection, viands* or *manna?*

Can *piquant* condiments assuage one's hunger?

Would you find *manna* at a *repast?*

Which usually offers more food, a *refection* or a *repast?*

---

a la carte
assuage
condiment
cuisine
culinary
deleterious
gastronomic
gourmand
manna
palatable
piquant
refection
repast
subsistence
viands

1. **a la carte** (ä-lə-kärt')—by the card or by the bill of fare. It is used to describe a meal that is ordered dish by dish, with each dish having a separate price. The opposite is *table d'hôte,* a complete meal of several courses offered at a fixed price.
   a. An *a la carte* dinner is usually more expensive than a complete dinner offered at a set price.
   b. The advantage of an *a la carte* meal is that you order and pay for only what you choose to eat.

2. **assuage** (ə-swäj')—to satisfy and slake; to lessen (pain or distress); allay; calm (passion); relieve. The Latin root *suavis* ("sweet") suggests that sweets play an important role in our eating habits.
   a. Upon our return from the arduous climb, we were treated to more than enough food to *assuage* our hunger.
   b. There was little anyone could say to the widow to *assuage* her grief.

3. **condiment** (kän'-də-mənt)—seasoning or relish for food, such as pepper, mustard, or sauce. The Latin root means "to pickle."
   a. Gourmets are very careful with the kinds and amounts of *condiments* used in the preparation of their food.
   b. It is no exaggeration to say that the search for *condiments* for the royal tables of Europe led to the discovery of the New World.

4. **cuisine** (kwə-zēn')—style of cooking or preparing food; the food prepared, as at a restaurant. In French it means "kitchen."
   a. Nowhere can you find as many restaurants offering international *cuisine* as in New York.
   b. The advertisement caught our eye because it claimed quite frankly that the restaurant had no atmosphere but offered an excellent *cuisine.*

5. **culinary** (kyōō'-lə-ner-ē, kul'-ə-ner-ē)—of the kitchen or cooking; suitable for use in cooking. *Culinary* comes from the Latin word for "kitchen" or "klin," *culina.*
   a. It is paradoxical that while a woman's place was once thought to be in the kitchen, the greatest *culinary* experts were men.
   b. These dishes are prepared with the finest *culinary* herbs.

6. **deleterious** (del-i-tîr'-ē-ə-s)—harmful.
   a. The school's asbestos was *deleterious* the pupils' health.
   b. We thought that Gary's testimony was *deleterious* to his case.

7. **gastronomic** (gas-trə-näm'-ik)—pertaining to the art and science of good eating; epicurean; pertaining to the enjoyment of food with a discriminating taste. *Gaster* is the Greek word for "stomach." *Gastronome* is the Russian name for a delicatessen.
   a. *Gastronomic* experts, like Craig Clayborne, have influenced our choice of foods.
   b. Television chefs have introduced the *gastronomic* delights of Oriental dishes to the Western household.

8. **gourmand** (goor'-mənd, goor'-mänd)—a glutton; a person with a hearty liking for good food and drink and a tendency to indulge in them to excess; a luxurious eater or epicure. *Gourmet* has only the second meaning, that is, a connoisseur in eating and drinking.
   a. Randolph was too much of a *gourmand* to appreciate rare and fragile flavors.
   b. It took a team of chefs to satisfy the *gourmand* appetite of Diamond Jim Brady.

9. **manna** (man'-ə)—food miraculously provided for the Israelites in the wilderness; divine and spiritual sustenance; anything badly needed that comes unexpectedly.
   a. The hard-pressed family regarded the unexpected bonus as *manna.*
   b. The doctor's assurance of a favorable prognosis was received by the patient like *manna* from heaven.

10. **palatable** (pal'-it-ə-b'l)—pleasing or acceptable to the taste; acceptable to the mind.
    a. The root, when properly cooked, was converted into a *palatable* and nutritious food.
    b. It took Darryl hours and several modifications to make his plan *palatable* to the rest of the committee.

11. **piquant** (pē'-kənt, -känt)—agreeably pungent or stimulating to the taste; pleasantly sharp or bitter; exciting agreeable interest or curiosity; stimulating.
    a. Joan had a delightful, *piquant* smile.
    b. Eleanor's columns are always *piquant* and sometimes blistering.

12. **refection** (ri-fek'-shən)—refreshment, especially with food or drink. *Refection* comes from a Latin word meaning "to restore" and refers to a light meal taken after a point of hunger or fatigue.
    a. After the lengthy speeches, the audience was anxious to partake of the *refection.*
    b. In our weight-conscious society, the grand *refections* at social gatherings challenge our will power and tempt us to gluttony.

13. **repast** (ri-past')—a meal; mealtime. Like other words in this list, *repast* has nonmaterialistic associations as well. *Pastor,* for example, is derived from the same Latin word *pascere* meaning "to feed."
    a. The Berensons preferred to be alone at the evening *repast.*
    b. How I envy people who are satisfied with a light *repast* of simple and nourishing food.

14. **subsistence** (sub-sis'-təns)—existence; means of support or livelihood, often the barest.
    a. Early pioneers to the Dakotas found a barren land providing no more than the barest *subsistence.*
    b. Without a skill or trade, Mr. Jenkins could not hope to reach a standard of living beyond a mere *subsistence* level.

15. **viands** (vī'-əndz)—foods of various kinds, especially choice dishes. The ultimate root is the Latin *vivere,* "to live."
    a. The grocery shelves were stocked with *viands* of the most exotic kind.
    b. To our surprise, the grizzled traveler pulled *viands* from his tattered knapsack that were unobtainable locally in the finest stores.

EXERCISES

I. Which Word Comes to Mind?

In each of the following, read the statement, then circle the word that comes to mind.

1. Catsup, curry, vinegar

    (a la carte, refectory, condiment)

2. Pennies from heaven

    (cuisine, manna, gourmand)

3. Living on the edge of poverty

    (subsistence, assuage, gastronomic)

4. Wake-up flavor

    (repast, deleterious, piquant)

5. "Something's cooking."

    (culinary, palatable, viands)

6. Gas fumes

    (condiments, deleterious, manna)

7. Italian, French, and Chinese

    (a la carte, subsistence, cuisine)

8. He eats as if food is going out of style

    (gastronomic, gourmand, viands)

9. The minister speaking to the grieving widow

    (assuage, a la carte, refection)

10. Refers to ways of serving

    (condiment, a la carte, palatable)

II. True or False?

In the space provided, indicate whether each statement is true or false.

_____ 1. *A la carte* refers to food brought to the table in a wagon.
_____ 2. *Assuage* refers to both hunger and thirst.
_____ 3. *Gourmand* can be used with a complimentary or derogatory connotation.
_____ 4. *Palatable* applies to foods that can be served on a plate.
_____ 5. *Gastronomic* describes a condition caused by excessive indulgence in foods that are rich in fats and carbohydrates.
_____ 6. *Viands* refer to choice dishes.
_____ 7. *A la carte* refers to payment for food rather than to types of food.
_____ 8. Both gourmet and gourmand describe food *connoisseurs*.
_____ 9. A repast is a snack; *refection* is a full meal.
_____ 10. The expression "Man does not live by bread alone" suggests that things other than food are *palatable*.

III. Find the Impostor

Find and circle the one word on each line that is not related to the other three.

1. repast	audible	nutritional	eatable
2. quench	assuage	determine	sate
3. sustenance	subsistence	essential	nourishment
4. palatable	pungent	savory	agreeable
5. banquet	refection	repast	relish

IV. Anagrams

In each of the following, add the letter indicated, then rearrange the letters to form the two new words whose definitions are given.

1. gourmand + e = a *scoundrel* and *condemn* _____
2. piquant + s = *to look obliquely* and *broadcast system* _____
3. viands = *forefront* and *divisions of the psyche* _____
4. refection + s = *sandbanks* and *gin and* _____
5. assuage + h = *estimate* and *expression of triumph or pleasure* _____

V. Matching

Match the word in column A with its correct definition in column B by writing the letter of that definition in the space provided.

A		B	
____	1. a la carte	a.	lover of food and drink
____	2. assuage	b.	divine food
____	3. condiment	c.	provocative
____	4. cuisine	d.	pacify
____	5. culinary	e.	meal
____	6. deleterious	f.	harmful
____	7. gastronomic	g.	choice dishes
____	8. gourmand	h.	style of cooking
____	9. manna	i.	existence
____	10. palatable	j.	suitable for cooking
____	11. piquant	k.	dish by dish
____	12. refection	l.	tasteful
____	13. repast	m.	flavor enhancer
____	14. subsistence	n.	refreshment
____	15. viands	o.	pertaining to the science of good eating

Unit IV
(Lessons 31–35)

Mini Review

I. Antonyms

Circle the word that most nearly expresses the *opposite* meaning of the word in capital letters.

1. MALAPROPISM: (a) epitaph (b) harangue (c) mot juste (d) undervalued
2. SENTENTIOUS: (a) angry (b) long-winded (c) shallow (d) sullen
3. CENSURE: (a) vigilance (b) negligence (c) innocence (d) approval
4. RECESSION: (a) inflation (b) depression (c) expansion (d) redemption
5. PERIPATETIC: (a) stationary (b) treacherous (c) enduring (d) reserved

II. Synonyms

Circle the word that most nearly expresses the *same* meaning as the word in capital letters.

1. CUISINE: (a) discomfort (b) manner of preparing food (c) familial relationship (d) sharpness of wit
2. ASSUAGE: (a) appease (b) endow (c) ogle (d) strengthen
3. TRAVERSE: (a) transplant (b) stretch (c) contemplate (d) cross
4. HEGEMONY: (a) culture (b) brevity (c) dominance (d) turning point
5. COUNTERMAND: (a) recall (b) order (c) disobey (d) overpower

III. Sentence Completions

Select those words from the group below that best fill the blanks.

bucolic   guttural   mellifluous   metaphor   refection   resonant   subversive   trek   wayfarer

1. The _____ music soothed his nerves after a tension-filled day.

2. Before endorsing Mr. Palemeri's candidacy, the committee questioned him vis-à-vis his reputed _____ connection with underworld figures.

3. Their trip to the state capital turned out to be quite a _____ ; first they got lost, then they had car trouble.

4. The ad showing a splattered egg has become an effective _____ for the brain of a drug addict.

5. Vito's _____ voice shook the opera house rafters.

Fun and Frolic

Why is a king well equipped to *regale* his subjects?

Would adding yeast to dough make it more *risible?*

Which is not likely to be *waggish*—a cat, a clown, or a tiger?

Which character trait makes a better friend, *bonhomie* or *insouciance?*

Might a *guffaw* turn up in a situation comedy?

---

antic
beguile
bonhomie
cajole
congenial
dalliance
divertissement
euphoria
guffaw
insouciance
regale
risible
roguish
squib
waggish

1. **antic** (an'-tik)—odd and funny; ludicrous; a playful or silly act, trick, prank, or caper. Shakespeare has Hamlet hide his real intent by assuming an *antic* disposition.
    a. How can we seriously consider Frank for the promotion when he is continually involved with such juvenile *antics?*
    b. Fletcher's *antics* may be fun to watch but I wouldn't want to be on the receiving end.

2. **beguile** (bi-gīl')—to charm; to divert attention in some pleasant way; to while away; to deceive.
    a. We often allow ourselves to be *beguiled* by false hopes and vain promises.
    b. To *beguile* the time, Carrie spent hours on the telephone.

3. **bonhomie** (bän-ə-mē', bän'-ə-mē)—frank and simple good-heartedness; a good-natured manner. The word is a combination of two French words meaning "good" and "man." *Bonhomie* was the name given to an order of begging friars and finally to French peasants in general.
    a. An affectionate *bonhomie* radiated from Mrs. Goren, endearing her to all she came in contact with.
    b. The alumni gathering was marked by the cheerfulness and *bonhomie* of a fraternity reunion.

4. **cajole** (kə–jōl')—to coax; wheedle.
    a. The T.V. executive attempted to *cajole* the audience into contributing money.
    b. Ingrid could always *cajole* Dad into letting her have the car.

5. **congenial** (kən-jēn'yəl)—sociable; having the same tastes.
    a. We love parties at the Perez house because they're *congenial* hosts.
    b. Because Arnie is so *congenial*, we get along beautifully.

6. **dalliance** (dal'-ē-əns, dal'-yəns)—a trifling away of time; amorous toying; flirtation. In *Hamlet,* Ophelia reminds her brother Laertes not to give her moral advice while he follows "the primrose path of *dalliance.*"
    a. Marco's short *dalliance* with the drug cult ended when he realized the terrible havoc it had wrought among its followers.
    b. Mrs. Farren warned her daughter that Steve's interest might be a mere amatory *dalliance.*

7. **divertissement** (di-vurt'-is-mənt, dī-ver-tēs-man')—a diversion or amusement; a short ballet or other entertainment performed between the acts of a play.
   a. The detective story has an honorable history as an intellectual *divertissement*.
   b. With the legalization of certain forms of gambling, lotteries have become a popular *divertissement*.

8. **euphoria** (yoo-fôr'-ē-ə)—a feeling of well-being or high spirits, especially one that is groundless, disproportionate to its cause, or inappropriate to one's life situation.
   a. Michael's *euphoria* was of a suspicious nature.
   b. Making the team in his sophomore year put Arnold into a state of *euphoria* that made it hard for him to settle down to his schoolwork.

9. **guffaw** (gə-fô')—a loud, coarse burst of laughter. This is an echoic onomatopoeic word. Laughs range from chuckles, giggles, and titters to snickers and *guffaws.*
   a. Mr. Bumble's loud *guffaw* could be heard above the din of the train station.
   b. As the clown continued his antics, the chuckles soon changed to howls and roars and *guffaws.*

10. **insouciance** (in-soo'-sē-əns)—calmness; freedom from anxiety; indifference.
    a. Disregarding the snickers around her, Alice walked to the stage with an elegant *insouciance* and delivered her speech.
    b. The diva's *insouciance* concealed a growing concern about her fading youth.

11. **regale** (ri-gāl')—to entertain by providing a splendid feast; to delight with something pleasing or amusing. The first meaning is related etymologically to the word *regal,* as it was customary for a king to treat his courtiers to sumptuous feasts.
    a. Washington hostesses must *regale* their guests with the best foods and good companionship if they wish to maintain their reputation in that competitive society.
    b. The purple mountains unfolding in grandeur to meet the rising sun were a sight to *regale* the eyes.

12. **risible** (riz'-ə-b'l)—able or inclined to laugh; laughable; funny. Most people are familiar with Leoncavallo's opera *Pagliacci,* in which the major character sings "Ride, Pagliacci." Our word *ridiculous* shows the close relationship to *risible.*
    a. "Heaven," said Christopher Morley, "is not for pallid saints but for raging and *risible* men."
    b. The manager was ordered off the field for his *risible* antics.

13. **roguish** (rō'-gish)—dishonest; unprincipled; pleasantly mischievous.
    a. With a *roguish* wink, the magician stepped into the box with the money he had "borrowed" and disappeared in a cloud of orange smoke.
    b. Blanche decided to return to her husband despite his *roguish* past.

14. **squib** (skwib)—a firecracker that burns with a hissing, spurting noise before exploding; a short, humorous satiric writing or speech; a short news item or filler.
    a. Teachers have become accustomed to being the subjects of versified *squibs* in yearbooks.
    b. Once famous and lionized, the old movie idol could not even rate a *squib* among the used-car ads.

15. **waggish** (wag'-ish)—roguishly merry; playful.
    a. A *waggish* disposition is not the best qualification for the position of class president.
    b. Albert's distorted idea of a *waggish* trick was to call in false fire alarms.

EXERCISES

I. Which Word Comes to Mind?

In each of the following, read the statement, then circle the word that comes to mind.

1. A pleasant intermission

   (insouciance, divertissement, euphoria)

2. The laughter of the Jolly Green Giant

   (guffaw, euphoria, dalliance)

3. A ten-course banquet

   (cajole, regale, risible)

4. Racy humor

   (bonhomie, waggish, beguile)

5. A satire

   (antic, roguish, squib)

6. Laughing at the breakup of the marriage

   (divertissement, insouciance, euphoria)

7. Tell funny anecdotes

   (congenial, regale, guffaw)

8. Can't be trusted

   (risible, roguish, euphoria)

9. A true friend

   (bonhomie, squib, waggish)

10. A raging passion that cooled

    (risible, dalliance, antic)

II. True or False?

In the space provided, indicate whether each statement is true or false.

_____ 1. You cannot trust a man with *bonhomie.*
_____ 2. A *waggish* person would be likely to indulge in *satire.*
_____ 3. A *dalliance* is a brightly colored flower.
_____ 4. The court jester entertained with his *antics.*
_____ 5. A *squib* is a variety of an octopus that has ten tentacles.

_____ 6. *Euphoria* is a ride on cloud nine.

_____ 7. A *guffaw* is to a smile as antic is to serious.

_____ 8. The natural reaction to a *risible* event is to burst into tears.

_____ 9. *Waggish* is a milder trait than its close synonym, roguish.

_____ 10. A regal personality is expected to *regale* his guests.

III. Missing Letters

Each word below has a missing letter. Fill in these missing letters and then rearrange them to form a word meaning "pixyish."

1. daliance
2. gufaw
3. divertissment
4. isouciance
5. squib

IV. Find the Words

Somewhere in this box of letters, reading up, down, across, or diagonally, five vocabulary words that were taught in this lesson are hidden. As you locate each one, draw a circle around it.

G	U	F	F	A	W
E	C	I	T	N	A
L	N	C	E	B	G
A	E	J	P	I	G
G	L	I	A	U	I
E	A	Y	R	Q	S
R	L	A	D	S	H

V. Matching

Match the word in column A with its correct definition in column B by writing the letter of that definition in the space provided.

<table>
<tr><td colspan="2">A</td><td colspan="2">B</td></tr>
<tr><td>_____</td><td>1. antic</td><td>a.</td><td>a short ballet</td></tr>
<tr><td>_____</td><td>2. beguile</td><td>b.</td><td>indifference</td></tr>
<tr><td>_____</td><td>3. bonhomie</td><td>c.</td><td>high spirits</td></tr>
<tr><td>_____</td><td>4. cajole</td><td>d.</td><td>ludicrous</td></tr>
<tr><td>_____</td><td>5. congenial</td><td>e.</td><td>coax</td></tr>
<tr><td>_____</td><td>6. dalliance</td><td>f.</td><td>sociable</td></tr>
<tr><td>_____</td><td>7. divertissement</td><td>g.</td><td>frolicsome</td></tr>
<tr><td>_____</td><td>8. euphoria</td><td>h.</td><td>lampoon</td></tr>
<tr><td>_____</td><td>9. guffaw</td><td>i.</td><td>boisterous laughter</td></tr>
<tr><td>_____</td><td>10. insouciance</td><td>j.</td><td>disreputable</td></tr>
<tr><td>_____</td><td>11. regale</td><td>k.</td><td>dawdling</td></tr>
<tr><td>_____</td><td>12. risible</td><td>l.</td><td>refresh with sumptuous food</td></tr>
<tr><td>_____</td><td>13. roguish</td><td>m.</td><td>deceive</td></tr>
<tr><td>_____</td><td>14. squib</td><td>n.</td><td>laughable</td></tr>
<tr><td>_____</td><td>15. waggish</td><td>o.</td><td>geniality</td></tr>
</table>

History and Government (II)

Is *suffrage* a matter of high tolerance to pain?

Who is opposed to progressive changes, the *reactionary* or the liberal?

Why does a vote count more in a democracy than in a *totalitarian* state?

What are the drawbacks to government *bureaucracy?*

Why would a *muckraker* be feared by people in high office?

anarchy
bourgeois
bureaucracy
demagogue
ethos
gerrymander
imperialism
Machiavellian
martial
muckraker
partisan
reactionary
schism
suffrage
totalitarian

1. **anarchy** (an'-ər-kē)—the complete absence of government; political disorder and violence; disorder in any sphere of activity. The anarchist opposes all direct or coercive government and proposes the voluntary association of people as the mode of organized society.
   a. The death of the king was followed by a period of *anarchy.*
   b. For some people liberty often means only license and *anarchy.*

2. **bourgeois** (boor-zhwä', boor'-zhwä)—typical of the social middle class; characterized by selfish concern for material comfort and for property values. *Bourgeois* virtues are thriftiness and a serious attitude toward life; its faults are a preoccupation with moneymaking and anxiety about respectability. It all depends on one's point of view.
   a. Communists say that all capitalists are *bourgeois.*
   b. The Martins were social climbers who followed a *bourgeois* mediocrity in their opinions and tastes.

3. **bureaucracy** (byoo-rä'-krə-sē)—a system that rigidly adheres to rules, forms, and routines. In American usage, the term is almost invariably derogatory unless the context establishes otherwise.
   a. We got tied up in red tape when we attempted to fight against the *bureaucracy.*
   b. In his election campaign, the candidate promised to streamline the *bureaucracy* and eliminate inefficiency.

4. **demagogue** (dem'-ə-gäg)—a leader who obtains power by means of impassioned appeals to the emotions and prejudices of the populace. In ancient Greece, the *demagogue* was the leader who championed the cause of the common people.
   a. Oversimplification and single-minded pursuit of an inflammatory issue are characteristics of the modern *demagogue.*
   b. The mayoral candidate seized upon the blackout to make a *demagogic* attack upon the ability of the incumbent.

5. **ethos** (ē'-thäs)—the disposition, character, or attitude that distinguishes a particular group, epoch, or region.
   a. From her youth, Althea Gibson had a distinctly athletic *ethos* about her, as if she might have majored in physical education.
   b. America has expressed its *ethos* in its basic allegiance to the principles of the Constitution.

6. **gerrymander** (jer'-i-man-dər, ger'-)—to divide an area into voting districts to give unfair advantage to one party in an election. The word comes from a reference to Elbridge Gerry, governor of Massachusetts, whose party redistricted the state in 1812, combined with *salamander,* because the map of Essex County, Massachusetts, seemed to resemble this animal after the redistricting.
   a. Federal law prohibits *gerrymandering* of school districts so that de facto segregation can be maintained.
   b. Only through a complex *gerrymander* was the entrenched union chief able to avoid a disastrous defeat.

7. **imperialism** (im-pir'-ē-al-iz'm)—the policy of extending the rule or authority of an empire or nation over countries, or of acquiring and holding colonies and dependencies.
   a. Communist Russia, like Nazi Germany before it, aimed at autocratic control and *imperialistic* expansion.
   b. It is conceivable that small nations can follow the path of *imperialism* through nuclear blackmail.

8. **Machiavellian** (mak-ē-ə-vel'-ē-ən, -vel'-yən)—acting in accordance with the principles of government in which political expediency is placed above morality; subtly or unscrupulously cunning or deceptive. Nicolo Machiavelli in *The Prince* expounded the doctrine of political expediency.
   a. Few people openly support the *Machiavellian* position that the end justifies the means.
   b. With *Machiavellian* cunning, the political newcomer gradually built a power base from which he hoped to seize power.

9. **martial** (mär'-shəl)—inclined or disposed to war; brave; warlike. The blood-red planet Mars was named after the Roman god of war.
   a. John Philip Sousa is the best known composer of *martial* music.
   b. When it became obvious that police were unable to contain the riot, *martial* law was declared to restore peace and order.

10. **muckraker** (muk'-rā-kər)—one who searches for and exposes real or alleged corruption and scandal. *Muckrake,* a rake for use on muck or dung, was first used in the work of Lincoln Steffens and his contemporaries.
    a. Who can feel safe if the *muckraking* journalists turn over every stone in a person's life?
    b. Unwilling to stoop to *muckraking* to discredit his opponent, Mr. Barios felt he could win on his own merit.

11. **partisan** (pärt'-ə-z'n, -s'n)—an adherent or supporter of a person, party, or cause; a member of an irregular troop engaged in harassing an enemy.
    a. *Partisans* in World War II, fighting against the Nazi occupation of their countries, carved a niche of honor and glory for their courage and determination.
    b. When the fabric of American society is disintegrating, it is useless and dangerous to play *partisan* politics.

12. **reactionary** (rē-ak'-shə-ner-ē)—a person who favors political conservatism or extreme rightism.
    a. *Reactionary* movements sometimes develop in response to unsuccessful or unhappy liberal politics.
    b. Aided by disunity and splintering among the progressives, the *reactionary* forces were able to achieve victory with their appeal for a return to "the good old days."

13. **schism** (siz'-əm, skiz'-əm)—a separation or division into factions. The term "The Great Schism" was used in connection with the Christian church to describe the split between the Western and Eastern sects.
    a. Despite their denials, a *schism* seemed to be developing between the president and the secretary of state.
    b. "Let there be no *schism* in our ranks," the prime minister admonished, "or we will fritter away our energies and strength in useless contention."

14. suffrage (suf'-rij)—the right to vote; a vote given in favor of a proposed measure or candidate.
   a. The U.S. Constitution guarantees that "no state shall be deprived of its equal *suffrage* in the Senate."
   b. The struggle for universal *suffrage* is behind us; ahead looms the battle to assure a decent standard of living for everyone.

15. totalitarian (tō-tal-ə-ter'-ē-ən)—of or pertaining to a centralized government in which those in control grant neither recognition nor toleration to parties of differing opinions.
   a. The children suffered under the *totalitarian* rule of the father in their patriarchal household.
   b. Almost all countries adopt *totalitarian* measures in war time.

EXERCISES

I. Which Word Comes to Mind?

In each of the following, read the statement, then circle the word that comes to mind.

1. The Confederacy votes to secede from the Union

   (martial, gerrymander, schism)

2. Vote the party line all the way

   (partisan, Machiavellian, reactionary)

3. Historically, some countries have tried to expand their territories.

   (anarchy, imperialism, bureaucracy)

4. The Amish object to TV and other modern inventions and conveniences

   (ethos, totalitarian, suffrage)

5. A spellbinding speaker

   (demagogue, muckraker, bourgeois)

6. Red tape and needless duplication

   (anarchy, reactionary, bureaucracy)

7. One form of investigative journalism

   (bourgeois, muckraker, gerrymander)

8. Usually associated with conservative isolationists

   (Machiavellian, reactionary, imperialism)

9. Tries to crush autonomous institutions

   (totalitarianism, ethos, martial)

10. The franchise

   (partisan, schism, suffrage)

II. True or False?

In the space provided, indicate whether each statement is true or false.

_____ 1. *Bourgeois* manners tend to be different from the manners of those who have been born with "a silver spoon in their mouth."

_____ 2. To *gerrymander* is to vote on the basis of issue rather than party.

_____ 3. *Martial* refers to a rank in the army.

_____ 4. A *Machiavellian* attitude could lead to power but also to unpopularity.

_____ 5. Anarchy is a form of government that is built upon *bureaucracy.*

_____ 6. *Anarchy* is a form of government that favors *gerrymandering.*

_____ 7. The *ethos* of a group is measured by its support of the government in power.

_____ 8. *Imperialism* follows the *totalitarian* approach.

_____ 9. "The Great *Schism*" ended the Papal monopoly over Christianity.

_____ 10. For *Machiavelli,* the bottom line is, Who wields the power?

III. Find the Impostor

Find and circle the one word on each line that is not related to the other three.

1. anarchy	narcissism	terrorism	nihilism
2. demagogue	instigator	pedant	agitator
3. partisan	coherent	zealot	adherent
4. schism	disjunction	fissure	quarry
5. Machiavellian	deceptive	artistic	sinister

IV. Mistaken Letters

In each of the words below, one letter is mistakenly used. Correct all the mistakes and use the discarded letters to form a word meaning "a basis for judgment."

1. ethas
2. boorgeois
3. marcial
4. gerrynander
5. mucknaker

V. Matching

Match the word in column A with its correct definition in column B by writing the letter of that definition in the space provided.

A	B
_____ 1. anarchy	a. one who appeals to the emotions
_____ 2. bourgeois	b. warlike
_____ 3. bureaucracy	c. right to vote
_____ 4. demagogue	d. disorder
_____ 5. ethos	e. one who exposes public misdeeds
_____ 6. gerrymander	f. system of beliefs
_____ 7. imperialism	g. supporter
_____ 8. Machiavellian	h. expansionism
_____ 9. martial	i. ultra-conservative
_____ 10. muckraker	j. conventional
_____ 11. partisan	k. breach
_____ 12. reactionary	l. deceitful
_____ 13. schism	m. belief in established routines
_____ 14. suffrage	n. total power of the state
_____ 15. totalitarian	o. divide into districts unfairly

Legal Language (III)

Should you be pleased to receive a *bequest?*

Is *altercation* related to alter (to change)?

Who would be likely to have an interest in *contraband?*

Would a labor leader necessarily welcome an *injunction?*

Why do consumer advocates use the phrase *caveat emptor?*

---

abnegation
abscond
affidavit
altercation
battery
bequest
cause célèbre
caveat emptor
codicil
contiguous
contraband
contumacious
disenfranchise
injunction
jurisprudence

1. **abnegation** (ab-nə-gā'-shən)—giving up of rights; self-denial.
    a. After years of *abnegation,* the timid relative decided to demand what was rightfully his.
    b. The *abnegation* of his citizenship was the painter's final move before going off to live in Tahiti.

2. **abscond** (əb-skänd', ab-)—to run away and hide in order to escape the law.
    a. When our trusted bookkeeper *absconded* with the money, I lost all faith in the human race.
    b. Because of adequate government insurance, we were not too concerned when the banker *absconded.*

3. **affidavit** (af'-ə-dā-vit)—a written statement made on oath, usually before a notary public. In Medieval Latin, the verb *affidare* meant "he has made an oath."
    a. In order to get the job, Maria needed an *affidavit* testifying to her character.
    b. When we checked into the salesman's *affidavits,* we found that they had all been forged.

4. **altercation** (ôl-tər-kā'-shən, al-)—a quarrel; an angry or heated dispute. Other synonyms are *spat* and *squabble. Wrangle* suggests a noisy dispute.
    a. When the *altercation* led to violence, the police were called.
    b. I hesitate to get involved in any *altercation* between a husband and his wife.

5. **battery** (bat'-ər-ē, bat'-rē)—a pounding; illegal beating. A person who commits *assault and battery* inflicts physical harm upon a victim; an emplacement for artillery; an array of similar things to use together, as "a battery of achievement tests"; baseball term for the pitcher and catcher; in electricity, a cell or cells that produce an electric current.
    a. Mrs. Grimes dropped the *battery* complaint when her assailant agreed to pay all the medical bills.
    b. It was hard to see how such a puny youngster could be accused of assault and *battery.*

6. **bequest** (bi-kwest')—something given by inheritance; a gift specified in a will. In Middle English, *bicewste* meant "a saying."
    a. The Academy Award winner always said that his acting talent was a *bequest* from his father.
    b. The *bequest* of $10 million allowed the university to go ahead with its plans for a new library.

7. **cause célèbre** (kōz sā-leb'r')—a celebrated law case, trial, or controversy.
   a. Let's settle this matter quietly before it becomes a *cause célèbre.*
   b. The famous Dreyfus Case was a genuine *cause célèbre* of the late nineteenth century.

8. **caveat emptor** (kā'-vē-at emp'-tôr)—let the buyer beware; one buys at his own risk. The implication is that the vendor is trying to sell inferior merchandise.
   a. The unscrupulous retailer followed the cynical policy of *caveat emptor.*
   b. None of the large department stores can afford to practice the doctrine of *caveat emptor.*

9. **codicil** (kod'-i-s'l)—an addition to a will; an appendix or supplement. The Latin word *codex* means "tree trunk" or a "wooden tablet covered with wax for writing."
   a. In an interesting *codicil,* Uncle Herbert set aside $10,000 for the care of his six cats.
   b. The outraged relatives went to court to try to get the offending *codicil* revoked.

10. **contiguous** (kən-tig'-yoo-wəs)—adjacent; touching.
    a. I wanted a wall built where Tom's property was *contiguous* to mine.
    b. Before the redesigning of the building, our offices were *contiguous.*

11. **contraband** (kän'-trə-band)—goods forbidden by law to be exported. This word was first used in the sixteenth century to refer to illicit trade with Spanish colonies.
    a. At Kennedy Airport, the customs officials make a thorough search for *contraband.*
    b. The *contraband* was discovered in the car trunk when the smugglers tried to cross the border.

12. **contumacious** (kän-too-mā'-shəs)—insubordinate; disobedient. Its original Latin meaning was "to swell up."
    a. The principal's *contumacious* behavior brought him headlines and disciplinary action.
    b. Our terrier used to be easy to manage but lately he has developed a *contumacious* personality.

13. **disenfranchise** (dis'-in-fran'-chīz)—to deprive of the rights of citizenship; to deprive of a privilege. This word is sometimes written as *disfranchise.*
    a. The punishment that the criminal fears the least is that he will be *disenfranchised.*
    b. Betty Friedan paid tribute to those feminists who had fought against the *disenfranchisement* of women.

14. **injunction** (in-junk'-shən)—a command or order; a court order stopping a person or group from carrying out a given action.
    a. Our attorney went into court to seek an *injunction* against the strikers.
    b. When I was a boy, no morning would be complete without my mother's injunction: "Brush your teeth!"

15. **jurisprudence** (joor'-is-proo-d'ns)—the science or philosophy of law; a system of laws.
    a. The law professor's religion was to worship at the shrine of *jurisprudence.*
    b. The proudest day of my father's life was when I became a Doctor of *Jurisprudence.*

EXERCISES

I. Which Word Comes to Mind?

In each of the following, read the statement, then circle the word that comes to mind.

1. When the financier could not be found, the scandal came to light

   (injunction, codicil, abscond)

2. A soldier is absent without leave

> *(contumacious, jurisprudence, disenfranchise)*

3. The plight of the whales attracts world-wide attention

> *(cause célèbre, caveat emptor, abnegation)*

4. Hidden weapons are discovered by the airport's X-ray machine

> *(contraband, contiguous, altercation)*

5. Relatives gather to hear the reading of the will

> *(battery, affidavit, bequest)*

6. Heavy artillery trained on the enemy

> *(altercation, battery, contraband)*

7. A notarized statement

> *(bequest, injunction, affidavit)*

8. Swore off smoking

> *(codicil, abnegation, disenfranchised)*

9. What the law requires

> *(jurisprudence, cause célèbre, affidavit)*

10. Smuggled goods

> *(abscond, contraband, caveat emptor)*

II. True or False?

In the space provided, indicate whether each statement is true or false.

_____ 1. When a dog displays its *contumacious* spirit, obedience training is often prescribed.
_____ 2. Merchants follow the policy of *caveat emptor* when competition is fierce.
_____ 3. Our houses are *contiguous,* and I wish we were closer together.
_____ 4. An important *codicil* is like the tail that wagged the dog.
_____ 5. Following the *altercation* on the field, both players were ejected.
_____ 6. *Contiguous* lines are necessarily parallel.
_____ 7. A *battery* is a weapon used by the Romans to shatter protection walls.
_____ 8. A thief might *abscond* to avoid prosecution.
_____ 9. An *altercation* is similar to a fracas.
_____ 10. A *cause célèbre* is a reason for a celebration.

III. Fill in the Blank

Insert one of the new words in the proper space in each sentence below.

1. The _____ specified that the heir marry within the faith.

2. In discovering that the watch he had bought from the street vendor had no mechanism, Fred learned the significance of _____ .

3. Some people live by whim and fancy, others by a rigorous _____ .

4. The charlatan's modus operandi was simple: ingratiate yourself with a rich widow, marry her, then _____ with the money.

5. To stop the flow of microchip technology out of the country, the government declared them _____ .

6. The _____ for the crucial game was changed at the last minute.

7. Ted wished he had remembered the warning, _____ , when he was offered the 80 percent discount for the "diamond" ring that turned out to be fake.

8. Pfc. Barton lost his one stripe when his _____ behavior was discovered.

9. The defense lawyer argued it was wrong to _____ his client because he had not renounced his former citizenship.

10. The judge threatened to issue a(n) _____ if the proposed strike plans were not withdrawn.

IV. What's the Antonym?

Which of the new words is most nearly *opposite* in meaning to the one provided?

1. compliant _____
2. reconciliation _____
3. permit _____
4. self-indulgence _____
5. empower _____
6. distant _____
7. legal trade _____
8. an insignificant case _____
9. money or property earned by one's labor _____
10. main section of a will _____

V. Matching

Match the word in column A with its correct definition in column B by writing the letter of that definition in the space provided.

<table>
<tr><td colspan="2" align="center">*A*</td><td colspan="2">*B*</td></tr>
<tr><td>_____</td><td>1. abnegation</td><td>a.</td><td>statement written under oath</td></tr>
<tr><td>_____</td><td>2. abscond</td><td>b.</td><td>a quarrel</td></tr>
<tr><td>_____</td><td>3. affidavit</td><td>c.</td><td>illegal beating</td></tr>
<tr><td>_____</td><td>4. altercation</td><td>d.</td><td>touching</td></tr>
<tr><td>_____</td><td>5. battery</td><td>e.</td><td>deprive of a privilege</td></tr>
<tr><td>_____</td><td>6. bequest</td><td>f.</td><td>famous law case</td></tr>
<tr><td>_____</td><td>7. cause célèbre</td><td>g.</td><td>self-denial</td></tr>
<tr><td>_____</td><td>8. caveat emptor</td><td>h.</td><td>system of laws</td></tr>
<tr><td>_____</td><td>9. codicil</td><td>i.</td><td>supplement</td></tr>
<tr><td>_____</td><td>10. contiguous</td><td>j.</td><td>an order</td></tr>
<tr><td>_____</td><td>11. contraband</td><td>k.</td><td>let the buyer beware</td></tr>
<tr><td>_____</td><td>12. contumacious</td><td>l.</td><td>gift specified in a will or testament</td></tr>
<tr><td>_____</td><td>13. disenfranchise</td><td>m.</td><td>disobedient</td></tr>
<tr><td>_____</td><td>14. injunction</td><td>n.</td><td>forbidden merchandise</td></tr>
<tr><td>_____</td><td>15. jurisprudence</td><td>o.</td><td>run away and hide</td></tr>
</table>

Philosophy and Logic

Does the *dogma* of a church have any relationship to its canons?

Why would a *utilitarian* reject "art for art's sake"?

Is a *syllogism* a foolish belief or a form of reasoning?

What is the ultimate goal of the *theosophists?*

What fallacy do the underprivileged see in *hedonism?*

---

aphorism
candor
credo
dogma
empirical
epistemology
fallacy
hedonism
pragmatism
predestination
syllogism
teleology
tenet
theosophy
utilitarian

1. **aphorism** (af'-ə-riz'm)—a brief statement of a principle; a tersely phrased statement of a truth or opinion.
   a. *Aphorisms,* like proverbs, may sometimes seem contradictory, but the wise person knows what counsel a particular situation calls for.
   b. Speeches that string together a list of *aphorisms* betray a lack of creativity.

2. **candor** (kan'-dər)—sincerity. *frankness*
   a. We found Sal's *candor* to be refreshing.
   b. Don's supposed *candor* was not appreciated by everyone.

3. **credo** (krē'-dō)—belief.
   a. The merchant's *credo* was to do unto others before they can do to you.
   b. A sound mind in a sound body is the Boy Scouts' *credo.*

4. **dogma** (dôg'-mə, däg'-)—a system of principles or tenets as of a church; prescribed doctrine; an established opinion or belief. *Dogmas,* derived from the Greek *dokein,* "to seem good," are sometimes put forth without adequate grounds and arrogantly or vehemently proclaimed.
   a. Despite efforts at detente, communist *dogma* assumes the ultimate eradication of capitalism.
   b. Modern pedagogy is based on the *dogma* that every child is educable.

5. **empirical** (em-pir'-i-k'l)—guided by practical experience and not theoretical.
   a. Much medical lore has had an *empirical* origin—centuries of trial-and-error groping after remedies.
   b. It is safer to be *empirical* and practical in dealing with reality.

6. **epistemology** (i-pis-tə-möl'-ə-jē)—the division of philosophy that investigates the nature, origin, methods, and limits of human knowledge.
   a. According to *epistemology,* it is impossible to transcend the confines of one's own civilization.
   b. *Epistemology* differs from ontology in that the former is concerned with knowledge, the latter with being.

7. **fallacy** (fal'-ə-sē)—an idea or opinion founded on mistaken logic or perception. There are several types of logical *fallacies:* the fallacy of accident, of composition, of division, of the antecedent, and of the consequence.
   a. Among some ardent admirers of Shakespeare, the *fallacy* exists that the bard was superhuman.
   b. Magellan and other explorers disproved the popular *fallacy* that the world is flat.

socism

8. **hedonism** (hēd'-'n-iz'm)—pursuit of or devotion to pleasure; the ethical doctrine that what is pleasant or has pleasant consequences is intrinsically good. In psychology, *hedonism* refers to the doctrine that behavior is motivated by the desire for pleasure or the avoidance of pain.
   a. The later Roman emperors were notorious for their *hedonism.*
   b. In the way she chose and cast off friends, Margaret was a perfect example of selfish *hedonism.*

9. **pragmatism** (prag'-mə-tiz'm)—the theory, developed by Charles S. Peirce and William James, that the meaning of a proposition or course of action lies in its observable consequences, and that the sum of these consequences constitutes its meaning; a method or tendency in the conduct of political affairs characterized by the rejection of theory and precedent, and by the use of practical means and expedients. A *pragmatic* person is practical and active rather than contemplative. He may also tend to be meddlesome and officious.
   a. *Pragmatism* takes the position that whatever works is right.
   b. Think tanks are a strange combination of *pragmatism* and idealism, not trying on the one hand to extract sunbeams from cucumbers, nor on the other hand to avoid pure speculation.

10. **predestination** (prē-des-tə-nā'-shən)—the doctrine that God has foreordained whatever comes to pass, especially the salvation or damnation of individual souls.
    a. Theologians have long struggled with the apparent contradiction between *predestination* and man's freedom of will.
    b. It is easy to attribute one's lack of ambition or success to some act of *predestination,* but there are many examples to prove to us that we are the "masters of our fate."

11. **syllogism** (sil'-ə-jiz'm)—in logic, a form of deductive reasoning consisting of a major premise (all men are foolish), a minor premise (Smith is a man), and a conclusion (therefore, Smith is foolish); a subtle or specious piece of reasoning. Opposed to *syllogistic* reasoning is inductive reasoning, known as the scientific method, which reasons from a part to the whole, from the particular to the general, or from the individual to the universal.
    a. A *syllogism* based on a false premise will of course lead to a mistaken conclusion.
    b. Francis Bacon, known as the father of the scientific method, rejected *syllogisms* in favor of the procedure of gathering sufficient facts through experiment before formulating a general principle by which to test further data.

12. **teleology** (tel-ē-äl'-ə-jē)—the doctrine that final causes exist; design, purpose, or utility as an explanation of any natural phenomenon. In philosophy, *teleology* looks upon natural processes as determined by the design of a divine Providence rather than as purely mechanical determinism.
    a. Darwinism and *teleology* both take into account design and utility in natural development but differ on whether this design is a temporal accident or an act of God.
    b. In ethics, *teleology* evaluates human conduct in relation to the end it serves; hence, behavior that has a beneficial purpose would be considered good.

13. **tenet** (ten'-it)—an opinion or doctrine held to be true.
    a. Observation and deduction are the two great *tenets* of the physical sciences.
    b. Political *tenets* are easily abandoned when the mood of the people changes.

14. **theosophy** (thē-äs'-ə-fē)—a system of philosophy or religion that proposes to establish direct, mystical contact with divine principles through contemplation or revelation. The doctrines of the modern Theosophical Societies incorporate elements of Buddhism and Brahmanism.
    a. As a believer in *theosophy,* the mahatma claimed superior wisdom and insight into the mastery of nature.
    b. Despite the U.N. and similar world-unifying attempts, we are far from attaining universal brotherhood, which is the goal of *theosophy.*

15. **utilitarian** (yoo-til-ə-ter'-ē-ən)—stressing the value of practical over aesthetic values. The theory of *utilitarianism,* proposed by Jeremy Bentham and John Stewart Mill, held that all moral, social, or political action should be directed toward achieving the greatest good for the greatest number of people.
    a. The original *utilitarians* believed that each individual was the best judge of his own welfare.
    b. Love of truth for its own sake is becoming rare in this hasty, *utilitarian* age.

EXERCISES

I. Which Word Comes to Mind?

In each of the following, read the statement, then circle the word that comes to mind.

1. How do we know what we know?

    (dogma, epistemology, pragmatism)

2. If *A* is *B* and *B* is *C,* then *A* is *C*

    (fallacy, credo, syllogism)

3. Buddy placed his cards on the table.

    (tenet, candor, teleology)

4. Don't do it; it might hurt

    (hedonism, aphorism, theosophy)

5. Daniel and Pearl forever

    (empirical, utilitarian, predestination)

6. Use it or lose it

    (utilitarian, aphorism, fallacy)

7. The quintessential principle that brooks no argument

    (theosophy, teleology, dogma)

8. Stated belief

    (theosophy, empirical, credo)

9. Respect for the old tried and true ways

    (candor, tenet, pragmatism)

10. Logic with a twist

    (teleology, syllogism, aphorism)

II. True or False?

In the space provided, indicate whether each statement is true or false.

_____ 1. A *pragmatist* and an *empiricist* are both more concerned with results than theories.

_____ 2. *A syllogism is a form of deductive reasoning.*

_____ 3. The explanation for the lion's mane, the elephant's trunk, the leopard's spots falls in the province of *teleology.*

_____ 4. A *tenet* is one of the ten basic principles of faith.

_____ 5. *Aphorism* is the belief that natural phenomena can be understood only by a study of original causes.

_____ 6. *Epistemology* is the science of letter writing.

_____ 7. The *empirical* approach relies on observation and experience to determine truth.

_____ 8. An assumption based on erroneous premises will inevitably be a *fallacy.*

_____ 9. *Theosophists* generally spend a great deal of time in contemplation.

_____ 10. *Tenets* are those who "dwell in the house of the Lord."

III. Find the Impostor

Find and circle the one word on each line that is not related to the other three.

1. empirical	teleology	utilitarian	predestination
2. document	dogma	tenet	doctrine
3. pragmatic	experiential	romantic	empirical
4. laconic	aphoristic	pointed	conjectural
5. hedonism	affliction	malaise	paroxysm

IV. Cryptogram

The first letters of each of the "words," below, when arranged in the proper order, spell out a vocabulary word from this lesson. The same is true for the second, third, and fourth letters. Find the four words. Hint: The initial letters of the words are in ETTS.

MHEY	LYYM	IOEL
RSOO	AHGS	IOLG
CPOI	ETTS	PELL

_____

_____

_____

_____

V. Matching

Match the word in column A with its correct definition in column B by writing the letter of that definition in the space provided.

	A		B
____	1. aphorism	a.	seek pleasure, avoid pain
____	2. candor	b.	fate
____	3. credo	c.	giving greatest happiness for most people
____	4. dogma	d.	brief statement of principle
____	5. empirical	e.	deductive reasoning
____	6. epistemology	f.	false notion
____	7. fallacy	g.	study associated with mysticism
____	8. hedonism	h.	based on observation
____	9. pragmatism	i.	belief in final causes
____	10. predestination	j.	sincerity
____	11. syllogism	k.	platform
____	12. teleology	l.	prescribed doctrine
____	13. tenet	m.	theory that results, not procedure, give meaning
____	14. theosophy	n.	belief
____	15. utilitarian	o.	study of the nature of knowledge

Beliefs and Religion

Is a *mantra* a hymn, a sacred object, or a clothing worm?

What do an *apostate,* an *infidel,* and a *blasphemer* have in common?

Is *apotheosis* a theory, a religious chant, or a glorification?

How does an *agnostic* differ from an atheist?

Does *theodicy* deal with a pilgrimage, the existence of evil, or the revelations in the Bible?

---

agnostic
apocalyptic
apocryphal
apostate
apotheosis
benediction
blasphemy
deist
infidel
mantra
ornithology
pantheism
raison d'être
sacrilegious
theodicy

1. **agnostic** (ag-näs'-tik)—a thinker who disclaims any knowledge of God. The agnostic does not deny God but denies the possibility of knowing Him.
    a. The *agnostic* position is midway between the atheist and the believer.
    b. The impassioned speaker claimed that faith, reason, and experience had shattered his *agnostic* beliefs.

2. **apocalyptic** (ə-päk-ə-lip'-tik)—pertaining to a revelation; foretelling imminent disaster and total destruction. *Apocalypse* refers to the last books of the New Testament.
    a. During the Cold War era, the two superpowers agreed to limitations on nuclear weaponry in order to avoid the *apocalyptic* horrors of a nuclear war.
    b. Books with an *apocalyptic* view of life find many readers in an age of violence.

3. **apocryphal** (ə-päk'-rə-f'l)—of questionable authority or authenticity; false or counterfeit. The *Apocrypha* includes the 14 books of the Septuagint found in the Vulgate but considered uncanonical by the Protestants because they are not part of the Hebrew Scriptures.
    a. The bookseller was careful to point out which works were regarded as authentic and which were *apocryphal.*
    b. *The Wisdom of Ben Sira,* although considered *apocryphal,* should be studied for its wisdom and good counsel.

4. **apostate** (ə-päs'-tāt)—one who forsakes his faith or principles.
    a. The Church excommunicated all *apostates* who professed the radically new doctrine.
    b. O'Connor's statement of support for the Republican nominee was taken to mean that he had become an *apostate* from his own party.

5. **apotheosis** (ə-päth-ē-ō'-sis)—deification; an exalted or glorified ideal.
    a. Elvis Presley was considered the *apotheosis* of the age of Rock and Roll.
    b. In their bestial and brutal policies, the Nazis reached the *apotheosis* of barbarism.

6. **benediction** (ben-ə-dik'-shən)—a blessing; an invocation of divine blessing, usually at the end of a religious service. A newly married man is called a *benedict,* suggesting that marriage brings to a bachelor many blessings.
    a. The gentle rain brought its *benediction* to the parched fields.
    b. His parents' *benediction* ringing in his ears, the young student departed for his first year in college.

7. **blasphemy** (blas'-fə-mē)—any irreverent or impious act or utterance.
   a. The outraged judge branded the witness's language an act of *blasphemy.*
   b. It is not *blasphemy* to question the motives of high officials.

8. **deist** (dē'-ist)—believer in the existence of God as the creator of the universe who after setting it in motion abandoned it, assumed no control over life, exerted no influence on natural phenomena, and gave no supernatural revelation. *Deism* is a natural religion based on human reason and morality.
   a. The *deist* views the world much like a giant clock that God wound up and now allows to run by itself.
   b. *Deistic* principles impose a sense of morality on the human race, but stop short of prescribing rituals and ceremonies.

9. **infidel** (in'-fə-d'l)—a person who does not believe in any religion; among Christians or Muslims, one who does not accept their particular beliefs. The word *infidelity* denotes unfaithfulness to moral or marital obligations.
   a. Those deemed *infidels* by the Inquisition were persecuted and often burned at the stake.
   b. In an atmosphere of tolerance and freedom from bigotry, the so-called *infidel* can still retain a position of dignity.

10. **mantra** (man'-trə)—a mystical formula of invocation or incantation in Hinduism and Buddhism. The word comes from *mens,* the Latin word meaning "mind," and the ancient Sanskrit word for "sacred counsel" or "formula."
    a. Upon entering the temple grounds, we heard the strange rhythms of the *mantra* coming from the inner chambers.
    b. His face suffused with serenity, the priest intoned the *mantra* as the worshippers listened respectfully.

11. **ornithology** (ôr-nə–thol'-ə-je)—the study of birds.
    a. The *ornithology* expert lectured on the history of the bald eagle.
    b. Josh raised pigeons as a young man, and his son now plans to major in *ornithology.*

12. **pantheism** (pan'-thē-iz'm)—the doctrine that the universe, conceived of as a whole, is God.
    a. According to *pantheism,* there is no God but the combined forces and laws that are manifested in the existing universe.
    b. Since *pantheism* tends to depersonalize God, identifying the Deity instead with nature, it could accommodate itself to and tolerate the worship of all gods at certain periods in the Roman Empire.

13. **raison d'être** (rē-zon' detr)—reason for existence.
    a. His *raison d'être* for the investment was pure greed.
    b. I'll need more of a *raison d'être* before I make my decision.

14. **sacrilegious** (sak-rə-li'-jəs)—disrespectful or irreverent toward anything regarded as sacred. The term is derived from the Latin *sacrilegium,* "one who steals sacred things," which of course is one form of *sacrilege.*
    a. The *sacrilegious* thieves stole the $500 that had been collected for charity.
    b. The change from Latin to the vernacular in church services as well as the relaxation of certain rules for the clergy has been regarded as *sacrilegious* by some traditionalists.

15. **theodicy** (thē-äd'-ə-sē)—a vindication of divine justice in the face of the existence of evil. *Theodicee* was the title of a work by Leibnitz in 1710. The word combines the Greek roots for "god" and "judgment."
    a. One of the arguments advanced for *theodicy* is that humans have only a limited view of life, whereas God sees everything.
    b. Theologians and philosophers, grappling with the *theodician* problem of the existence of evil in a world created by a Perfect Being, have asserted that good would not be recognizable without evil.

EXERCISES

I. Which Word Comes to Mind?

In each of the following, read the statement, then circle the word that comes to mind.

1. In the Middle Ages this would have brought the harshest punishment

    (theodicy, blasphemy, apocryphal)

2. God and nature are synonymous

    (benediction, pantheism, apocalyptic)

3. This person could be a Christian, Muslim, or Jew, depending on what you are

    (infidel, mantra, apotheosis)

4. An attempt to explain why God permitted the rise of Hitlerism

    (theodicy, apostate, sacrilegious)

5. Belief in the existence of God

    (agnostic, infidel, deist)

6. The absolute best of its kind

    (apotheosis, sacrilegious, apocryphal)

7. Doomsday is coming

    (blasphemy, apocalyptic, mantra)

8. The universe is God

    (agnostic, pantheist, apotheosis)

9. A blessing

    (mantra, benediction, blasphemy)

10. An unauthorized version

    (sacrilegious, apocryphal, blasphemy)

II. True or False?

In the space provided, indicate whether each statement is true or false.

_____ 1. The *apocryphal* writings have been universally accepted as part of the Bible.

_____ 2. An *apostate* is one who has changed his religious beliefs.

_____ 3. *Pantheists* emphasize the importance of religious services.

_____ 4. The *sacrilegious* person holds a place of honor in the community of believers.

_____ 5. The *apocalyptic* view is definitely pessimistic.

_____ 6. The *agnostic* is inclined to say, "Thank God for my blessings."

_____ 7. The *apostate* finds solace in his mantra.

_____ 8. *Ornithology* is for the birds.

_____ 9. *Sacrilegious* and *blasphemous* behavior is typical of an apostate.

_____ 10. *Mantras* are part of the worship in Buddhism and Hinduism.

III. Synonyms or Antonyms

Find and circle the two words on each line that are either synonyms or antonyms.

1. apostate	apocryphal	heretic	biblical
2. blasphemous	apotheosis	degradation	occult
3. infidel	mantra	religion	invocation
4. canonical	apocryphal	apocalyptic	orthodox
5. laity	benediction	denominational	anathema

IV. Matching

Match the word in column A with its correct definition in column B by writing the letter of that definition in the space provided.

A	B
_____ 1. agnostic	a. profanity
_____ 2. apocalyptic	b. prophetic
_____ 3. apocryphal	c. one who doesn't know God
_____ 4. apostate	d. atheist
_____ 5. apotheosis	e. one who forsakes his faith
_____ 6. benediction	f. mystical incantation
_____ 7. blasphemy	g. belief that God is the universe
_____ 8. deist	h. questionable or fictitious
_____ 9. infidel	i. blessing
_____ 10. mantra	j. vindication of God
_____ 11. ornithology	k. deification
_____ 12. pantheism	l. purpose of existence
_____ 13. raison d'être	m. one who believes God has a hands-off policy toward life
_____ 14. sacrilegious	n. impious
_____ 15. theodicy	o. the study of birds

Review

**Unit IV
(Lessons 31–40)**

A. The Out-of-Place Word

In each of the following groups, find and circle the one vocabulary word that is out of place. You should be able to explain what the other three words have in common.

1. mellifluous, beguile, safari, assuage
2. palatable, renascent, cuisine, regale
3. apotheosis, infidel, blasphemy, sacrilegious
4. injunction, countermand, mantra, gainsay
5. deist, pantheism, theosophy, pragmatism
6. benediction, apostate, anarchist, pharisaical
7. safari, wanderlust, trek, hegira
8. fallacy, malapropism, apostate, simile
9. guffaw, paradigm, onomatopoeia, guttural
10. censure, muckraker, harangue, aspersion

B. Rearranging Words

Rearrange the following groups of words using the first letter of each word to spell out one of the words in this unit.

1. fallacy, recession, abnegation, abscond, imperialism, semantics

   _____

2. oligarchy, deist, gastronomic, anarchist, muckraker

   _____

3. squib, insouciance, cause célèbre, metaphor, subsistence, hedonism

   _____

4. risible, theosophy, suffrage, anarchist, predestination, euphoria

   _____

5. epistemology, landmark, subversion, mellifluous, infidel, injunction

   _____

C. Making the Right Connection

In each of the following, which word best describes the person or thing named? Circle the correct answer.

1. A language expert

   (mantra, polyglot, oxymoron, demagogue)

2. Light entertainment

   (euphoria, peonage, divertissement, portmanteau)

3. A government representative

   (plenipotentiary, votary, schism, partisan)

4. Hotel accommodations

   (apostate, concierge, tenet, bureaucracy)

5. A food expert

   (codicil, teleology, gourmand, safari)

6. Property boundaries

   (caveat emptor, dalliance, landmark, condiment)

7. A way to quench your thirst

   (squib, panegyric, tandem, viands)

8. Someone who would appreciate your hospitality

   (argot, wayfarer, cuisine, surrogate)

9. Someone to discredit your opponent

   (muckraker, gobbledegook, refection, bourgeois)

10. A substitute

    (proxy, threnody, oligarchy, jargon)

D. Making Pairs

From the group below, find the pairs of words that have something in common and record them in the spaces provided. You should be able to find nine such pairs. List them numerically using the same number for each pair.

simile _____	waggish _____	codicil _____	repast _____
tenet _____	utilitarian_____	canon _____	pragmatism __
refection _____	surrogate _____	badinage_____	jargon _____
oligarchy _____	bequest _____	metaphor _____	argot _____
proxy _____	totalitarian _____		

E. Cliché Time

Which of the words from this unit fit into the following familiar expressions? Choose the correct word from the choices given and record it in the space provided.

1. Don't cast any _____

   (semantics, aspersions, viands, braggadocio)

2. In the _____ of the underworld

   (censure, bathos, jargon, cuisine)

3. To order _____

   (harangue, squib, dalliance, a la carte)

4. A _____ delight

   (surrogate, culinary, martial, contiguous)

5. The basic _____ of his argument

   (subsistence, fallacy, affidavit, hustings)

6. The _____ seized by the customs inspector

   (contraband, paradigm, bathos, mantra)

7. Fed up with government _____

   (peonage, subversion, bureaucracy, votary)

8. Vote by _____

   (tandem, ethos, proxy, bequest)

9. With _____ guile

   (apocryphal, piquant, apocalyptic, Machiavellian)

10. To _____ her grief

    (assuage, beguile, censure, countermand)

Vocabulary Roundup

We learn vocabulary words in many different ways. Although memorizing a word's meanings is a traditional technique, we gain real ownership when we are able to use the words intelligently in all forms of communication. That is why this book has offered you a host of sample sentences as models. Below you will find a series of interesting articles worth discussing in class or with friends. The articles contain words in context—words that you should be familiar with at this point.

We hope you enjoy the material in this summary section and profit from the way the words in bold print are used.

Late Again

A friend of mine lived across the street from her elementary school, yet she was frequently late. I often tell my **dilatory** wife that the 8 P.M. show will start at 7:30 just to make sure that she'll be ready in time. The famous actress Marilyn Monroe was **untrammeled** about her lateness to the set, causing the film company executives to tear their hair out, even the **glabrous** ones.

According to psychiatrists, such habitual lateness is not an accident. Some blame it on boredom, or resentment of authority, or insecurity because of low achievement. The tardy individuals are often quite **ingenious** in accounting for their inability to show up on time or to produce material on the date it was promised. Some are **contrite**, whereas others are **flippant** about it, wondering why the rest of society is so uptight about a little lateness.

A university professor has been studying the **pathology** of habitual lateness and the failure to meet deadlines. In the process he has collected some juicy alibis, including the **antediluvian** chestnut "My dog ate my homework." Here are some of the classic explanations he found:

- "Whenever we're on time, the curtain is sure to be delayed."
- "My mother threw my alarm clock at my stepfather and broke it."
- "We wallpapered the foyer and I couldn't find the front door."
- "Someone slipped invisible ink into my pen, and the homework disappeared."
- "A snowflake got into my watch."

Although many of the culprits are addicted to their tardiness, some **miscreants** may wish to reform. The experts suggest the following:

- Realize that those you love may be hurt by your continual lateness.
- As a New Year's resolution, decide to change your ways and avoid the **censure** of your friends.
- Keep an account of your daily activities; review it to see where you could save time.
- Prioritize.
- Set your watch ahead so that you might "fool" yourself into being on time.

For personal reasons, however, you may not want to be on time. In that connection, note the **waggish** quotation from E. V. Lucas's *365 Days and One More*: "I have noticed that the people who are late are often so much jollier than the people who have to wait for them."

Surveillance for Safety

"Smile, you're on digital camera!"

In the schools of Biloxi, Mississippi, that sentence has special relevance because there are **omniscient** cameras in every classroom and hallway, enabling principals and other administrators to keep an eye on what's happening throughout the building.

The horror stories of violence in U.S. schools led Biloxi educators to install the new surveillance system in all of its 500 classrooms, stairwells, and cafeterias. The huge sums of money required for the innovation came from the revenues of the gambling casinos, a fixture in the Gulf Coast community.

"It's like a truth serum," Principal Laurie Petrie said. "When we have an **altercation** in class between a couple of **bellicose** pupils—a he-said, she-said situation, 9 times out of 10 all we have to do is ask the children if they want us to go back and look at the camera, and they fess up."

A *New York Times* article on school safety told the Biloxi story while referring to the hundreds of schools across the country where similar surveillance technology is making its appearance.

Some civil libertarians are up in arms over the Biloxi experiment and are **chary** about the new technology, claiming there is no **empirical** evidence to support the value of the investment. Paul Abramson, a school design consultant, fired off a **salvo**: "Kids are kids. What are we telling them when we put them under surveillance?"

And a lawyer for the Electric Frontier Foundation labeled Biloxi's cameras "a Kafka-esque civil liberties nightmare," referring to the measure as **draconian** and unnecessary.

Is the camera's presence an "Orwellian intrusion on the sanctity of the classroom," or is it helping to protect youngsters, improve discipline, and raise test scores as Biloxi administrators claim? One of the teachers was worried that the surveillance would ruin the **esprit de corps** that now exists between the teachers and the administration. "I know the **jargon**," he sniffed. "They say it's for wholesome purposes such as security, but I figure it's just another **craven** plot by the principal to keep tabs on us."

Controversial Valedictorian

In 2003, people in the United States were edgy about the aftermath of the war to remove the dictator Saddam Hussein from power in Iraq. The daily reports about American soldiers being slain by guerrillas inflamed the public to think unkind thoughts about that part of the world. Some Muslims who were U.S. citizens were the objects of persecution although, in fact, they were completely loyal and thoroughly opposed to terrorism.

The top seniors at a Colorado high school had been invited to compete for the honor of delivering the valedictory address at their commencement exercises. The winner was Minoo Bahadani, an eighteen-year-old who had grown up in Baghdad and had come to Colorado several years earlier. Minoo, living with her uncle, was a straight-A student whose Muslim parents remained in Iraq, where her father was a judge. She covered her head with the traditional scarf that Muslim women wear, but that was not **palatable** for some of her classmates, or for many faculty members.

The school's rules for selecting a valedictorian were quite clear: the senior with the highest academic average would, **ipso facto**, be the winner who would address the audience at graduation time. However, Jack Leahy, a **mercurial** math teacher whose nephew had been killed in Iraq, took an **acidulous** view of the situation. He organized an **appellate** faculty committee that came up with an **ad hoc codicil** that a valedictorian must have spent at least three years in the high school. That eliminated Minoo who had entered the school only two years earlier.

Although some members of the community were pleased with that legalism, others were outraged. "Minoo won fair and square," one student said. "She's the top kid in our class, and we shouldn't hold her religion or place of birth against her."

The **demure** Minoo was gracious, however. "A rule is a rule," she said, "and I'm happy to accept it." But Ellen Wermuth, Minoo's English teacher, was angry and ashamed of what she viewed to be a **pusillanimous** decision. In a **harangue** against her fellow educators, she threatened to transfer if Minoo were bypassed.

What is your opinion of the case?

Conquering Childbed Fever

A great puzzle for a nineteenth-century Hungarian-born doctor, Ignaz Philipp Semmelweis, was that the mortality rate for pregnant women at the Hospital of the University of Vienna was 25 percent. How was it possible, he wondered, that one out of four mothers died at the modern facility, whereas the survival rate for those who gave birth in the street or in rural homes unattended by trained **gynecologists** was much higher. In fact, it had reached the point in the Austrian capital where a **generation** of women preferred to deliver their babies anywhere but in the hospital because of the incidence of childhood or **puerperal** fever. This fever was a cruel disease that started with chills, an **abscess**, an escalating fever, and abdominal swelling. Once these symptoms appeared, death was sure to follow. Semmelweis was depressed, but he vowed to find the answer.

The death of one of his colleagues led Semmelweis to the answer. That doctor had cut his finger while performing an autopsy, and the infection resulted in a horrible death that was labeled "cadaveric poisoning." The postmortem showed that the dead man had suffered from meningitis, phlebitis, and lymphangitis—the same killers of Vienna's expectant mothers. Semmelweis focused on the **etiology** of the disease, tracing the typical obstetrician's day: mornings were spent in the dissecting room, followed by tours of the maternity wards. However, doctors rarely washed their hands after the autopsies.

After Semmelweis ordered maternity ward doctors and their students to scrub their hands in a chlorine antiseptic solution, the spectre of childbed fever disappeared. Surprisingly, many **churlish** doctors representing the medical **hierarchy** resented Semmelweis's targeting of them as the **perpetrators** of childbed fever, and they cast **aspersions** on his theory. Semmelweis was shaken by their criticism, but he refused to be an **apostate**, standing by his findings even though his career was threatened.

There are many questions that remain unanswered about Semmelweis's ironic death in 1865. Confined to an asylum for the insane, he performed as an assistant at an operation, infecting himself and dying of blood poisoning. But recent research pointed to Alzheimer's disease, syphilis, and a brutal case of assault and **battery** at the hands of asylum guards.

Dr. Sherwin Nuland told of Semmelweis's ordeal in *The Doctor's Plague*, describing him as the **archetype** of the ideal physician who felt a great obligation to help suffering people.

"I Only Regret…"

One of the most familiar quotations in the **martial** annals of American history is Nathan Hale's "I only regret that I have but one life to lose for my country."

As most students know, Captain Hale was **incarcerated** by the British and then hanged in 1776 after admitting to serving as a spy. Now, a manuscript donated to the Library of Congress appears to solve the mystery of Hale's capture and execution more than two hundred years ago. The document, written by Consider Tiffany, a Connecticut resident and British sympathizer, tells of how Hale was trapped by a British officer, Major Robert Rogers.

Hale, a Connecticut schoolteacher, was a member of George Washington's Colonial Army who volunteered to go behind the enemy's lines to gain information about British strength and military plans. But he would have flunked as a C.I.A. agent in that **epoch** because the **loquacious** Hale **hobnobbed** with a total stranger, Major Rogers, and blabbed about his mission.

Wearing civilian clothes and being less than **circumspect**, Hale attracted Rogers's attention and all but announced his purpose as a Mata Hari precursor. The British officer, who pretended to be a spy himself, subsequently invited Hale to a **conclave** at his quarters where, disregarding protocol, Hale openly engaged in the kind of subversive talk whose **denouement** was his arrest.

Furthermore, no self-respecting spy would have incriminating papers in his possession, but Hale was a neophyte at the game, and it cost him his life. In an article in the Library of Congress's *Information Bulletin*, James Hutson questioned Hale's inexperience: "How could anyone on a secret mission be so stupid, so naïve, or so credulous to be taken in by a perfect stranger and then to disclose the object of his mission to several more perfect strangers?"

Although Nathan Hale's performance as an undercover agent was a total failure, his **landmark panegyric** of pride in the new country remains a glorious tribute to his beloved America.

The Italian Navigator

"The Italian Navigator has reached the New World."
"And how did he find the natives?"
"Very friendly."

The seemingly innocent telephone conversation between two university professors in December 1942 was in code because of wartime secrecy. Nevertheless, the **mot juste** was one of the most famous messages in modern history, because its meaning was that the **debonair** Italian scientist Enrico Fermi and his team of physicists had achieved a controlled chain reaction. Its significance was that the Atomic Age with all its promise and potential terror was an actuality.

At that time there was a furious transatlantic race between German and American scientists to manufacture an atom bomb. Had the Nazis beaten us to its development, the entire history of the twentieth century would have been affected. But the 1938 Nobel Prize winner, Enrico Fermi of Rome, had settled in the United States and gained President Franklin Roosevelt's **benediction** to undertake an all-out effort in atomic energy research. Fermi understood the dual threats of fascist and Nazi **demagogues**, and he applied his genius to winning the global competition to build the ultimate weapon.

Fermi's project took shape on an abandoned squash court under the stands of Stagg Field, the University of Chicago's stadium. When the brave volunteer, who could have been **immolated**, **nonchalantly** removed a cadmium rod (the safety catch) from an aperture in the graphite bricks and uranium chunks that constituted the **amorphous** "pile," the chain reaction took place just as Fermi had **augured**. The **accolades** from the forty-two witnesses were spontaneous. One of Fermi's assistants (anticipating a Hiroshima?) wrote, "We knew that with the advent of the chain reaction the world would never be the same again."

The Italian Navigator had sailed a perilous voyage, but he landed safely, and the natives were friendly indeed.

Murder Most Foul

Lord Dunsany, a nineteenth-century Irish dramatist and writer, was a World War I hero, winning medals for bravery in combat, but readers cherish his memory for his excellence as a storyteller.

His chilling tale "Two Bottles of Relish" appears in dozens of collections of short stories, and is the work of a master of the art form. It is narrated by Smithers, a traveling salesman whose product, Num-numo, was a popular relish for meat dishes. In Smithers's own words, "It isn't the story you'd expect from a small man like me, yet there's nobody else to tell it. Those that know anything of it besides me are all for hushing it up."

Smithers was sharing a London flat with a brilliant man named Linley. Both men had become interested in a notorious mystery in a nearby **bucolic** town—the disappearance of a beautiful blonde named Nancy Elth. Scotland Yard police had made a **Herculean** effort to solve what they believed to be a murder. They suspected that her boyfriend, Seeger, had something to do with it, but they were unable to find a **cadaver** or crack the case.

One of the reasons Seeger had aroused the suspicions of his neighbors was that he was a dedicated vegetarian at a time when few Englishmen were attracted to that kind of **cuisine**. Furthermore, Nancy's bank account had been emptied, and Seeger was suddenly flush with money.

With matters at an **impasse**, Smithers read a police report that mentioned Seeger's purchase of a couple of bottles of Num-numo. He told that to the clever Linley, who was also intrigued by the information that Seeger had cut down twelve trees in his garden just after Nancy had disappeared. A **polygraph** might have helped the police, but it hadn't been invented at that time.

The story turned on Seeger's **deposition** that he had purchased two bottles of Num-numo, the relish that was good on meat but not on salads or vegetables. Linley put two and two together, using that bit of **minutiae**, and solved the crime for the police, who were stymied by the **conundrum** of why Seeger expended energy in cutting down those trees.

Lord Dunsany ends the horror story with Linley's **pièce de résistance** explanation: "Solely in order to get an appetite."

Shades of Hannibal Lecter!

Poems to Ponder

Many adults who remember lines of poetry they read in high school can usually recall "Miniver Cheevy, born too late, / Scratched his head and kept on thinking; / Miniver coughed, and called it fate, / And kept on drinking." The famous poem is by Edwin Arlington Robinson, and it reminds us of all the "losers" we have known who developed comfortable alibis to explain their failures.

A better-known Robinson poem, and one that cultivates a mystery, is "Richard Cory," the wealthy **grandee** who was the envy of all the **bourgeois** townspeople but "Went home and put a bullet through his head." Countless English classes have mulled over the **inscrutable** Cory's **coup de grâce** decision to commit suicide, seeking to understand the **dichotomy** of why anyone who had everything to live for would decide to take his own life.

Some suggest that Cory may have had an incurable cancer or an apocalyptic view of the world, was making atonement for some secret sin, or was driven by some bête noire; others offer embezzlement and impending arrest or unrequited love as reasons for the suicide. Even boredom, a lack of challenges, and not having any new worlds to conquer are all possibilities for students to ponder.

Why, we ask, didn't Robinson give us the answer? Is this another "Lady or the Tiger" teaser? Since poets rarely explain anything, it's up to the reader to imagine the secrets of Mr. Cory, who "glittered when he walked."

Are there clues in the poem that might lead us to understand the aberrant decision of the man who was "richer than a king"? Not really. But we are intrigued by the hopelessness of Richard Cory's fate, wondering whether he might have been a clone of Miniver Cheevy.

Buddha, the Enlightened One

One day more than five hundred years before the birth of Christ, a young Indian prince rode out among his people in a jeweled chariot. As a result of what he saw, his whole life was altered, as well as the lives of subsequent hundreds of millions of his followers.

Prince Siddhartha Gautama had led a sheltered life, preparing for the day when he would succeed his father on the throne. The horrors he viewed on the road left him lachrymose with guilt over the misery that affected his people. It led him to exchange his lavishly embroidered robe for the yellow robe of a monk, renouncing his heritage to beg for alms to help his poverty-stricken brethren.

According to the legend, after six years of wandering and enduring physical hardships the contrite Siddhartha came to a massive tree (the Bo tree). For forty-nine days and nights he remained incommunicado beneath the tree, taking neither food nor water, asking for atonement and searching within his soul for the pathway to peace and contentment. During those seven weeks of contemplation, Siddhartha underwent a metamorphosis—he became the Buddha, or the Enlightened One.

He sent a bevy of his disciples to spread the message that salvation is attainable through enlightenment. He censured those who ignored the suffering of the poor, stressing his credo and his discovery of the Four Noble Truths:

1. Suffering on this earth is de rigueur and unavoidable.
2. Man's desire for wealth and power lead to the suffering of others.
3. To abolish suffering, we must discard avaricious goals, eliminating "me" and "mine" from our vocabulary.
4. The middle path can lead us to nirvana, the state of peace and joy.

Today there are close to 500 million Buddhists in almost every part of the world. His philosophy has a universal appeal, and images of Buddha adorn shrines and temples everywhere, revealing a figure in complete repose, supremely calm, devoid of passion.

You Must Remember This . . .

Did you ever have the risible experience of going into a room and not remembering why you went there? People who are on in years frequently complain of such memory loss, but now, even young people report similar incidents.

People in their forties and fifties who suffer memory lapses (Where are my car keys? Is my dental appointment for Monday or Wednesday?) have begun to quail at the possibility of the onset of Alzheimer's, a disease that remains quiescent in one's early years but breaks out as people age. Some entrepreneurs have cashed in on the fear of addled brains, producing a magnitude of books, tapes, and films on how to overcome forgetfulness. Paula Oleska conducts a popular workshop called "Brain Upgrade" in which participants engage in a series of activities to heighten their ability to remember names, words, and numbers. And Fred Chernow, a New York educator, has enjoyed free Caribbean junkets in exchange for his shipboard seminars on memory retention.

Many baby boomers have flocked to Gary Small's training workshops at the Center for Aging in Los Angeles. Small places the onus for forgetfulness on personal stress, poor nutrition, and lack of sleep, and a Virginia **gerontologist**, Paul Mellor, offers six tips to sharpen memory:

1. Tell yourself why you are going into another room. For example, "I'm heading for the kitchen to get some bottled water."
2. When introduced to a new person, repeat his name several times.
3. When parking your car in a garage, use a memory device such as "four west," establishing that you are parked on the west side of the fourth floor.
4. Misplaced your glasses? Put them in the same place ten times in a row.
5. Getting travel directions? Ask for landmarks (City Bank on your left) and always repeat what you have heard.
6. If you tend to lose your train of thought on the phone, make a list of topics ahead of time and cross each off as you cover it. You will find that **therapeutic**.

Got it? Now repeat the six suggestions.

Double Standard?

Suppose your school's star basketball player was failing several academic subjects and couldn't participate in the city's championship game unless he passed.

As you might imagine, dilemmas such as that have occurred on hundreds of high school and college campuses. They have been resolved in different ways, of course. Tutors have been provided to help the weak student, teachers have been pressured into raising the star's marks—or the athlete has actually been barred from the competition.

In many colleges, sports have become big business. They bring in considerable revenue from television, as well as gifts from wealthy alumni who are sports fans. That money is often desperately needed to fund other programs, so the school might suffer if the superstar were ineligible to play.

Several years ago, a Virginia university had a basketball player **par excellence**, Nancy Lieberman, who had won **accolades** for her ability to put the ball through the hoop. However, Lieberman received a failing mark in English, making her ineligible to play. She was **disconsolate**. Her coach told Lieberman's professor that the women's sports program kept the athlete so busy (a **bevy** of games had been played on the road by the **peripatetic** team) that Lieberman missed classes and had little time to read her assignments. The coach added that Lieberman had been recruited to play basketball on a full scholarship, and that the school's bureaucracy should take that into consideration. The **lissome** Lieberman, asked to comment on the **imbroglio**, explained, "If we have a big game, it's hard for me to sit down and concentrate on poetry."
  But the English teacher was **obdurate**.

"If Nancy were a male," the coach claimed, "they would have **countermanded** the teacher's decision to flunk her; Nancy's mark would have been raised without a fuss. It's a double standard; there's no **equity**."

We can be sure of one thing: as women make strides in areas once closed to them, they will experience the same problems that men have faced.

Cheating in School—A Growing Phenomenon

As the story goes, a weak student was able to get good grades on his math tests by copying the answers from a bright pupil who sat in the next row. Nothing unusual about that—it happens all the time. But when the brainy neighbor wrote, "I don't know" next to an algebra question, and the sad sack wrote, "Me neither," the cheater was caught and **ostracized**.

We know that academic cheating has become a **cause célèbre** throughout our various school systems. It takes place in many different forms: sneaking a peek at a classmate's test paper, copying material from someone else's work and passing it off as your own (**plagiarism**), buying term papers or the answers to the same old tests that lazy professors have been giving year in and year out, and so on.

Pedants, of course, must be more vigilant so that anyone attempting to pass in a **purloined** paper cannot get away with it. If students were asked to write essays in class all term long, the instructors would become familiar with their ability and not easy to hoodwink with a canned paper that was cribbed from the Internet. One needn't be a professional **shamus** to detect such a con game.

Professor Mark Edmundson, author of *Teacher: The One Who Made the Difference,* reported that almost 40 percent of the students he polled had been involved in **tawdry** "cut and paste" plagiarism, borrowing whole paragraphs from published works without giving attribution to the source. A company called Direct Essays, according to Edmunson, promises access to more than 100,000 high-quality term papers. From all reports, business is booming. The troubling thing about this situation is that many cheaters don't think they are doing anything wrong. "It's much **ado** about nothing," one student declared **blithely**. "What's the big deal?" he added. Then, in a **nolo contendere** defense, he pleaded that paying for a term paper is **immaterial**. "The important thing is that I learned a lot from the paper I bought, and isn't that justification for what I did?"

A Family Crisis

Mr. Roberts had assigned his Honors English class a composition dealing with a family crisis, and he was moved by the personal dramas revealed in their work. The Philadelphia high school teacher read the following one to his students:

*At Easter time my parents visited a cousin in Laguna Woods, California. After three days of socializing, my mother had some labored breathing and was taken to a local clinic. The **internist** who read my mom's X-ray found congestive heart failure, a **harbinger** of the major illness to come, and he recommended immediate hospitalization. She was driven to Mission Hospital in Mission Viejo and placed on a ventilator. For eleven days my mom was **comatose**, heavily sedated while the machine breathed for her. The doctors had no clue as to the **etiology** of the disease, but the pulmonologist in charge advised my father to consider a hospice because of the seriousness of her condition. In short, he was dubious about her survival.*

*But, wonder of wonders, her X-rays began to improve, and she was removed from the Intensive Care Unit. However her blood work showed that she was sharply anemic, and an **oncology** specialist was called in to deal with it. He ordered a bone marrow **biopsy** and three days later gave my father the bad news—she had an acute case of leukemia, the cancer packed into her bone marrow. With a **baleful** expression, the physician told Dad of three options: (1) do nothing, watchful waiting, or (2) give her a massive dose of morphine and remove the breathing tube to allow for a peaceful death in a few hours, or (3) start an aggressive chemotherapy treatment.*

*Naturally, my father chose the chemo, and the oncologist followed quickly with two weeks of **diurnal** injections. A biopsy brought the **euphoric** news that the cancer was in remission—but before the family could celebrate, the oncologist gave the bad news: her bone marrow was radically depleted by the chemo, and without the necessary platelets and blood cells that provide for clotting and fighting against infection, my mother would be a ripe target for a fatal pneumonia.*

*While that information was devastating, the **coup de grâce** was yet to come. The oncologist summoned my father, my sister, and our cousin to a conference where he announced that Mom had an incurable disease called Graft versus Host. She would break out in a terrible body rash, followed by a spike in temperature up to 105° and would face uncontrollable bleeding. My father called that the worst day of his life.*

In the next weeks there was no rash, stable temperature, no sign of bleeding. The Graft versus Host was a false diagnosis, thank God! But the powerful chemo had left my mother with neuromyopathy, an extreme weakness in her hands and feet. She could no longer walk or use her swollen hands to care for herself.

There's more to the story but I believe I have satisfied the assignment about a family crisis. The happy ending is that she is making progress in recovery, profiting from physical and occupational therapy. Having defied a couple of doctors, she is growing stronger every day.

Better Luck Next Time

Every week, religiously, Tony Colon, a poor resident of his town's **barrio**, bought a Mega Million ticket at his neighborhood 7-Eleven store. He never expected to win, and he was absolutely correct. In fact, many weeks went by, and Tony never got a single number right. Even a **benediction** over tickets by an obliging priest didn't help.

Of course he scanned the listing of winning numbers in the newspaper before he turned to the sports pages. It wasn't with a sense of excitement that Tony read the winning numbers aloud, because all his life whenever he reached out for the brass ring, it always eluded his grasp. Almost every week the newspapers carried stories of the window washer, elevator operator, or shoe salesman who had hit it big. Their smiling faces in front of the magnified checks for $50 million stared out at Tony and taunted him with "Better luck next time, sucker!" But Tony, whose career was always the **antithesis** of those who had good luck, continued on his jinxed path.

If that was all that ever happened to the ill-fated Mr. Colon, we would not have turned our attention to him at this time. But over his buttered bagel one frosty morning the earth moved. At least it seemed that way, because when Tony idly perused the Mega Million box, his heart began to race ahead wildly, and he nearly slid off his chair. A **deus ex machina** had come down to cast some sunshine into the poor man's life.

He put his ticket on the kitchen table and reviewed the numbers 8, 10, 26, 34, 35—and then, unbelievably, the mega ball 2 turned up. The match was perfect! Tony had the golden ticket (slightly greasy now), and it was a blockbuster because there had not been a winner for the previous two weeks. The jackpot was huge.

Now what? Whom could Tony tell of his great good fortune? He had no family, no close friends, not even down at the warehouse—no one with whom to share the celebration. There was his widowed landlady, who cast a loving eye in his direction whenever his Social Security check arrived. Can't tell that Venus flytrap, Tony thought. Perhaps the bartender on the corner, but surely Tony couldn't take him into his confidence about the incredible **bonanza**. No, there was no one.

Tony called the **barrister** from the Knights of Columbus who had once helped him get prescription medicine that was costly. He'd have some good advice for the old man, but Tony couldn't reach the lawyer directly and didn't want to leave any real information on his phone message unit.

The smartest thing, Tony thought, was to get down to 7-Eleven and find out how one goes about collecting the zillions that were coming to him. The **denouement** of this unhappy/happy/unhappy tale is shocking. Excited, his clothing **awry**, Tony was scurrying across a major intersection when he happened to **careen** in front of a **behemoth** of a garbage truck and expired on the street as the winning ticket slipped from his hand and blew into the sewer drain.

Was there any other way this story could have ended?

Going to the Mat

Charley Kropinicki was a Little League **elite** first baseman at age ten, and he later excelled at swimming and track as a high school sophomore. For a sixteen-year-old, he was remarkably strong, having practiced weight lifting with his father, a professional bodybuilder. Charley also ran the anchor leg on Thomas Jefferson's prizewinning relay team, and everyone assumed that he would be showered with athletic scholarship offers from a prestigious Ivy League college.

So it came as a shock when he tried out for the wrestling squad and was turned down by Coach Al (Tank) Biagio, who explained that school rules prohibited Charley from engaging in any contact sport because he had only one kidney. "It would be **deleterious** to his health," Biagio said.

"I'd love to have Charley wrestle for Jefferson," Biagio told the young man's parents, "but we're concerned about his welfare. If your son got hurt in a wrestling match, his life could be in jeopardy."

The Kropinickis had brought Charley up to believe that he wasn't handicapped in any way despite having lost a kidney in a childhood accident. Mr. Kropinicki was **disconsolate** by what he called an **authoritarian** action, saying, "I want Charley to be treated like everyone else. If his mother and I are willing to have him wrestle, knowing there is some danger involved, we think the school should respect our wishes."

The case developed into a **cause célèbre**. Charley's father tried to get the principal to **countermand** Biagio's ruling, but the administrator supported the coach, who was merely enforcing district policy. And the school's doctor agreed with the decision, citing cases of young wrestlers who had suffered serious injuries.

"Of course there's a risk," said the **feisty** Mrs. Kropinicki, "but the greater risk would be to Charley's normal development and his self-esteem. We're going to court seeking **appellate** justice. This is no **fait accompli** just yet."

How would you **adjudicate** this matter?

Final Review Test

ANTONYMS

For each of the fifty questions below, choose the best answer and blacken the corresponding space. Each question consists of a capitalized word followed by five choices. Pick the word or phrase that is most nearly OPPOSITE in meaning to the word in capital letters. Since some of the answers are fairly close in meaning, consider all the choices before deciding which is best.

Example

TALL: (A) huge (B) high (C) short (D) sad (E) rich ⒶⒷ●ⒹⒺ

---

1. **CONTUMACIOUS:** (A) obedient (B) sinful (C) considerate (D) tearful (E) stiff ⒶⒷⒸⒹⒺ

2. **QUIXOTIC:** (A) lively (B) urbane (C) adventurous (D) warlike (E) practical ⒶⒷⒸⒹⒺ

3. **SATURNINE:** (A) obvious (B) youthful (C) talented (D) vengeful (E) cheerful ⒶⒷⒸⒹⒺ

4. **TAWDRY:** (A) sweet (B) sour (C) tasteful (D) trustworthy (E) sleepy ⒶⒷⒸⒹⒺ

5. **BELLICOSE:** (A) ancient (B) peaceful (C) slow (D) inquisitive (E) trembling ⒶⒷⒸⒹⒺ

6. **COMPLAISANT:** (A) impolite (B) slick (C) rugged (D) hesitating (E) rare ⒶⒷⒸⒹⒺ

7. **CONVIVIAL:** (A) ruthless (B) hostile (C) studious (D) nervy (E) tardy ⒶⒷⒸⒹⒺ

8. **CRAVEN:** (A) brave (B) dull (C) infallible (D) original (E) succinct ⒶⒷⒸⒹⒺ

9. **LACHRYMOSE:** (A) tortured (B) unwise (C) ingenious (D) intolerant (E) jolly ⒶⒷⒸⒹⒺ

10. **CORNUCOPIA:** (A) foot ailment (B) sadness (C) ship's mast (D) shortage (E) doldrums ⒶⒷⒸⒹⒺ

11. **HERCULEAN:** (A) unintelligible (B) puny (C) mythical (D) furtive (E) intolerable ⒶⒷⒸⒹⒺ

12. **EXTROVERT:** (A) imitator (B) pious person (C) braggart (D) lout (E) withdrawn person ⒶⒷⒸⒹⒺ

13. **RENEGADE:** (A) partisan (B) recluse (C) fugitive (D) loyalist (E) veteran ⒶⒷⒸⒹⒺ

14. ANTEBELLUM: (A) serene   (B) post war
(C) incorruptible   (D) previous   (E) subsequent

Ⓐ Ⓑ Ⓒ Ⓓ Ⓔ

15. DIURNAL: (A) investigative   (B) somber
(C) nightly   (D) unconditional   (E) chaotic

Ⓐ Ⓑ Ⓒ Ⓓ Ⓔ

16. EON: (A) fleeting moment   (B) mortal thing
(C) light year   (D) land mass   (E) oration

Ⓐ Ⓑ Ⓒ Ⓓ Ⓔ

17. EPHEMERAL: (A) eroded   (B) permanent
(C) blasé   (D) robust   (E) repetitious

Ⓐ Ⓑ Ⓒ Ⓓ Ⓔ

18. SVELTE: (A) resistant   (B) obese
(C) humid   (D) curved   (E) inane

Ⓐ Ⓑ Ⓒ Ⓓ Ⓔ

19. COMATOSE: (A) lively   (B) stubborn
(C) rugged   (D) tenacious   (E) dour

Ⓐ Ⓑ Ⓒ Ⓓ Ⓔ

20. DICHOTOMY: (A) degree   (B) advice
(C) inversion   (D) harmony   (E) opening

Ⓐ Ⓑ Ⓒ Ⓓ Ⓔ

21. EXHUME: (A) invent   (B) nurture
(C) cover up   (D) reject   (E) tranquilize

Ⓐ Ⓑ Ⓒ Ⓓ Ⓔ

22. CIRCUMSPECT: (A) sightless   (B) monstrous
(C) troublesome   (D) obtuse   (E) careless

Ⓐ Ⓑ Ⓒ Ⓓ Ⓔ

23. DEMURE: (A) imaginative   (B) fruitful
(C) brash   (D) sinister   (E) vocal

Ⓐ Ⓑ Ⓒ Ⓓ Ⓔ

24. FLACCID: (A) strong   (B) stern
(C) severe   (D) sacrificial   (E) sacred

Ⓐ Ⓑ Ⓒ Ⓓ Ⓔ

25. FLIPPANT: (A) solemn   (B) stable
(C) deceitful   (D) corrosive   (E) two-faced

Ⓐ Ⓑ Ⓒ Ⓓ Ⓔ

26. FLORID: (A) ambiguous   (B) pale
(C) businesslike   (D) doubtful   (E) cool

Ⓐ Ⓑ Ⓒ Ⓓ Ⓔ

27. GLABROUS: (A) objectionable   (B) weighty
(C) imperceptible   (D) hairy   (E) devious

Ⓐ Ⓑ Ⓒ Ⓓ Ⓔ

28. INTRANSIGENT: (A) beneficial   (B) rotund
(C) malicious   (D) flexible   (E) morose

Ⓐ Ⓑ Ⓒ Ⓓ Ⓔ

29. INSCRUTABLE: (A) understandable   (B) vicious
(C) salient   (D) concerned   (E) ambitious

Ⓐ Ⓑ Ⓒ Ⓓ Ⓔ

30. MEGALOPOLIS: (A) unknown locale   (B) plateau
(C) slope   (D) deserted area   (E) small nation

Ⓐ Ⓑ Ⓒ Ⓓ Ⓔ

31. DRACONIAN: (A) tyrannical   (B) mild
(C) topical   (D) out of tune   (E) fabulously wealthy

Ⓐ Ⓑ Ⓒ Ⓓ Ⓔ

32. LICENTIOUS: (A) surreptitious   (B) prudish
(C) illegal   (D) savage   (E) grasping

Ⓐ Ⓑ Ⓒ Ⓓ Ⓔ

33. **MERETRICIOUS:**   (A) unworthy   (B) thoughtful
(C) forgiving   (D) logical   (E) plain   Ⓐ Ⓑ Ⓒ Ⓓ Ⓔ

34. **MUTABLE:**   (A) dull   (B) constant
(C) rosy   (D) proud   (E) horrid   Ⓐ Ⓑ Ⓒ Ⓓ Ⓔ

35. **NOXIOUS:**   (A) wholesome   (B) rusty
(C) gentle   (D) abrasive   (E) meddlesome   Ⓐ Ⓑ Ⓒ Ⓓ Ⓔ

36. **PUSILLANIMOUS:**   (A) approving   (B) carping
(C) brave   (D) receptive   (E) glowing   Ⓐ Ⓑ Ⓒ Ⓓ Ⓔ

37. **IMMATERIAL:**   (A) relevant   (B) thin
(C) suspicious   (D) moot   (E) temporary   Ⓐ Ⓑ Ⓒ Ⓓ Ⓔ

38. **GAUCHE:**   (A) critical   (B) tactful
(C) vehement   (D) commonplace   (E) onerous   Ⓐ Ⓑ Ⓒ Ⓓ Ⓔ

39. **ASKEW:**   (A) circuitous   (B) rigid
(C) contemplative   (D) straight   (E) timorous   Ⓐ Ⓑ Ⓒ Ⓓ Ⓔ

40. **CHARY:**   (A) unscrupulous   (B) cheap
(C) careless   (D) willful   (E) bombastic   Ⓐ Ⓑ Ⓒ Ⓓ Ⓔ

41. **PUERILE:**   (A) mature   (B) antiquarian
(C) ghastly   (D) significant   (E) enraged   Ⓐ Ⓑ Ⓒ Ⓓ Ⓔ

42. **SEDULOUS:**   (A) terminal   (B) lavish
(C) corpulent   (D) lazy   (E) distraught   Ⓐ Ⓑ Ⓒ Ⓓ Ⓔ

43. **AD HOC:**   (A) litigious   (B) sub rosa
(C) truncated   (D) of moderate means   (E) permanently established   Ⓐ Ⓑ Ⓒ Ⓓ Ⓔ

44. **DILATORY:**   (A) prompt   (B) constructive
(C) hopeful   (D) contracted   (E) skeptical   Ⓐ Ⓑ Ⓒ Ⓓ Ⓔ

45. **GENTEEL:**   (A) profitable   (B) irreligious
(C) charitable   (D) coarse   (E) synthetic   Ⓐ Ⓑ Ⓒ Ⓓ Ⓔ

46. **JOCUND:**   (A) classical   (B) informed
(C) disagreeable   (D) solitary   (E) vengeful   Ⓐ Ⓑ Ⓒ Ⓓ Ⓔ

47. **LOQUACIOUS:**   (A) careless with words   (B) benevolent
(C) willing to negotiate   (D) moody   (E) silent   Ⓐ Ⓑ Ⓒ Ⓓ Ⓔ

48. **TENUOUS:**   (A) substantial   (B) beyond doubt
(C) modest   (D) threatening   (E) deaf to all pleas   Ⓐ Ⓑ Ⓒ Ⓓ Ⓔ

49. **CENSURE:**   (A) trial   (B) approval
(C) lack of concern   (D) critique   (E) evaluation   Ⓐ Ⓑ Ⓒ Ⓓ Ⓔ

50. **ANTEDILUVIAN:**   (A) decrepit   (B) restored
(C) modern   (D) lacking in culture   (E) ambulatory   Ⓐ Ⓑ Ⓒ Ⓓ Ⓔ

SENTENCE COMPLETIONS

Select the words that best fill the blanks.

1. We are entering into an _____ of great volatility in the stock market.
   (a) accolade   (b) epoch   (c) odyssey   (d) eon   (e) augury

2. When it comes to a question of increasing my allowance, Dad is _____ .
   (a) agnostic   (b) bucolic   (c) hermetic   (d) intractable   (e) tendentious

3. Phyllis entertained us with one delightful _____ after another about her school days.
   (a) vignette   (b) narcissism   (c) junket   (d) rubric   (e) censure

4. The funeral _____ brought tears to the eyes of millions of television viewers.
   (a) salvo   (b) gerontology   (c) mantra   (d) dirge   (e) archetype

5. To make their offer _____ , the bank gave out free toasters.
   (a) waggish   (b) untrammeled   (c) palatable   (d) venal   (e) gauche

6. In such an important matter, it was necessary for us to be quite _____ .
   (a) circumspect   (b) ephemeral   (c) apocalyptic   (d) stygian   (e) vulpine

7. Elvis Presley's _____ mansion is visited by thousands of tourists each year.
   (a) genteel   (b) palatial   (c) peripatetic   (d) glabrous   (e) minatory

8. The angry _____ started with a seemingly innocent remark by the taxi driver.
   (a) nihilism   (b) altercation   (c) benediction   (d) blasphemy   (e) eclat

9. The poorly educated baseball player was notorious for his _____ .
   (a) hustings   (b) non sequiturs   (c) Machiavellianisms   (d) mot justes   (e) cul-de-sacs

10. Following a one hour _____ about cleaning his room, Bobby promised his parents to do better.
    (a) accolade   (b) bequest   (c) fait accompli   (d) lien   (e) harangue

11. The one minor benefit of Matthew's diet is that he no longer is regarded as a _____ .
    (a) lothario   (b) gourmand   (c) votary   (d) bête noire   (e) cyclopean

12. Although an amateur student of insect life, Kyra was pleased to be called an _____ .
    (a) atavist   (b) entomologist   (c) endocrinologist   (cl) ophthalmologist   (e) apostate

13. Before the _____ of the play, most of the audience had guessed the murderer.
    (a) tenet   (b) dichotomy   (c) codicil   (d) refection   (e) denouement

14. During the presidential campaign we were treated to one _____ after another on the topic of the economy.
    (a) philippic   (b) parvenu   (c) paradigm   (d) insouciance   (e) apotheosis

15. The scandal was of _____ interest, quickly forgotten by the public.
    (a) aberrant   (b) ephemeral   (c) indeterminate   (d) empirical   (e) teeming

16. In a _____ mood, the angry prizefighter smashed dishes and broke windows.
    (a) venal   (b) dilatory   (c) jocund   (d) truculent   (e) piquant

17. Sharon could endure the _____ of society, but her family's aloofness was of greater concern.
    (a) threnody   (b) solecism   (c) ostracism   (d) bequest   (e) bonhomie

18. Overcome by _____ feelings, Roger sent a dozen roses to his secretary.
    (a) contrite   (b) lissome   (c) empirical   (d) authoritarian   (e) vulpine

19. When the _____ polished the stones, they gleamed with a breathtaking brilliance.
(a) beadle   (b) cosmetologist   (c) epidemiologist   (d) graphologist   (e) lapidary

20. After the exhausting _____ through the wilderness, his disciples were famished and dehydrated.
(a) hegira   (b) malaise   (c) oligarchy   (d) wanderlust   (e) salvo

21. The editor called it hypocritical when he heard so many _____ statements coming from the crooked businessmen.
(a) vacuous   (b) sententious   (c) tenuous   (d) pedantic   (e) renascent

22. Most of the senate voted to _____ their colleague for his inflammatory remarks.
(a) mulct   (b) deign   (c) beguile   (d) censure   (e) purloin

23. When our canoe entered the tunnel, we were plunged into _____ darkness.
(a) amorphous   (b) bilious   (c) stygian   (d) diurnal   (e) flaccid

24. The scholar was upset to learn that his _____ research failed to be comprehended by the reading public.
(a) arcane   (b) captious   (c) apochryphal   (d) edacious   (e) imperious

25. We agreed that the _____ window display was totally out of place on the elegant boulevard.
(a) obtuse   (b) meretricious   (c) moot   (d) contiguous   (e) bicameral

26. Charles was _____ about the possibility of someone forging his name on an incriminating document.
(a) circumspect   (b) paranoid   (c) intractable   (d) picayune   (e) demure

27. _____ experts warn that time is running out on forestalling the erosion of the earth's delicate environment.
(a) Philistine   (b) Seismology   (c) Oncology   (d) Avant-garde   (e) Ecology

28. Dickens' character Mr. Scrooge is the stereotype of the _____ miser.
(a) sardonic   (b) supercilious   (c) pusillanimous   (d) obdurate   (e) mercurial

29. The law imposing penalties for frivolous suits should dampen the _____ instincts of opportunists.
(a) litigious   (b) puerile   (c) sub rosa   (d) ambivalent   (e) vacuous

30. His parents decided to raise him in a tight disciplinary regimen instead of a _____ environment.
(a) genteel   (b) venal   (c) tenuous   (d) gauche   (e) laissez-faire

31. The teacher urged Hector to submit the _____ of his life in Puerto Rico to a magazine.
(a) fait accompli   (b) rubric   (c) scintilla   (d) vignette   (e) hegira

32. "This _____ ," said the suave jeweler "will cost you only $10,000."
(a) condiment   (b) repast   (c) codicil   (d) mantra   (e) bauble

33. Adopting _____ tone, the preacher proceeded to deliver his standard fire and brimstone sermon.
(a) a sacrilegious   (b) an oracular   (c) an agnostic   (d) an empirical   (e) an antic

34. Beverley has an instinct for knowing when to be _____ and when to be accommodating.
(a) palatable   (b) apocalyptic   (c) utilitarian   (d) recalcitrant   (e) partisan

35. The congressman refused the generous campaign contribution knowing that it would entail
_____ .
(a) a schism   (b) a subsistence   (c) a quid pro quo   (d) a divertissement   (e) an altercation

36. Gertrude was so _____ over the loss of her job, she briefly even contemplated suicide.
(a) disconsolate   (b) apocryphal   (c) mellifluous   (d) pragmatic   (e) roguish

37. With his _____ logic, Ben could blur the distinction between fact and fancy.
(a) piquant   (b) renascent   (c) polyglot   (d) tenuous   (e) sinuous

38. Ophelia praised Hamlet as the _____ of perfection.
(a) microcosm   (b) iota   (c) paradigm   (d) leitmotif   (e) argonaut

39. We must admire the ability to pack a ton of wisdom into _____ phrase.
(a) a homeric   (b) a Promethean   (c) a non compos mentis   (d) a sententious   (e) an indeterminate

40. When I could not take part in the debate, I sent a _____ .
(a) apostate   (b) martial   (c) tandem   (d) venal   (e) surrogate

41. The proliferation of nuclear and chemical weapons necessitates _____ decision to end this threat to human survival.
(a) a froward   (b) a landmark   (c) a nolo contendere   (d) an ad hoc   (e) a Machiavellian

42. The homeless need help beyond mere _____; they need to be rehabilitated to a life with hope.
(a) bureaucracy   (b) suffrage   (c) subsistence   (d) aphasia   (e) manna

43. The _____ of drugs is short-lived and life threatening.
(a) euphoria   (b) subversion   (c) bathos   (d) onus   (e) fallacy

44. A(n) _____ regime is likely to deprive the people of hope, pride, and humanity.
(a) contraband   (b) bourgeois   (c) reactionary   (d) totalitarian   (e) subliminal

45. Many people in a democracy fail to exercise their hard-won _____ .
(a) portmanteau   (b) subsistence   (c) suffrage   (d) anarchy   (e) jurisprudence

46. Ted was shattered to learn that the _____ effectively shut him out from any part of his uncle's estate.
(a) cause célèbre   (b) benediction   (c) ethos   (d) codicil   (e) plebiscite

47. The selfish person adheres to the _____ that the world revolves around him or her.
(a) canon   (b) aspersion   (c) tenet   (d) smidgen   (e) impasse

48. In the realm of human conduct, injustice is _____ .
(a) omniscient   (b) sacrilegious   (c) mercurial   (d) amorphous   (e) truculent

49. Much to his surprise, the _____ received an indeterminate sentence.
(a) wayfarer   (b) gourmand   (c) infidel   (d) muckraker   (e) miscreant

50. The secret of Carla's scintillating _____ was that it was carefully rehearsed.
(a) larceny   (b) magnitude   (c) repartee   (d) censure   (e) wanderlust

ANSWERS TO EXERCISES

Lesson 1: Words from Proper Names

I. 1. philippic   2. jingoism   3. maverick   4. quixotic   5. procrustean   6. tawdry   7. lothario   8. maverick
    9. sybarite   10. philippic

II. 1. T   2. T   3. F   4. T   5. F   6. F   7. T   8. F   9. T   10. T

III. 1. nemesis   2. maverick   3. quixotic   4. tawdry   5. philippic   6. jingoist   7. spoonerism   8. sybarite
    9. lothario   10. saturnine

IV. 1. maverick   2. philippic   3. tawdry   4. saturnine   5. quixotic   6. protean   7. philanderer   8. sybarite
    9. jingoist   10. procrustean

V. 1. c   6. n   11. o
    2. j   7. m   12. f
    3. d   8. b   13. a
    4. g   9. l   14. h
    5. i   10. e   15. k

Lesson 2: Appearances and Attitudes (I)

I. 1. contrite   2. churlish   3. avaricious   4. dyspeptic   5. bilious   6. bellicose   7. lachrymose
    8. craven   9. contrite   10. churlish

II. 1. F   2. T   3. T   4. T   5. F   6. T   7. T   8. F   9. T   10. T

III. 1. lachrymose   2. craven   3. captious   4. bellicose   5. convivial   6. avaricious   7. complaisant
    8. dyspeptic   9. baleful   10. bumptious

IV. 1. bellicose   2. lachrymose   3. dyspeptic   4. complaisant   5. churlish   6. bilious   7. bumptious
    8. churlish   9. craven   10. avaricious

V. 1. d   6. a   11. f
    2. e   7. n   12. b
    3. h   8. c   13. k
    4. o   9. l   14. g
    5. m   10. j   15. i

Lesson 3: Words About Groups

I. 1. rapprochement   2. caste   3. camaraderie   4. hobnob   5. ecumenical   6. cortege   7. cabal
    8. genealogy   9. liaison   10. detente

II. 1. F   2. T   3. T   4. T   5. T   6. T   7. T   8. F   9. F   10. T

III. 1. echelon   2. liaison   3. hobnob   4. esprit de corps   5. cortege   6. cabal   7. rapprochement
    8. genealogy   9. hierarchy   10. elite

IV. 1. elite   2. esprit de corps   3. camaraderie   4. ecumenical   5. hobnob   6. rapprochement   7. hierarchy
    8. caste   9. camaraderie   10. clandestine

V.	1. d		6. m		11. e
	2. o		7. j		12. b
	3. l		8. b		13. c
	4. h		9. g		14. i
	5. k		10. n		15. a

Lesson 4: Sounds Italian

I.   1. largo   2. salvo   3. imbroglio   4. bravura   5. staccato   6. vendetta   7. libretto   8. fortissimo
9. contralto   10. virago

II.   1. F   2. F   3. F   4. T   5. T   6. T   7. T   8. F   9. T   10. T

III.   1. imbroglio   2. bravura   3. staccato   4. libretto   5. crescendo   6. vendetta   7. salvo   8. falsetto
9. bravura   10. staccato

IV.   1. adagio   2. contralto   3. vendetta   4. crescendo   5. fortissimo   6. staccato   7. crescendo
8. falsetto   9. virago   10. imbroglio

V.	1. f		6. k		11. e
	2. o		7. n		12. i
	3. a		8. b		13. d
	4. h		9. g		14. m
	5. c		10. j		15. l

Lesson 5: Job and Professions

I.   1. osteopath   2. graphologist   3. entomologist   4. dermatologist   5. ornithologist   6. alienist
7. internist   8. lapidary   9. pharyngologist   10. ophthalmologist

II.   1. T   2. F   3. T   4. T   5. F   6. T   7. T   8. F   9. T   10. T

III.   1. cosmetologist   2. entomologist   3. osteopath   4. ornithologist   5. dermatologist   6. pharyngologist
7. lapidary   8. alienist   9. graphologist   10. ophthalmologist

IV.   adagio

V.	1. d		6. f		11. g
	2. o		7. j		12. i
	3. h		8. c		13. k
	4. b		9. l		14. n
	5. a		10. e		15. m

Unit I Mini Review (Lessons 1–5)

I.   1. b   2. c   3. b   4. d   5. c

II.   1. b   2. d   3. a   4. d   5. a

III.   1. acidulous   2. lachrymose   3. staccato   4. libretto   5. rapprochement

Lesson 6: Mythology (I)

I.   1. erotic   2. cornucopia   3. iridescent   4. herculean   5. bacchanal   6. narcissism   7. Adonis   8. iridescent   9. odyssey   10. phoenix

II.   1. T   2. T   3. F   4. T   5. F   6. T   7. F   8. T   9. T   10. T

III.   1. dramatic   2. baccalaureate   3. metallic   4. corpulent   5. erotic

IV.   1. cornucopia   2. herculean   3. phoenix   4. iridescent   5. odyssey   6. Olympian   7. Adonis   8. narcissism   9. Cassandra   10. cupidity

V.
1. m	6. b	11. k
2. h	7. n	12. c
3. a	8. o	13. d
4. j	9. f	14. l
5. g	10. i	15. e

Lesson 7: Social Sciences

I.   1. euthanasia   2. epidemiology   3. aberrant   4. demography   5. trauma   6. extrovert   7. schizophrenia   8. authoritarian   9. euthanasia   10. anthropomorphism

II.   1. F   2. F   3. T   4. F   5. T   6. T   7. F   8. T   9. T   10. F

III.   1. trauma   2. euthanasia   3. authoritarian   4. aberrant   5. demography   6. schizophrenia   7. psychopath   8. extrovert   9. epidemiology   10. catharsis

IV.   1. authoritarian   2. aberrant   3. subliminal   4. extrovert   5. archetype

V.
1. h	6. k	11. j
2. c	7. a	12. e
3. g	8. m	13. f
4. o	9. b	14. l
5. n	10. d	15. i

Lesson 8: From Sunny Spain

I.   1. torero   2. mañana   3. machismo   4. bonanza   5. desperado   6. renegade   7. siesta   8. flotilla   9. bravado   10. aficionado

II.   1. T   2. T   3. T   4. T   5. F   6. T   7. F   8. T   9. T   10. F

III.   1. afficionado   2. siesta   3. flotilla   4. barrio   5. torero   6. bravado   7. lariat   8. mañana   9. desperado   10. flotilla

IV.   1. bravado   2. renegade   3. mañana   4. machismo   5. desperado   6. bonanza   7. siesta   8. hacienda   9. grandee   10. barrio

V.
1. j	6. m	11. l
2. a	7. c	12. g
3. f	8. d	13. i
4. b	9. n	14. e
5. o	10. k	15. h

Lesson 9: Time on Our Hands

I.   1. antediluvian   2. anachronism   3. atavism   4. biennial   5. augury   6. score   7. ephemeral
     8. epoch   9. antebellum   10. diurnal

II. 1. T   2. T   3. T   4. T   5. T   6. T   7. F   8. T   9. F   10. T

III. 1. anachronism   2. biennial   3. antebellum   4. epoch   5. generation   6. antediluvian   7. augury
     8. ephemeral   9. eon   10. diurnal

IV. 1. anon   2. epoch   3. antediluvian   4. ephemeral   5. diurnal   6. anachronism   7. biennial
     8. antebellum   9. eon   10. atavism

V.   1. f   6. o   11. a
     2. h   7. e   12. m
     3. n   8. l   13. j
     4. b   9. k   14. c
     5. d   10. i   15. g

Lesson 10: Short but Challenging Words

I.   1. eke   2. mete   3. quail   4. tryst   5. bane   6. shunt   7. svelte   8. knell   9. roil   10. thrall

II. 1. T   2. F   3. T   4. T   5. F   6. T   7. T   8. T   9. T   10. T

III. 1. O   2. S   3. U   4. S   5. O

IV. 1. meek   2. meter   3. motor   4. stele   5. roil

V.   1. l   6. f   11. a
     2. d   7. o   12. n
     3. h   8. i   13. g
     4. j   9. m   14. e
     5. c   10. k   15. b

Unit I Review (Lessons 1–10)

A.   1. nemesis   2. thrall   3. philippic   4. odyssey   5. anachronism
     6. lachrymose   7. echelon   8. siesta   9. palladium   10. lapidary

B.   1. jingoist   2. adagio   3. cortege   4. lariat   5. solecism

C.   1. osteopath   2. graphologist   3. cortege   4. cabal   5. dermatologist
     6. genealogy   7. lapidary   8. ophthalmologist   9. tercentenary   10. maverick

D.   lothario-philanderer   acidulous-dyspeptic
     augury-Cassandra   esprit de corps-camaraderie
     renegade-desperado   herculean-protean
     ornithologist-phoenix   elite-Olympian
     libretto-contralto   bacchanal-sybarite

E.   1. bane   2. crescendo   3. Pyrrhic   4. staccato   5. elite

Lesson 11: Medical Science

I. 1. simian   2. carcinogen   3. mastectomy   4. comatose   5. arteriosclerosis
    6. biopsy   7. cadaver   8. malingerer   9. prosthesis   10. therapeutic

II. 1. T   2. T   3. F   4. T   5. T   6. T   7. T   8. F   9. T   10. F

III.

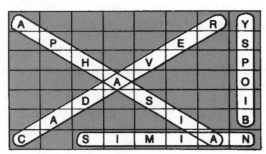

IV. bane, eke

V. 1. n   6. l   11. i
    2. k   7. j   12. a
    3. f   8. o   13. m
    4. g   9. h   14. d
    5. e   10. b   15. c

Lesson 12: Animal World

I. 1. saurian   2. vulpine   3. vixen   4. bestial   5. ursine   6. venomous   7. equine   8. feline
    9. leonine   10. bovine

II. 1. F   2. F   3. T   4. F   5. F   6. T   7. F   8. F   9. F   10. F

III. 1. equity   2. feline   3. vexing   4. terrain   5. fowl

IV. 1. risen   2. nix   3. bone   4. Nile   5. saran

V. 1. l   6. e   11. g
    2. i   7. n   12. k
    3. d   8. c   13. o
    4. a   9. b   14. h
    5. m   10. f   15. j

Lesson 13: Countdown—Words with Numbers

I. 1. dichotomy   2. protocol   3. millennium   4. penultimate   5. nihilism   6. atonement   7. decimate
    8. Decalogue   9. quintessence   10. bicameral

II. 1. F   2. T   3. F   4. T   5. T   6. T   7. T   8. F   9. T   10. F

III. 1. protocol   2. atonement   3. decimate   4. nihilism   5. primeval   6. dichotomy   7. quintessence
     8. penultimate   9. bicameral   10. millennium

IV. 1. untrammeled   2. primeval   3. penultimate   4. dichotomy   5. nihilism   6. atonement
    7. decimate   8. ambiguous   9. protocol   10. bicameral

V. 1. g   6. l   11. m
    2. k   7. f   12. c
    3. j   8. i   13. n
    4. a   9. h   14. e
    5. b   10. d   15. o

Lesson 14: Legal Language (I)

I. 1. intestate   2. deposition   3. appellate   4. perjury   5. incommunicado   6. collusion   7. exhume
    8. lien   9. tort   10. litigation

II. 1. F   2. F   3. T   4. T   5. T   6. T   7. F   8. T   9. F   10. F

III. 1. adjudicate   2. deposition   3. lien   4. litigation   5. collusion   6. equity   7. incommunicado
     8. tribunal   9. perjury   10. intestate

IV. 1. exhume   2. perjury   3. equity   4. incommunicado   5. tort

V. 1. d   6. h   11. o
    2. k   7. l   12. m
    3. i   8. n   13. e
    4. a   9. g   14. c
    5. j   10. b   15. f

Lesson 15: Appearances and Attitudes (II)

I. 1. circumspect   2. imperious   3. intractable   4. flippant   5. demure   6. feisty   7. ingenious
    8. dolorous   9. glabrous   10. intransigent

II. 1. T   2. F   3. F   4. T   5. T   6. F   7. T   8. T   9. T   10. F

III. 1. ingenious   2. feisty   3. imperious   4. circumspect   5. flippant   6. intransigent or intractable
     7. demure   8. dolorous   9. dispassionate   10. florid

IV. 1. circumspect   2. effete   3. glabrous   4. intractable or intransigent   5. florid
    6. dispassionate   7. demure   8. ingenious   9. flippant   10. feisty

V. 1. f   6. c   11. m
    2. a   7. e   12. b
    3. o   8. n   13. g
    4. d   9. h   14. i
    5. k   10. j   15. l

Unit II Mini Review (Lessons 11–15)

I.   1. d   2. a   3. b   4. a   5. b

II. 1. c   2. b   3. d   4. d   5. d

III. 1. saurian   2. litigation   3. collusion   4. carcinogen   5. millennium

Lesson 16: Mystery and the Occult

I.   1. shamus   2. soothsayer   3. pallor   4. purloin   5. polygraph   6. inscrutable   7. conundrum
     8. illusion   9. ritual   10. arcane

II. 1. F   2. F   3. T   4. T   5. T   6. T   7. T   8. F   9. T   10. T

III. 1. thaumaturgy   2. ritual   3. polygraph   4. arcane   5. conundrum   6. alchemy   7. shamus
     8. pallor   9. purloin   10. inscrutable

IV. beadle

V.   1. g   6. m   11. b
     2. a   7. k   12. j
     3. d   8. i   13. l
     4. f   9. o   14. n
     5. h   10. e   15. c

Lesson 17: Size and Shape (I)

I.   1. infinitesimal   2. megalopolis   3. minimize   4. peccadillo   5. titanic   6. Lilliputian
     7. minutiae   8. palatial   9. picayune   10. vista

II. 1. F   2. F   3. F   4. F   5. F   6. T   7. T   8. T   9. T   10. T

III. 1. infinitesimal—titanic (A)   4. picayune—unbiased (A)
     2. swarming—teeming (S)   5. exaggerate—minimize (A)
     3. amplitude—range (S)

IV. 1. c   6. j   11. l
     2. a   7. b   12. e
     3. i   8. d   13. g
     4. o   9. k   14. h
     5. f   10. m   15. n

Lesson 18: Words with Tales Attached

I.   1. proletariat   2. ostracism   3. draconian   4. epicurean   5. accolade   6. conclave   7. sycophant
     8. rigmarole   9. junket   10. dirge

II. 1. F   2. T   3. F   4. F   5. F   6. F   7. T   8. T   9. T   10. T

III. 1. O   2. S   3. U   4. U   5. S

IV. 1. dirge   2. draconian   3. ostracism   4. rigmarole   5. sycophants   6. juggernaut   7. accolades
     8. proletariat   9. conclave   10. epicurean

V. 1. n   6. k   11. a
    2. c   7. o   12. f
    3. b   8. g   13. d
    4. e   9. h   14. l
    5. i   10. j   15. m

Lesson 19: Of Loves and Fears and Hates

I. 1. hydrophobia 2. acrophobia 3. misogynist 4. triskaidekaphobia 5. xenophobe
    6. claustrophobia 7. Francophile 8. paranoid 9. philately 10. misanthropy

II. 1. F 2. F 3. T 4. T 5. F 6. F 7. T 8. T 9. T 10. T

III. 1. xenophilia 2. philanthropy 3. bibliophobia 4. acrophilia 5. Francotriskaidekaphilia

IV.
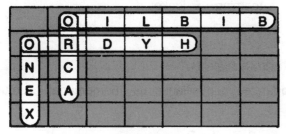

V. 1. b   6. a   11. l
    2. j   7. c   12. d
    3. i   8. g   13. m
    4. e   9. h   14. f
    5. o   10. n   15. k

Lesson 20: Science — "Ology" Words

I. 1. ecology 2. gerontology 3. necrology 4. paleontology 5. cardiology 6. toxicology
    7. archaeology 8. cardiology 9. seismology 10. toxicology

II. 1. T 2. T 3. F 4. F 5. F 6. T 7. T 8. T 9. T 10. T

III. 1. No 2. Yes 3. No 4. Yes 5. No 6. Yes 7. No 8. Yes 9. No 10. No

IV.
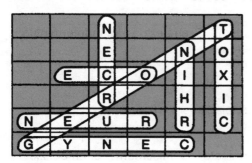

V. 1. c   6. m   11. e
    2. f   7. b   12. g
    3. a   8. d   13. k
    4. j   9. i   14. o
    5. h   10. l   15. n

Unit II Review (Lessons 11–20)

A. 1. quatrain   2. equity   3. alchemy   4. bovine   5. etiology
    6. tautology   7. vulpine   8. purloin   9. amplitude   10. elfin

B. 1. conclave   2. lupine   3. comatose   4. titanic   5. decimate

C. 1. cadaver   2. equity   3. soothsayer   4. bibliophile   5. prosthesis
    6. misanthropist   7. simian   8. accolade   9. megalopolis   10. aficionado

D. circumspect-demure   Lilliputian-infinitestimal
    peccadillo-picayune   Russophobe-misanthropist
    intractable-intransigent   flaccid-effete
    tort-litigation   Decalogue-decimate
    titanic-amplitude   tribunal-adjudicate

E. 1. pallor   2. inscrutable   3. incommunicado   4. teeming   5. junket

Lesson 21: Appearances and Attitudes (III)

I.   1. omniscient   2. noxious   3. minatory   4 obdurate   5. pusillanimous   6. mercurial   7. mutable
     8. licentious   9. obtuse   10. nonchalant

II. 1. F   2. F   3. T   4. T   5. T   6. F   7. T   8. F   9. T   10. F

III. 1. mercurial   2. omniscient   3. mutable   4. licentious or libidinous   5. nonchalant   6. noxious
     7. pusillanimous   8. meretricious   9. officious   10. jejune

IV. 1. minatory   2. jejune   3. noxious   4. pusillanimous   5. obdurate   6. jejune   7. omniscient
     8. nonchalant   9. meretricious   10. licentious

V.   1. h   6. k   11. j
     2. g   7. b   12. i
     3. o   8. n   13. l
     4. a   9. e   14. m
     5. c   10. d   15. f

Lesson 22: Legal Language (II)

I.   1. amicus curiae   2. arson   3. extradition   4. plagiarism   5. embezzle   6. indeterminate
     7. plagiarism   8. miscreant   9. embezzle   10. immaterial

II. 1. F   2. T   3. T   4. T   5. F   6. T   7. F   8. F   9. T   10. T

III. 1. larceny   2. probation   3. arson   4. extradition   5. plagiarism   6. amicus curiae
     7. barrister   8. larceny   9. embezzle   10. perpetrator

IV. 1. immaterial   2. incarcerate   3. litigious   4. indeterminate   5. miscreant   6. embezzle
     7. miscreant   8. litigious   9. indeterminate   10. incarcerate

V.   1. e   6. a   11. g
     2. n   7. c   12. d
     3. h   8. m   13. f
     4. b   9. j   14. i
     5. l   10. o   15. k

Lesson 23: Foreign Terms (I)

I.   1. non compos mentis   2. coup de grâce   3. junta   4. non sequitur   5. avant-garde
     6. fin de siècle   7. laissez-faire   8. bon mot   9. sine qua non   10. gauche

II. 1. T   2. F   3. T   4. T   5. T   6. F   7. T   8. T   9. T   10. F

III. 1. non sequitur   2. deus ex machina   3. cul-de-sac   4. junta   5. fin-de-siècle
     6. bête noire   7. bon mot   8. cul-de-sac   9. sine qua non   10. gauche

IV. 1. sine qua non   2. gauche   3. non compos mentis   4. avant-garde   5. fait accompli
     6. non sequitur   7. laissez-faire   8. fait accompli   9. bête noire   10. gauche

V.   1. l   6. a   11. f
     2. e   7. n   12. m
     3. h   8. b   13. g
     4. o   9. c   14. i
     5. k   10. d   15. j

Lesson 24: En Français

I.   1. sangfroid   2. tour de force   3. tête-à-tête   4. repartee   5. ingenue
     6. denouement   7. impasse   8. malaise   9. vignette   10. coiffure

II. 1. T   2. T   3. F   4. T   5. T   6. T   7. T   8. T   9. T   10. T

III. 1. tête-a-tête   2. entrepreneur   3. repartee   4. vignette   5. ingenue   6. impasse
     7. élan   8. éclat   9. coiffure   10. malaise

IV. 1. éclat   2. impasse   3. sangfroid   4. vignette   5. malaise   6. élan   7. entrepreneur
     8. denouement   9. ingenue   10. tour de force

V.   1. h   6. k   11. o
     2. n   7. a   12. e
     3. b   8. d   13. g
     4. m   9. f   14. i
     5. j   10. c   15. l

Lesson 25: Crossword Puzzle Words

I.   1. bauble   2. chary   3. aperture   4. aims   5. ado   6. onus   7. nabob
     8. acrid   9. addled   10. amulet

II. 1. F   2. F   3. F   4. T   5. T   6. T   7. F   8. T   9. T   10. T

III.

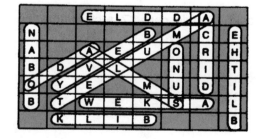

IV. taper, ilk, hay, ban, bonus

V. 1. o   6. i   11. d
    2. b   7. l   12. m
    3. e   8. k   13. c
    4. g   9. a   14. j
    5. n   10. h   15. f

Unit III Mini Review (Lessons 21–25)

I.   1. c   2. d   3. a   4. b   5. c

II. 1. c   2. d   3. b   4. d   5. b

III. 1. blithe   2. addle   3. entrepreneur   4. habeas corpus   5. bevy

Lesson 26: Mythology (II)

I.   1. calliope   2. myrmidon   3. oracular   4. thespian   5. Promethean   6. siren
     7. homeric   8. paean   9. stygian   10. terpsichorean

II. 1. T   2. F   3. T   4. F   5. F   6. T   7. T   8. T   9. F   10. T

III. 1. harpy—termagant (S)   2. obdurate-stubborn (S)   3. myrmidon—servant (S)
     4. awkward—terpsichorean (A)   5. puny—homeric (A)

IV. paean

V. 1. k   6. c   11. d
    2. n   7. l   12. i
    3. g   8. m   13. f
    4. b   9. o   14. j
    5. a   10. h   15. l

Lesson 27: Appearances and Attitudes (IV)

1.   1. sardonic   2. sleazy   3. prolix   4. restive   5. ribald   6. recalcitrant   7. voluptuous
     8. pertinacious   9. sedulous   10. pedantic

II. 1. T   2. F   3. F   4. T   5. T   6. T   7. F   8. F   9. T   10. T

III. 1. supercilious   2. voluptuous   3. pretentious   4. pertinacious   5. pedantic   6. pretentious
     7. prolix   8. sleazy   9. sedulous   10. ribald

IV. 1. sedulous   2. puerile   3. prolix   4. restive   5. ribald   6. quiescent   7. recalcitrant
     8. supercilious   9. voluptuous   10. prolix

V. 1. i   6. a   11. l
    2. m   7. k   12. h
    3. f   8. d   13. b
    4. o   9. g   14. c
    5. n   10. j   15. e

Lesson 28: Foreign Terms (II)

I. 1. bon vivant   2. ad hoc   3. nolo contendere   4. leitmotif   5. quid pro quo
    6. de facto   7. leitmotif   8. savoir faire   9. gemütlich   10. a capella

II. 1. T   2. T   3. T   4. F   5. T   6. T   7. T   8. T   9. F   10. F

III. 1. nolo contendere   2. vis-à-vis   3. de facto   4. a cappella   5. par excellence
     6. ad hoc   7. bon vivant   8. quid pro quo   9. de facto   10. gemütlich

IV. 1. bon vivant   2. gemütlich   3. sub rosa   4. ad hoc   5. savoir faire
    6. savoir faire   7. par excellence   8. bon vivant   9. sub rosa   10. pièce de résistance

V. 1. h   6. e   11. d   16. p
    2. a   7. b   12. f
    3. m   8. n   13. g
    4. c   9. o   14. l
    5. k   10. i   15. j

Lesson 29: Appearances and Attitudes (V)

I. 1. bucolic   2. ambivalent   3. dilatory   4. crotchety   5. loquacious
    6. jocund   7. dudgeon   8. splenetic   9. ambivalent   10. tendentious

II. 1. T   2. F   3. T   4. T   5. F   6. T   7. F   8. T   9. T   10. F

III. 1. vacuous   2. tendentious   3. ambivalent   4. bucolic   5. froward
     6. bucolic   7. tendentious   8. venal   9. jocund   10. dilatory

IV. 1. dilatory   2. truculent   3. splenetic   4. genteel   5. venal
    6. froward   7. disconsolate   8. ambivalent   9. genteel   10. vacuous

V. 1. c   6. a   11. f
    2. j   7. b   12. g
    3. d   8. i   13. n
    4. k   9. l   14. h
    5. o   10. e   15. m

Lesson 30: Size and Shape (II)

I. 1. magnum opus   2. gargantuan   3. lissome   4. tenuous   5. sinuous
    6. micrometer   7. serpentine   8. scintilla   9. copious   10. smidgen

II. 1. T   2. T   3. T   4. T   5. F   6. T   7. T   8. T   9. F   10. T

III. 1. magnitude   2. microcosm   3. serpentine   4. micrometer   5. magnum opus
     6. scintilla   7. tenuous   8. sinuous   9. gargantuan   10. amorphous

IV. 1. tenuous   2. gargantuan   3. macrocosm   4. amorphous   5. lissome
    6. serpentine   7. lissome   8. magnitude   9. microcosm   10. magnum opus

V. 1. a   6. l   11. k
    2. i   7. c   12. g
    3. o   8. f   13. b
    4. j   9. n   14. d
    5. e   10. h   15. m

Unit III Review (Lessons 21–30)

A. 1. pusillanimous   2. bucolic   3. non sequitur   4. pontifical   5. qui vive   6. sinuous   7. gauche
   8. officious   9. miscreant   10. amulet
B. 1. nabob   2. arson   3. iota   4. venal   5. vignette
C. 1. tête-à-tête   2. barrister   3. omniscient   4. terpsichorean   5. ingenue
D. voluptuous—libidinous   pontifical—oracular
   impasse—cul-de-sac   miscreant—perpetrator
   iota—scintilla   jocund—gemütlich
   mercurial—mutable   bon mot—mot juste
   bilk—embezzle   homeric—Promethean
E. 1. crotchety   2. ad hoc   3. mercurial   4. larceny   5. voluptuous

Lesson 31: Language

I. 1. threnody   2. malapropism   3. onomatopoeia   4. bathos   5. panegyric   6. malapropism
   7. bathos   8. metaphor   9. polyglot   10. oxymoron

II. 1. T   2. F   3. F   4. F   5. F   6. T   7. T   8. F   9. F   10. T

III. 1. literary   2. legacy   3. panorama   4. paradox   5. paradigm

IV.

V. 1. e   6. b   11. n
   2. o   7. j   12. k
   3. c   8. g   13. f
   4. m   9. l   14. h
   5. d   10. a   15. i

Lesson 32: Speech

I. 1. jargon   2. aspersion   3. guttural   4. mellifluous   5. gainsay   6. badinage   7. resonant
   8. countermand   9. bombast   10. jargon

II. 1. T   2. T   3. F   4. T   5. T   6. T   7. F   8. F   9. F   10. T

III. argot

IV. 1. glorification—aspersion (A)   2. mellifluous—soft (S)   3. timidity—braggadocio (A)   4. gainsay—deny (S)
    5. rhapsodic—bombastic (S)

V. 1. m   6. g   11. b
   2. a   7. n   12. e
   3. o   8. i   13. j
   4. c   9. f   14. k
   5. l   10. h   15. d

Lesson 33: History and Government (I)

I.   1. peonage   2. canon   3. plebiscite   4. plenipotentiary   5. recession   6. canon
     7. reprisal   8. votary   9. hegemony   10. renascent

II. 1. F   2. T   3. T   4. F   5. T   6. F   7. F   8. T   9. F   10. T

III. tryst

IV.
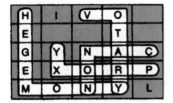

"scattered"

word:

oligarchy

V.   1. f   6. d   11. b
     2. k   7. m   12. l
     3. o   8. a   13. c
     4. n   9. h   14. e
     5. i   10. j   15. g

Lesson 34: Travel

I.   1. hustings   2. portmanteau   3. landmark   4. safari   5. tandem   6. traverse   7. hegira
     8. hustings   9. peripatetic   10. portmanteau

II. 1. T   2. T   3. T   4. F   5. F   6. T   7. T   8. T   9. F   10. T

III. 1. parabolic   2. valediction   3. trek   4. travail   5. anticipate

IV.
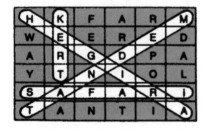

"scattered"

word:

wayfarer

V.   1. a   6. i   11. e
     2. o   7. d   12. m
     3. l   8. f   13. j
     4. n   9. g   14. h
     5. k   10. b   15. c

Lesson 35: Foods and Taste

I.   1. condiment   2. manna   3. subsistence   4. piquant   5. culinary   6. deleterious   7. cuisine
     8. gourmand   9. assuage   10. a la carte

II. 1. F   2. T   3. T   4. F   5. F   6. T   7. T   8. T   9. F   10. T

III. 1. audible   2. determine   3. essential   4. pungent   5. relish

IV. 1. rogue, damn   2. squint, p.a.   3. van, ids   4. reefs, tonic   5. guess, aha

V. 1. k   6. f   11. c
    2. d   7. o   12. n
    3. m   8. a   13. e
    4. h   9. b   14. i
    5. j   10. l   15. g

Unit IV Mini Review (Lessons 31–35)

I.   1. c   2. b   3. d   4. c   5. a

II. 1. b   2. a   3. d   4. c   5. a

III. 1. mellifluous   2. subversive   3. trek   4. metaphor   5. resonant

Lesson 36: Fun and Frolic

I.   1. divertissement   2. guffaw   3. regale   4. waggish   5. squib   6. insouciance   7. congenial
     8. roguish   9. bonhomie   10. dalliance

II. 1. F   2. T   3. F   4. T   5. F   6. T   7. T   8. F   9. T   10. T

III. elfin

IV.

V. 1. d   6. k   11. l
    2. m   7. a   12. n
    3. o   8. c   13. j
    4. e   9. i   14. h
    5. f   10. b   15. g

Lesson 37: History and Government (II)

I.   1. schism   2. partisan   3. imperialism   4. ethos   5. demagogue   6. bureaucracy   7. muckraker
     8. reactionary   9. totalitarianism   10. suffrage

II. 1. T   2. F   3. F   4. T   5. F   6. F   7. F   8. T   9. T   10. T

III. 1. narcissism   2. pedant   3. coherent   4. quarry   5. artistic

IV. canon

V. 1. d   6. o   11. g
    2. j   7. h   12. i
    3. m   8. l   13. k
    4. a   9. b   14. c
    5. f   10. e   15. n

Lesson 38: Legal Language (III)

I.   1. abscond   2. contumacious   3. cause célèbre   4. contraband   5. bequest   6. battery
     7. affidavit   8. abnegation   9. jurisprudence   10. contraband

II. 1. T   2. F   3. F   4. T   5. T   6. F   7. F   8. T   9. T   10. F

III. 1. bequest   2. caveat emptor   3. jurisprudence   4. abscond   5. contraband   6. battery
     7. caveat emptor   8. contumacious   9. disenfranchise   10. injunction

IV. 1. contumacious   2. altercation   3. injunction   4. abnegation   5. disenfranchise   6. contiguous
     7. contraband   8. cause célèbre   9. bequest   10. codicil

V. 1. g   6. l   11. n
    2. o   7. f   12. m
    3. a   8. k   13. e
    4. b   9. i   14. j
    5. c   10. d   15. h

Lesson 39: Philosophy and Logic

I.   1. epistemology   2. syllogism   3. candor   4. hedonism   5. predestination
     6. utilitarian   7. dogma   8. empirical   9. pragmatism   10. syllogism

II. 1. T   2. T   3. T   4. F   5. F   6. F   7. T   8. T   9. T   10. F

III. 1. utilitarian   2. document   3. romantic   4. conjectural   5. hedonism

IV. empirical, theosophy, teleology, syllogism

V. 1. d   6. o   11. e
    2. j   7. f   12. i
    3. k   8. a   13. n
    4. l   9. m   14. g
    5. h   10. b   15. c

Lesson 40: Beliefs and Religion

I.   1. blasphemy   2. pantheism   3 infidel   4. theodicy   5. deist   6. apotheosis   7. apocalyptic
     8. pantheist   9. benediction   10. apocryphal

II. 1. F   2. T   3. F   4. F   5. T   6. F   7. F   8. T   9. T   10. T

III. 1. apostate—heretic (S)   2. apotheosis—degradation (A)   3. mantra—invocation (S)
     4. canonical—orthodox (S)   5. benediction—anathema (A)

IV. 1. c   6. i   11. o
     2. b   7. a   12. g
     3. h   8. m   13. l
     4. e   9. d   14. n
     5. k   10. f   15. j

Unit IV Review (Lessons 31–40)

A. 1. safari 2. renascent 3. apotheosis 4. mantra 5. pragmatism 6. benediction 7. wanderlust
    8. apostate 9. paradigm 10. harangue
B. 1. safari 2. dogma 3. schism 4. repast 5. simile
C. 1. polygot 2. divertissement 3. plenipotentiary 4. concierge 5. gourmand 6. landmark 7. viands
    8. wayfarer 9. muckraker 10. proxy
D. simile-metaphor   oligarchy-totalitarian
    repast-refection   waggish-badinage
    pragmatism-utilitarian   surrogate-proxy
    jargon-argot   bequest-codicil
    tenet-canon
E. 1. aspersions 2. jargon 3. a la carte 4. culinary 5. fallacy 6. contraband 7. bureaucracy 8. proxy
    9. Machiavellian 10. assuage

Final Review Test

Antonyms

1. A	11. B	21. C	31. B	41. A
2. E	12. E	22. E	32. B	42. D
3. E	13. D	23. C	33. E	43. E
4. C	14. B	24. A	34. B	44. A
5. B	15. C	25. A	35. A	45. D
6. A	16. A	26. B	36. C	46. C
7. B	17. B	27. D	37. A	47. E
8. A	18. B	28. D	38. B	48. A
9. E	19. A	29. A	39. D	49. B
10. D	20. D	30. D	40. C	50. C

Sentence Completions

1. B	11. B	21. B	31. D	41. B
2. D	12. B	22. D	32. E	42. C
3. A	13. E	23. C	33. B	43. A
4. D	14. A	24. A	34. D	44. D
5. C	15. B	25. B	35. C	45. C
6. A	16. D	26. B	36. A	46. D
7. B	17. C	27. E	37. E	47. C
8. B	18. A	28. D	38. C	48. B
9. B	19. E	29. A	39. D	49. E
10. E	20. A	30. E	40. E	50. C

INDEX

The page number refers to the page on which the definition of the new word appears.